The SHAKEN SNOW GLOBE

FINDING HAPPINESS BEYOND MY WHITE PICKET FENCE

KRISTY DOMINIAK

This is a work of creative nonfiction. While all the stories in this book are true, some names and identifying details have been changed to protect the privacy of the people involved.

Edited by Pamela Murphy McCormick and Jennifer Hall

Cover and Interior by Publish Pros (www.publishpros.com)

For my "Forever and Always"

CHAPTER 1

Time For Me To Fly

I am a "good girl," a strong girl, a girl who feels guilty wanting more out of her so-called picture-perfect life. But, I do. I crave so much more.

But, what do I need?

I had been asking myself this question for years, yet I filled my time with more and more stuff to perpetuate the busyness and ignore the emptiness I felt. As a stay-at-home mom with my youngest of three children off to preschool, I had time on my hands.

Time is what I didn't need or want!

Having another baby was out of the question. Three was more than enough for this only-child to handle. How was I going to ignore the guilt that my life felt unfulfilled?

Stop the mind wandering!

I should be relieved to be sitting on an indented cushion in cramped quarters, breathing stale air, not dwelling on my isfied and lackluster life. I was escaping, even if only fo weekend.

1

"Kristy, how am I going to fit this? The compartment is full."

Chloe was still standing, trying to find space in the over-head compartment for her Louis Vuitton carry-on. She was my best friend and the one woman that understood me—and I her. Despite our vastly different upbringings, we were both stuck at the same point in our lives—housewives. Or was it stay-at-home moms? I couldn't keep track of the labels. All I knew was that we were both on the same spinning hamster wheel desperately trying to get off and find meaning—or at least excitement—in our monotonous lives.

With our children being in school full time, Chloe and I began enjoying the luxuries of our bank accounts. After all, we deserved a little break from the houses we were managing to be someone other than wife and mother.

Didn't we?

Lunches, pedicures and shopping were meaningless mind es-capes, a way to feel alive. When these escapes were not enough to fill my "happy quota," I graduated to "Girls' Night Out" and ignored the guilt of leaving my husband, Patrick, home alone with our three small kids. Maybe ignore wasn't accurate, it was more like numbing the guilt with the first cocktail. Either way, Girls' Night became my one joy outside of my children. Patrick, being the supportive husband he was, encouraged my girl time. As he put it, "No one's happy unless mamma's happy!" And he was right!

My life after cooking, cleaning, paying bills, chauffeuring kids and tending to my husband became all about the temporary es-cape of Girls' Night. The once a month outings became more and more frequent, until once a week wasn't even enough. Girls' Night was the one time I was happy and free from the unappreciated life of a homemaker. Don't get me wrong. Time together with girl-s is important, but, when you're only happy planning the e, that's a problem, even if I didn't see it like that at the

Those nights surrounded by girlfriends made me feel like *the girl* I once knew—a vivacious, head-turning woman who could discuss more than kids, PTA and PMS. Not that I didn't love being a mom, I just yearned for the break of being someone other than *the wife* and responsible mother of three. I was convinced my husband, Patrick, reaped the benefits of the woman that went out with the girls. At least she wore something other than sweatpants and the scent of fresh pine and bleach. If he was lucky, the sexy, sassy woman he had fallen in love with would awaken him upon her tipsy return. Meanwhile, the tired out stay-at-home mom was nowhere to be found. I think we both longed for this woman more, and, thus, Girls' Night became routine.

How did I get here?

My first crush was the summer before my freshman year of high school on Brooks Lake in a small Michigan town. Brian was two grades ahead of me. He had motored over with his best friend, Patrick, who stepped one foot off the wobbly aluminum craft onto the dock to stop from crashing into it. Despite a few dirt smudges from working in the Christmas tree fields earlier in the day, Patrick seemed to be a clean-cut, skinny kid with piercing green eyes, sun-streaked locks and full, kissable lips.

Brian tried to introduce us, but Patrick was preoccupied with securing the boat so the wind wouldn't take it away. He remained determined, though appeared a bit frazzled from their less than graceful approach.

He glanced up, flashed a boyish grin and eventually stood up and said, "Nice to meet you."

As I moved forward to show off my best flirtatious smile—I was young and still perfecting that—my hip nudged his side, knocked him off balance and plunged him into the cool water—clothes and all.

As Patrick came up for air, I giggled.

"Nice to meet you, too. You OK?" I asked.

Brian shook his head.

"So, now you've met Kristy!" he added.

We spent the rest of the summer on or near the lake water-skiing, swimming and just hanging out talking on the docks. I didn't have to worry about impressing Patrick and Brian, as they both were the epitome of the boy-next-door persona. I could just be myself, unlike the girls who were always changing friendship rules and expectations. Life always seemed to be a competition with girls, but not with Patrick and Brian. Both could handle me winning almost every jet ski race or scurry out to the raft. After that first summer, reliable Patrick became a fixture in my life—*the* fixture.

The captain's announcement lurched me back to my mundane reality.

"Our flight to Texas will last approximately three and a half hours. Weather in Houston is currently a comfortable 75 degrees."

The passengers in the cabin seemed to collectively sigh in relief at just the thought of the warmth to come.

It was the last weekend of a snow-filled February. Actually, all Februarys in Northern Michigan are snow-filled. Chloe and I were escaping the frozen tundra for an eagerly anticipated, hot week-end to visit our friend, Danielle, who had moved to the Lone Star State. "Escaping" was an interesting word choice, but I wasn't quite ready to address that. Instead, I focused on my excitement to wear my staple wardrobe item—cowboy boots—without being a spectacle. What better place than Texas?

Danielle moved there when she lost her lucrative job up north. In order to keep her family in the lifestyle to which they had grown accustomed, Danielle felt she had to accept another high paying executive position, even if that meant moving without her family. Chloe and I knew Danielle's adjustment would be difficult and wanted her to know that, even if the miles separated us, she was still a valued friend. It was just the excuse we needed for another girls' weekend. Escaping the dead of a Michigan winter was an added bonus.

My mind drifted to our last unforgettable outing a few months earlier.

CHAPTER 2

Don't Cha

"How have I never done this?" I inquired to Chloe as she waltzed past the mile long line wrapped around the corner leading to a Chicago nightclub.

"You have been sheltered, haven't you? Stop worrying and stay close," she replied, while confidently strutting to the front of the line.

She whispered to the stone-faced man dressed in black behind the red velvet rope, while handing him something. Before I realized what was happening, we were whisked under the rope and escorted up a back stairwell by another equally intimidating guy. The tall, dark and handsome twenty-something, who brought up the rear, grabbed my waist to steady me from falling when my platform shoe missed the step.

Where did he come from?

He, too, was in all black with one of those secret service-like spiraled wires running down the back of his ear. I felt like a celebrity, a far cry from wiping noses and serving spaghetti the night before.

A stunning woman appeared in a trendy black pantsuit. She extended her hand to Chloe, as she met us at the top of the stairs. We were now inside a dimly lit room with clean lines and shiny metal rails. Bass pounded—thump, thump, thump—and lights flashed all around us. The woman escorted us up a second winding staircase. At the top, four more beefy men in black with ear pieces stood at attention next to a wall of smoky glass. On the other side of the thin walkway was a gold rail that saved clumsy me from falling two stories to the dance floors below. Below us was quite an aquarium of creatures, oblivious to the over-sized fish bowl in which they were displayed. The men stepped aside, and an opening appeared in the glass. Then, we were escorted into another dimly lit room with a long glass bar, circular leather couches and an area set-up for a band. Our attractive female escort introduced Chloe to our two personal waitresses who brought us full bottles—not drinks—and the attractive, "hot" guy who helped me earlier stood guard at our roped off table, preventing unwelcome guests. The eye candy acting as our bodyguard was a bonus, but this prissy girl knew better than to touch. Ogling this exotic land, I wondered why I hadn't done this before I was tied to a ring.

Who lived this kind of life?

I was thirty-five and had never been exposed to this scene, not even in college which was only an hour or so drive from here. Well, maybe that doesn't count as I did attend the *ever Catholic* University of Notre Dame where dorm buildings are still separated by sex and the code of conduct states fornication by a student will result in expulsion. As the consummate "good girl," I would never break that rule or any other. I had worked too hard at playing it straight so I could escape my hometown of 1,500. Life was a simple philosophy for me—follow the rules and life will reward you. So far, so good.

"Are those two Chicago Bulls players over there?" I inquired.

"How would I know? You're the basketball fan, not me," Chloe responded, while she mixed her vodka red bull. "It's my birthday and we're here to celebrate! I'm not worried about anyone else, unlike you. Have a drink and relax."

She knew me all too well. I was anxious, noticing everyone and everything.

Did I miss something? People my age and older were hanging out in a club, spreading money around, partying. This is what celebrities did on television, NOT Midwest housewives!

Based on the attention we were drawing, I did not feel like a housewife, and, I must say, my ego was getting a much needed boost.

Despite Chloe's comfort, she wasn't a regular in this scene either. Chloe came from humble beginnings and just so happened to marry a tie-dye wearing surgeon. He was gifted in his profession and loved what he did—maybe too much. His career did provide loads of discretionary income, and, since he had no time to spend it, Chloe spread enough wealth for the both of them. She was a generous soul, which was probably why we had been treated like royalty from the start of the evening. A part of me envied her worldly experiences and sense of adventure.

Chloe led an intriguing life in her twenties—traveling around the world with the military, putting herself through college, working as a paramedic and dealing with some tough family issues. She embodied the term "strong girl." Chloe's strength came from living hardships, whereas mine came from Catholic rules.

Rules had been my compass. I didn't think I was doing anything wrong, but my Catholic guilt made me question being in this nightclub, drinking and sharing the life of these people. The Chicago nightlife was a far cry from the usual small bar that is home to our Girls' Nights. There I felt in control with my harmless flirting and bold personality, but this place was much more unpredictable. Thank goodness I was with Chloe. She was fearless and didn't care what other people were doing or what they thought. She was comfortable with herself, and I loved that about her. Chloe was my safety harness, giving me the freedom to explore without breaking any rule. It was exhilarating!

Had the destination of my righteous path been worth not exploring this wild side of life during my single days? Hadn't I earned a right to peek at the wild side of life I had avoided? I wasn't doing anything against my Catholic values. I was merely getting a glance at the glamorous chaos of a fast paced life.

After some drinks, mindless dancing and eye-popping scenes, I slipped into the guarded bathroom to call Patrick. Yes, guarded. That was a first for me. A burly bodyguard-type stood near the entrance of a long hallway with multiple ornate steel doors guarding single bathroom units and one line for both men and women. I wasn't sure I wanted to know why there was a guard or unisex accommodations, but the private marble escape did provide a quiet place for a quick phone call.

"Hey, Hon. You still awake?"

"I am now," Patrick answered, yawning into the phone. "How's it going?"

"This place is crazy...private bathrooms, pro basketball players, money and a bunch of old people. I feel like I'm in a movie. These places really do exist. It's wild! Beautiful, young, half-dressed women everywhere, and, surprisingly, men are still talking to me, Miss Boring Housewife," I said jokingly.

"Of course they're talking to you. They're not blind!" Patrick responded. "You getting your dancing fix?"

"Like you have to ask."

"Good. Get it out of your system so I don't have to dance for a long, long time. And save me some money, while you're at it, as I'm sure those men who can't have you are trying to buy you drinks."

"You're funny," I spouted, wishing sometimes that Patrick had at least one jealous bone in his body.

"How are the kids?" I asked.

"Sleeping, of course. It's 3 in the morning!"

"Oh, yeah. Sorry. Forgot the time change thing."

"Kristy, it's still 2 o'clock in the morning there," Patrick added.

"Oh, you're right! I guess the time got away from us. It's just so interesting to watch the people...young with old...old with young... girl hanging on girl...the outfits. It's beyond my scope."

"Well, be safe, and stay out of trouble. I'm going back to sleep. Love you."

"Love you, too," I whispered before hanging up.

Patrick was dependable—my best friend—even before Chloe. Patrick and I had known each other since we met at the lake when I was thirteen years old, and he was your typical "boy next door" in most every way, including his boyish good looks. I confided in him about everything.

As I exited the bathroom, Chloe pushed her way to the front of the line. The guard reached out to stop her, but Chloe dismissed him with a simple "I'm with her" as she pushed me back into the bathroom. What she didn't see was the beautiful, late twenty-some-thing blonde in a pinstriped skirt and a one-too-many-buttons-un-done blouse who stumbled in behind us. The blonde shut the door.

"Thanks. I just couldn't wait any longer," she noted.

"No worries," Chloe replied, un-phased that another woman was sharing the bathroom with us.

The blonde continued to converse with us like she had known us for years. Now, I know women often go to the restroom in groups, but, to me, this time felt a little too close-quartered. Chloe went about her business, while the woman rambled on about how she worked in the loop of Chicago, had a kid and ended up here after work with her boss and a few co-workers. As she continued fussing her fingers through her wild mop of tangled blonde waves, she kept repeating how stunning the two of us were. She was shocked that we could have six kids between us and insisted we had to be her age. I observed a sad edge to her and, despite her smiling face, her skin looked more distressed in the bathroom lighting.

"C'mon...join me. We could have a lot of fun together," she said, as she reached to stroke Chloe's sleek chestnut locks, envying its color.

She seemed a bit desperate to be with us as she parroted her invitation to have a drink with her. Chloe, seemingly unaffected, deflected her invitation and coolly moved past her toward the exit yet still engaged her in chatter. I looked up to follow her out and the scene in front of me played out in slow motion as the woman stuck her well-manicured, extra-long fingernail up to Chloe's nose.

I sobered at the reality of what was happening. My pulse skyrocketed.

Is that cocaine I am seeing mounded on her nail? What have I gotten myself into?

This small town girl had never even seen weed—maybe smelled it at a concert—but I had never come this up-close and personal with an illegal substance. The closest I have been to drugs was hearing about Chloe's experiences trying to rescue people from hardcore drugs before her life as a surgeon's wife. This was more than I bargained for.

I wanted out.

Nonchalantly, Chloe said, "Put that away. That stuff will kill you."

The woman stared at her with inquisitive eyes.

Chloe continued, "You don't need that. Let me tell you something...I have a friend that did stuff like that, and it ruined her. I don't touch it and neither should you."

I had never seen Chloe so convicted, so opinionated. That was always my job. This was different. Her objection didn't reject the woman. In fact, her tone was nurturing, showing disapproval of the act but not of her. I don't know if I would have been able to distinguish the two even if I had tried sober. Chloe's passion and pain on the subject were transparent—a rare glimpse into my friend's heart. This was a world she had escaped and a world I could not understand.

It was a trip I didn't necessarily want to repeat. However, I must admit I enjoyed being out of my well-constructed box and was excited for another escape from my mundane life. I was able to forget the monotony of being a stay-at-home mom, if only for the weekend.

I could handle the drinking, the aggressive men and watching other's immoral behavior. However, I was unprepared for the bathroom encounter. I was left feeling a bit dirty, as if I had read a tabloid and didn't want anyone to witness my guilty pleasure.

CHAPTER 3

History In The Making

Over the loud speaker the shrill voice of the flight attendant interrupted my daydream.

"Please turn off all electronics and fasten your seat belts. We will be pushing back from the gate momentarily."

I turned to Chloe, who was messing with her purse under the seat in front of her.

"Can you believe we are getting away again after our last adventure?" I asked.

"Hopefully, no crazy, bisexual, drug addicts this time," Chloe snickered. "That was a bit over the top."

"Slightly," I said, snickering back.

"I'm more surprised Patrick let you out of the house after you spilled all the beans from our last excursion. If I told 'Mr. Surgeon' all of the gory details, I would get a lecture on how irresponsible we were for just being there."

"You know we have no secrets. He trusts me," I said proudly. "Besides, I couldn't keep my mouth shut if I tried."

"Isn't that the truth?" Chloe jabbed.

"Hey!"

So, OK, it was the truth. My mouth could get me in trouble. I was out-spoken and opinionated, I kept nothing to myself. Patrick knew all my secrets, including 'the incident' with the Sheriff. (More on this later.) He had known this only child for more than 20 years and knew how I ticked. A small smile formed on my lips as I reflected on the evolution of my relationship with Patrick.

Transitioning to high school was much easier with Patrick to lean on like a big brother. It didn't matter if I was dating the Captain of the Varsity Basketball team or forgetting my jacket on a blustery day, Patrick was always looking out for my well-being—lending his ear or his sweatshirt.

At the end of my freshman year, and contrary to the calendar, the wind whipping across the high school parking lot felt as if winter was hanging on. Patrick and I sprinted against the howl to his shiny, red Mustang, his pride and joy—and my way to escape. Each day we would avoid the scary food in the cafeteria for the better fare at the local convenience store. We had 20 minutes for our ritual lunch break. Patrick had earned enough as a dish boy during the school year and trimming Christmas trees in the summer to buy his own car. I admired his work ethic. Even though my parents' rules forbid me to ride in a car with a boy until I was sixteen, I wasn't too worried about our lunchtime ritual. After all, he was just a friend, and my parents adored him. I figured the rule was their way of ensuring I wasn't doing anything I wasn't supposed to be doing in a car with a boy, and "it" wasn't about to happen with Patrick. So, in my mind, the rule didn't really apply here.

On this particular day, my girlfriend, who would often go with us to lunch, was absent, leaving us alone in his Mustang. Between bites of that youthful staple, Pecan Swirls, Patrick sprung it on me.

"Would you like to go to prom with me?" he asked with his boyish grin.

"Prom?"

"Yea, prom. Don't act so surprised. Who else would I ask?"

"I don't know...but I'm not allowed to date 'til I'm sixteen. You know my parents."

I rolled my blue eyes for dramatic effect.

"Your parents will make an exception for me. I'm that nice boy who hangs around," he bragged.

"Well, aren't you cocky?" I objected. "Remember, this is my mother we're talking about."

"Yes, but she already agreed to it...if you do."

"What? Wait! You asked my mother?"

I didn't know whether to be irritated or impressed by his boldness. My mother was like a pitbull and confronting her took some guts. Either way, I had underestimated him.

"Of course I did. So, will you go with me or not?"

"I can't believe she agreed to this."

"Well, there's one stipulation. But, I've already covered that if you say yes."

"And that is...?" I inquired, waiting for him to finish explaining.

Patrick knew I wouldn't answer his question without all the details mapped out.

"We have to double date, and your friend Rachelle agreed to go with the Columbian exchange student. So...are you in?"

"Go to prom, huh...for real?"

I looked at him with skeptical eyes but didn't pause long enough for him to answer.

"Of course I'll go. What freshman doesn't want to go to prom with an upperclassman? I can't believe you pulled it off with my parents," I said with a full smile.

We laughed all the way back to the school at the thought of Rachelle taking one for the team and agreeing to go to the dance with the exchange student. The whole thing reminded us of the movie "Sixteen Candles" where the short exchange student has a voluptuous date for prom and poor Molly Ringwald is stuck watching them with her less than optimal date.

Back at school, the shock of my parents agreeing to let me go to prom—even if it was a double date—distracted me from science class.

Were these the same parents that wouldn't let me ride to rent a movie with Patrick on a Saturday afternoon? The only explanation I could muster is they weren't worried about hanky-panky. This was Patrick after all. Or maybe we both underestimated his charm.

This relationship shift also changed thought patterns. For example, while I was getting dressed for the prom in a short white dress with a big black sash tied around the waist I wondered if the black sash would be eliminated in the years to come, leaving me standing in all-white as a bride.

Could Patrick be the man of my dreams?

I had never viewed Patrick as Prince Charming, since he wasn't much for sharing emotions, but we did have an amazing friendship. I could tell him anything, and he wasn't too hard on the eyes either. Giddiness sent a shiver through me—maybe even a bit of nervousness. Patrick was to be my first "car date." Heck, he'd be my first "date date." His devotion to me made me pause and thin—maybe?

Patrick had the great smile, was Catholic, flexed fabulous running calves for a skinny guy, but he still needed a little work in the emotional arena. Time was on his side. It was only high school, after all. He was more handsome than I remembered, all dressed up in his tux. I assumed dancing wasn't his strong suit, but, then again, I didn't think dating was either. I don't know if it was the hype of the night, the fancy clothes, or his boyish charm, but, as we were saying goodnight on my front porch steps, I let my best friend kiss me.

Big mistake!

The kiss was not what I was hoping for. It was nice but not like the one I conjured up in my dreams. My heart sank, wondering if Patrick's good manners interfered with his ability to open up or if he just wasn't interested in the type of connection I craved. Either way, I reverted to my comfort zone—Patrick as best friend—while I dated upperclassman jocks. He never showed hurt over my wanting to stay just friends and kept hanging out with me without pursuing more. He treated me like one of the guys—just the way I liked things, at least at that time.

I was saddened a bit by the thought of what was missing in my life—a passionate pursuit.

Chloe's voice brought me back to present. Her frustration with her emotionally disconnected husband was bubbling over, a topic to which I could relate. As the force of the take-off held us tight in our seats, we could no longer hear ourselves talk. Chloe and I were as far away from first class as you could get. Our silent laughs grew as we realized the irony of sitting next to the smelly toilets in the last row as we pondered our so-called "picture perfect lives." We craved so much more.

Were we just being greedy?

We had this same conversation repeatedly. The unspeakable guilt we were feeling for being unsatisfied trapped us. We knew we had been following a road map to living, but the so-called "good life" wasn't enough. What should we be doing to find our personal passions for living? For the first time, I had a plan—a really good plan for both of us.

The flight attendant asked us if we wanted a drink. Even though it was only 10 am, Chloe and I ordered two tiny bottles of rum and a Diet Coke. We figured it would help the stench, and I hoped it would loosen Chloe up to my idea.

I began my relentless "Kristy chatter" about an organization called CHADD, my latest and greatest plan to date. The acronym stood for Children and Adults with Attention/Hyperactivity Deficit Disorder. Since there was no local chapter of the National Organization of CHADD in Traverse City, I believed this was the perfect support group to start. I hoped—maybe, just maybe—this would be the purpose we were both craving outside of wifedom and motherhood. I wasn't giving her an opportunity to say no and was using tactics I learned from my father, the proverbial salesman. He would not let me ask a direct yes or no question from the day I could first talk. For example, instead of "Can we go out for ice cream?" he'd make me ask "Can we go out for ice cream now or in twenty minutes?" His tactics were well applied, but Chloe was still a tough egg to crack. At least I had the whole trip to convince her about CHADD.

Chloe excused herself to use the bathroom or perhaps escape my ramblings. Trying to calm my overzealous state, I adjusted my seat a little and gazed out the frosted glass window at the snow-covered land we were leaving. Sipping on my drink, I reflected back on how I got to this point in my life.

I thought maybe after high school Patrick would prove to be the man of my dreams—until my hopes of Patrick being "him" were shattered the summer he left for college.

Patrick's graduation from high school was upon us. I couldn't believe my best friend was leaving me. We were in my parent's kitchen sitting on wooden bar stools drinking lemonade, while gazing out the window at the newly budding trees.

"Last night...it happened," Patrick stated coyly.

"What?"

My naivety spilled out.

"You know...'it'."

"What is 'it'?"

I didn't want to hear what I was hearing.

"Last night at the cabin, we had a few drinks...and, after the party died down, she came into my bedroom and 'it' happened."

"With her?"

My face couldn't hide my loathing. She wasn't good enough for him. Her beauty and popularity couldn't mask her reputation. My heart sank like a bobber under the surface of the lake, suffocating.

Couldn't she have been at least a long-term girlfriend, instead of a meaningless hookup? At least then I might be able to accept she was worthy of his gift and not simply a result of his physical weakness. Patrick knew I valued strength in waiting, yet he chose her.

My fisherman had lost the fight to reel me in, cutting his line. Catching me must not have been worth the trouble or he would have kept on fighting, despite the fact that I didn't want to be caught, yet.

"That was disappointing," Chloe said, as she sat down.

She couldn't have chosen a more appropriate word for what I was thinking, but I knew Chloe was referring to the unmaintained bathroom and not Patrick's prior actions. I redirected my disappointed thoughts to the future and resumed my chatter about the potential of CHADD for the remainder of our flight.

CHAPTER 4

Sounds Like Life To Me

I pushed the revolving door. A wave of Texas heat greeted us as I shed my layers. My purse bumped off my suitcase and spewed its contents across the sidewalk. Scrambling on my hands and knees to corral the items, I reached for my rolling lipstick and bumped into a cowboy boot. The boot shifted to the left, stopping my lipstick. I raised my head up from the ground to encounter a man's grinning face in my personal space. I gasped. The stranger grabbed my lipstick then extended his hand to help me off the ground.

"You OK, Miss."

His deep accent sent tiny tingles up my spine.

I think I'm going to like Texas.

The beeping of a horn pulled me from my moment. Our friend, Danielle, pulled up to the curb in her shiny, black Lexus.

Having witnessed my akward Texas welcome, Chloe shook her head at me and smiled.

"Kristy antics already?"

I jabbed back at her, giggling, "Hey, that wasn't my fault. He approached me. I'm focused this trip. I don't need any empty flirting to distract myself from what will never be. I'm moving on to bigger and better ideas...like CHADD...hint, hint."

I double elbowed her in the arm, trying to drum up a reaction to the plan I described to her on the plane. When that didn't work, I continued my ramblings, while she put my bags in Danielle's trunk.

Danielle chose a quiet restaurant for dinner, so we could catch up on life. The restaurant was a unique wine boutique where the walls were lined with bottles of all shapes and sizes. The cozy place was a nice change of pace from our usual who's who type restaurant and was conveniently located just around the corner from her apartment. Danielle had to work in the morning, so she was taking the evening in strides.

Since moving to Texas, Danielle had buried herself in her career. She beamed with pride over her accomplishments at work and brushed over her sadness from being separated from her family. She was good at compartmentalizing things, and I couldn't blame her as she had been dealt a tough hand early in life. She bounced from foster home to foster home—one tale more tragic than the next. Chloe and she shared stories from their pasts that were unimaginable to me. Compared to the two of them, my childhood was as boring as one could get. I guess this is why I cherished them both so much. They were far more resilient and adventurous than I could ever be.

"You're rather quiet tonight," Danielle said to me. "What's wrong? You're not even peppy with the hot waiter."

"Nothing, I'm just pondering what's next for my life. You both have lived boldly, and...well...I've lived...boring and predictably."

"Boring isn't so bad when you consider the alternative," Chloe interjected.

"Really?" I spouted. "At least you have memories of passionate relationships before your marriage to hang on to."

"Yeah, but now I know what I'm missing," she rebutted.

"So, you're telling me you would rather go your whole life without than to have at least once experienced 'that' feeling?"

I didn't leave her time to answer.

"Flirting is as good as it gets for me, and the thought of that now sucks! I need to find something more meaningful in my life."

Danielle redirected the conversation.

"Didn't you just tell me how much positive feedback you received after your speech on ADHD awareness in the Catholic schools?"

"Yeah."

"Well, that's a start to something more meaningful," Danielle added.

"It's funny you brought that up. That's exactly what I have been telling Chloe," I said, smirking in Chloe's direction.

Although most of the locals deemed February the "off-season" and despite the 80 degree temperatures, Danielle still had to put in few hours at the office. Her rigorous work schedule allowed little time for her own pleasure during the week. Chloe and I didn't mind. In fact, we looked forward to some poolside R&R.

Danielle said she would have time off on the weekend to entertain us, and, with plenty of excitement planned, I knew a little rest by the pool would do me some good. I wasn't much for holding my liquor and keeping up with the two of them multiple days in a row would prove to be a challenge.

We were the only ones poolside at Danielle's apartment—the perfect place for us Northern Michigan girls needing a thaw after not having felt the warmth of the sun for six months. Chloe broke the silence, embracing us, while basking under the clear blue Texas sky.

"So I've been thinking about what you were saying on the plane. I think it may work," Chloe said.

Did she just say what I think she said?

"Really?" I responded.

I couldn't contain my excitement. I started rambling,

"I thought for sure you wouldn't be open to people knowing your personal business. You're always so private, plus you barely asked me any questions on the plane about starting a chapter of CHADD."

"How could I get a word in edge wise? You talked the entire flight," she snickered.

OK, she gets this one.

Pondering my journey thus far, and having decided where I was headed, I wanted Chloe to agree to my plan. I needed her approval, so I chattered the entire flight trying to convince her why CHADD was the right venture for us to escape the unappreciated life of a homemaker. Chloe had great attention to detail and would be a perfect organizer behind the scenes—a place she liked to be unless she was drinking. I, on the other hand, liked to be front and center—as an only child would—and my gift of gab would serve well as the facilitator. I hoped by pursuing this cause we would find the passion and purpose we were searching for in our lives.

Chloe and I had up close and personal experiences with attention deficit hyperactivity disorder—ADHD. The diagnoses and treatment changed the direction of my child's life for the better—once Patrick and I overcame society's stereotyping and my fear of imperfect labels, that is.

Brooke, my middle child who was named after the lake where Patrick and I met, was diagnosed with ADHD two years earlier at the age of six. Once treated, she began to soar academically and her self-esteem grew by leaps and bounds. I shared Brooke's story with anyone who would listen and thought the time was right to formalize my efforts for public awareness and support.

Brooke was independent from an early age. She was the baby who did not want to be cuddled or rocked to sleep, crying until she was placed in her crib. By the time she was school age, she was hit or miss with her ABC's and 123's. Although she struggled to look adults into the eyes, Brooke was social and active. The opinion was that she was choosing not to apply herself and compete with her older brother, Seth, the star student. Her reading level in the first grade was below a kindergarten level, so Patrick and I decided to intervene. We discovered, of all things, she had ADHD. Despite her outward confidence and independent nature, her self-esteem was in the dumpster. She was masking her struggles, and, once treated, the light bulb ignited. Her reading scores skyrocketed in a year's time to a fourth grade level. She became a success story of early diagnosis in spite of society's demonic description of the disorder as an overused excuse for behavior issues and lack of parental control.

I believed this cause could be a perfect fit for both me and Chloe, filling the void that Girl's Nights Out couldn't. The yummy attention from my empty flirting hadn't been enough to refuel my tank. Instead, it made me more frustrated with the reality of my life.

CHADD might be just what we girls needed to escape the day-to-day doldrums of our lives. Maybe CHADD would also supply the passion and purpose for which I was searching.

CHAPTER 5

Why Don't We Just Dance?

What was I thinking? rushed into my mind, as the peanut shells crunched under my bronze cowboy boots. This was another foreign territory like Chloe's birthday adventure but the polar opposite of Chicago—big hats, pointed boots, wrangler jeans lined up at the bar and people promenading in a big circle around the floor to a strange twang.

Earlier in the limousine, my over-anxious mouth spoke before my naïve mind processed what I was saying.

"Forget the nightclub. Let's go for today's perfect trifecta. We survived our first rodeo and first country music concert, so let's go dance our first two-step before we fly back to reality tomorrow."

I followed Danielle as she paraded us around the rim of the dance floor where couples were moving in unison like sleek race cars around a track. At that point, I realized the day's liquid courage had worn off. I felt the numerous eyes penetrating my walk. It may have been because we were a rainbow of sassy in a sea of neutral, but I didn't recognize that at the time. Danielle sported a sexy, bright red, sequined halter top with matching high-heeled boots, Chloe wore a low-cut cobalt shirt accenting her beautifully round chest, and I donned a swingy, probably too short in retrospect, tie-dyed green cotton dress with my shiny bronze cowboy boots. I guess we didn't look like true cowgirls. It was more like *Charlie's Angels* down to our complementary hair color—Danielle's chocolate, Chloe's crimson and my dirty blonde.

Ahhhh! Bartender straight ahead!

Finally something familiar—the bar! A big hat blocking my path startled me.

I heard a strong Southern accent say, "Miss, would you like to dance?"

How did I miss this cowboy's approach?

"No," I blurted out, before even seeing his wide smile and broad shoulders.

The moment I spoke I wanted to take it back.

Who was talking?

I don't say no. My goal was to come here and learn new dances. I tried to salvage my negative response. The words stumbled out of my mouth.

"Uh...I mean...I don't know how...I...uh...this isn't my kind of music. I...I might step on you 'cuz I don't know what I'm doing."

What's up with my nerves?

He locked eyes with mine, dominating the moment. His stare never wavered. He rubbed the bottom of his chin as if doubting the answer—not in an arrogant way, but as if he knew something about me I didn't.

He finally spoke with a half-smile.

"Maybe later then, Miss."

And with a tip of his hat, he walked away.

"Who are you?" Chloe said with a puzzled look. "Why didn't you dance with him?"

"I don't know. Can you believe it, Chlo, I said *No*? What is wrong with me? I don't say No...What'd he look like? I was stuck on that smile and yet stammered out a No. Who am I? I love to dance, I don't get nervous and I'm an innocent flirt. That's who I am! I wasn't voted 'most likely to be on *The Dating Game* because I'm shy, why didn't I just..."

"Kristy, slow down. Get a drink. This Texas heat must be more than you can handle," Chloe said as she laughed, and we walked towards the bar.

Danielle had a drink waiting for us. As I grabbed it, I was still bemoaning my earlier reaction to the grinning cowboy.

I wasn't alone in my head for more than a sip or two when I saw a towering, 6'4", broad-shouldered cowboy approaching. He spoke with a deep drawl.

"Hello, Miss. I'm Earl. Would you like to dance?"

Did he just say Earl? It sounded so...country. That's a name I had never encountered before. Wow! Cowboys sure aren't like the men in the Midwest.

This time, I confidently responded, "I thought you'd never ask. I have to warn you though. I have no idea how to two-step...but, if you're brave enough to teach me, I'm all yours."

My bubbly, bold self had returned—thank goodness! *This* is the girl I knew. Earl led me by my diamond-adorned left hand to the speeding dance "track." As I glanced back at my friends with a satisfactory smile, I noticed the first cowboy leaning against the bar with his wide grin and his eyes still on me. Before I had time to process my actions, I was spinning and moving with the crowd of couples with Earl leading me. I loved to dance, but this style had been off my radar. I didn't even like country music—never really listened to it. I was more of a Top 40 person. But that day was a day of firsts.

I settled into a groove, enjoying the innocent escape, when Earl joked.

"So much for being a rookie. You handled the track like a veteran...that is, once you gave up trying to drive."

I smirked and glanced up, while continuing to move to the umpteenth song I didn't recognize. Looking over Earl's shoulder, my eyes locked onto those of the rejected cowboy. He was dancing in our shadow but staring at me. His skeptical eyes and playful grin persisted, as if to say *I thought you couldn't dance?* As we realized we were having a conversation with our gaze, while in the arms of others, we both chuckled.

What was it about this cowboy?

Men don't affect me like this—must be guilt. Here I am dancing with tall, dark and handsome Earl, and the guy with the smile has hijacked my attention.

Where was my usual force field for blocking the effects of charm?

He isn't even THAT tall—at least not as tall as Earl, who possesses the basketball player's frame I adore.

The remorse of rejecting the smiling cowboy lingered, not because I cared what he thought, but because I'm never nervous around men. I would never give a man what most men *really* want, so dealing with the opposite sex had always been easy for me. Tonight, cowboys were simply a means to an end—my learning to two-step. As Earl continued to tow me around, my mind couldn't escape what a hypocrite I was for saying no to "Mr. Smiley."

Days before the trip, I was sitting around my kitchen island dispensing advice on boys and life to Amanda and Morgan, two stunning teenage girls in my neighborhood who would loiter after finishing with their babysitting jobs. Morgan asked my opinion as to whether she should go to her senior prom with this boy, who she said was "not her type." I didn't hesitate to give her my opinion, as I was full of opinions.

"I think you should say yes to someone who has the courage to ask you out. Life is all about experiences. Date all the boys that ask, but that is all you should be doing with them. Stay strong and true to finding your one and only Prince Charming. Plus, you never know if you are the girl to change the way the shy boy thinks of himself or if his friend might be 'the one.' Give everyone a chance."

This is how I had lived my life—pure, yet open to the possibilities of all people. My picture perfect life with the amazing husband was proof to these young girls that my philosophy succeeded in achieving what they strived for, happiness within the white picket fence. As an only child, I loved feeling like their big sister with worldly wisdom.

So, not understanding my earlier freeze up with the grinning cowboy, the honorable thing was to right my wrong.

What did I have to be afraid of anyway?

As the music turned slow, Earl and I took a break back at the bar where Danielle and Chloe were still perched.

"I thought we came here to learn to dance? Get out there!" I insisted.

They both ignored me, so I stuck Earl on them.

"Earl, get one of these ladies on the floor."

I grabbed Earl's hand and pushed him toward Chloe and Danielle, as I introduced him to the girls. Then, I climbed onto the brass footrest of the bar, leaned over its lacquered wood and flagged the bartender for a beer. The cold was refreshing in my sweaty palm—sweaty from dancing, not nerves.

At least this is what I told myself.

Confidence usually wasn't an issue for me, as "assertive" was my middle name.

I walked over to the grinning cowboy.

CHAPTER 6

That's How Country Boys Roll

The brim of his hat shadowed his eyes, but his smile could be seen for miles. Its warmth may have been enough to melt a few hearts but not mine. I was only interested in dancing with him and righting my wrong from earlier in the evening. His shoulders were broad and well defined, and his commanding presence turned heads. He wasn't as tall as I usually preferred, but he was still a suitable height for dancing.

"I think I owe you this," I said apologitically, pointing to the cold beer. "You were kind enough to ask me to dance, and I froze."

Grinning like a Cheshire cat, he replied, "No, Miss, I believe you rejected me because you said you couldn't dance."

"That wasn't an excuse. It was the truth. I'm not from here, and I've never two stepped in my life!"

Somehow I found myself on the defensive.

"It didn't look that way as you twirled around with your 7 foot giant. And I know you're not from here," he harassed, while still smiling that intoxicating grin.

"No, really. We had just walked in, and you caught me off guard. To be honest, I don't care for this twangy music. It's not my thing."

"Looks like you're Mr. Giant's thing though," he said as he nodded in the direction of Earl, now glaring our way.

"I'm not with him," I said. "I'm just a Midwest girl on a girls' weekend, learning this country thing. Nothing more, nothing less."

I extended the peace offering.

Accepting the beer, he lightly grasped my hand with his other and said, "I'm Chad. Nice to meet you, Miss."

His hand lingered as his eyes penetrated mine. He bent over and kissed my hand. I held my breath as he looked over and tipped his hat in Earl's direction. Based on Earl's expression, he took the bait, and we both erupted in laughter. Boy, these cowboys are forward, yet polite, and not deterred by the shiny diamond on the third finger of my left hand. My thoughts were interrupted by a familiar sound.

Could that really be Kid Rock's All Summer Long?

"Now, this is my kind of music!"

I grabbed his hand, spilling his beer, and pulled him toward the dance floor as I shouted, "I'm Kristy!"

I charged against the emptying dance floor, pulling Chad with me. The two-steppers were headed to the refueling station. Chloe and Danielle were also pushing their way through the exiting crowd with Earl. We yelled the lyrics in unison...

"It's summer time in Northern Michigan!"

Our anthem in a country music bar in Texas? Who knew?

It was time to show these country folk real dancing. We sang and moved our bodies to the familiar tune. To my surprise, Chad hung in there with us—along with Earl. Two more pop songs played, and Chad and I continued to dominate the dance floor, while the rest of the rabble refueled. When the country vocals returned, Chad grabbed my hand and took charge before Earl could.

"Not bad for a country boy," I teased.

Unlike with Earl, our eyes connected, while dancing. It was a strange encounter for me. I was uncomfortable, yet not to the point of looking away.

"How long have you been married?" Chad inquired.

His question startled me, because, despite my holding my left hand in his face earlier, I had deemed him oblivious to its luster.

"Twelve years," I answered.

"And he lets you out?"

His nose crinkled, while still smiling.

"Yeah, he trusts me. We've known each other...forever. He knows I'm a harmless flirt. I'm the proverbial 'good girl.' So, don't get any ideas," I joked. "Plus, he doesn't have a jealous bone in his body. As a matter of fact, he knows I'm on this peanut-shell covered floor learning to two-step with whoever will teach me. Dancing isn't his thing...but he knows it's mine."

"Well, Kristy. It's my thing too," Chad responded, while dipping me.

Back upright and to distract me from the fluttering in my chest, I inquired. "So, what's your story? Who comes to the bar alone and chooses to dance with a married me when there are all these single beauties in the room?"

His face became serious, and I worried I had asked the wrong question.

"You're safe," he said.

I must have appeared perplexed, or he just needed to vent because he continued.

"I just came to dance, and the ring means no strings."

He held his breath for a moment.

I could feel his heart beating. I wanted to believe it was from our dancing.

"Drinking and dancing are my prescription for trying to forget my cheating ex-wife," he added.

I brushed over his deepness.

"So it's not my overwhelming beauty?" I sarcastically asked, trying to break his spell on my eyes and the seriousness of the moment.

"Your beauty..." he started. "Proves I can survive this."

His expressionless face maintained eye contact.

Somewhere deep within me, at a level I didn't even realize existed, I could feel a connection to his sadness. Our eyes locked like magnets to metal. My opinionated, tell-it-like-it-is voice was lost.

Our intense eye trance broke with the release of Chad's chest exhaling his trapped air, as he tried to revert back to our playful banter. Chad's accent reverberated in my ear as he spoke.

"That is until you decide to reject me again and dance with him."

His deep blue eyes darted in Earl's direction.

"Hey, it's your fault for catching me off guard," I teased before slugging his shoulder. "And we're dancing now, aren't we?"

"I guess we are, Miss Kristy."

His lips crooked with an adorable smirk.

My heart skipped with panic as he lifted me from the ground, spun me and dipped me. When I caught my breath, I couldn't stop giggling. This cowboy—the first to rattle my cage—was dismantling my well-constructed armor. I struggled to gain my composure, thinking it must be the drinks or the strange twang coming from the speakers. Either way, I had underestimated the impact of a country music bar.

Dancing the two-step with Chad freed my spirit. Scary as it was, I didn't want to stop. Chad's strong arms protected me from the speeding traffic weaving around us, and I settled into his arms like a peaceful Sunday afternoon drive.

Time stood still.

A tap on my shoulder startled me.

"Come on! Danielle's outside. Let's go!"

There was Chloe, on the track alone, trying to coax me off.

"What?" I responded with a wrinkled brow as I kept dancing.

"Let's go!" Chloe said, now blocking traffic.

"I'm not ready to go. All weekend, you both have been telling me I'm not myself, to perk up and get my bubbly back. Well, look! I have. So tell her I'm not ready yet," I insisted as I nodded to Chad to keep dancing.

"Shouldn't you go?" he asked with a furrowed brow.

With a coy smile, I changed the direction of the conversation.

"What? Are you already tired of this Northern girl that can't dance?"

Chad grasped my hand tighter and picked up our pace around the track. As we sunk back into our natural rhythm, my mind searched to define this unfamiliar feeling.

Was my ego so desperate for stroking that I would give up all sensibility and chose a stranger over friends?

My mind jumped to the irony of Chloe trying to coax me out of the bar. She was the night owl.

I stole a few more unrecognizable songs, before Chloe returned.

"Come on! Danielle's done."

What slipped out of my mouth shocked me.

"I'm not leaving unless he's comin'."

Chad's jaw dropped, flabbergasted by my bluntness.

Indifferent to my words, Chloe continued.

"I don't care who comes, as long as we go."

I paused in his eyes, still dumbfounded at my remark, not sure how to suck it back in. Yet part of me didn't want to. There was something about him I couldn't put my finger on and that bothered me. I was always dead on at seeing through people. For some unexplainable reason, I got lost in him.

Before I knew it, Chad, Chloe and some of Danielle's co-workers were in the limo, headed back to Danielle's temporary apartment. I had quit drinking hours before when I had handed the apology beer to Chad. I must have sensed tonight would not be a night to have clouded vision.

And I was right.

CHAPTER 7

Kiss A Girl

As we followed the occupants of the limo up the stairs toward Danielle's apartment, my brain halted my steps. This innocent flirt would be crossing boundaries if I took a strange cowboy into the personal space of an apartment. My heart was already speaking a foreign language which was bad enough.

"Hey, Danielle, isn't there a bar we could go to nearby?" I asked as she fumbled with her keys, trying to open the door of her apartment.

"I think there is a little bar around the corner that might still be open. It's across the street from the wine boutique where we had dinner the other night."

After managing to open the door, Danielle tossed the keys down the open air stairwell to where I was standing. Out of instinct, I reached for the keys, catching them in midair, and bobbled backwards against Chad's chest as his hands clutched my waist.

"Baby, you've got to be careful!" he warned.

Chad's voice dripped with concern for my well-being like that of a protective father grabbing his child's hand and pulling her back from the street. My backside sank into him, and I felt safe under his strong grip.

"Go ahead. Take my car. I'm out!" Danielle insisted as a mischievous smile lit up her face.

I didn't care what she was thinking. I was on a mission to demystify the cowboy and stay in God's good graces. I hadn't crossed a line yet, but, then again, I *never* had "feelings" before like I did that night.

"Chloe?" I asked, only half-hoping she would serve as a buffer.

However, she was already at the kitchen island mixing drinks.

At my request, Chad and I took a detour to the bar Danielle had suggested. At least there we would be out in public with our private conversation.

The atmosphere at the bar was low-key compared to where we had met earlier. There were a few tables of people scattered throughout, and the bar was full. Chad escorted me to a small table in the corner, pulled out my chair and smiled that mesmerizing grin.

Yep, we were much safer here.

The waitress approached, and Chad ordered two beers and a glass of water. We bantered back and forth getting lost in conversation.

"So, how long have you been divorced?" I pried.

"Divorce was final six months ago, today."

He set his drink on the table. The froth from his beer glossed his upper lip forcing me to take a deep breath to stay focused.

"It's ugly. Sixteen years of marriage, and she cheats."

He paused revealing more pain in his eyes.

"And with a tattooed guy none-the-less," he continued. "Who would have thought she would have thrown us all away for some graffiti covered loser?"

I connected with the resentment in his voice. Chad was clean-cut, handsome and as polite as they come.

Why do good guys always come in last?

His emotions crashed into my heart, and my chest tightened with each word.

"This is not how I imagined my life," he added. "I don't believe in divorce, yet here I am. She took my life AND my three boys with her. I wasn't prepared for this. Catholics are supposed to love 'til death do us part."

He's Catholic too? The list of coincidences kept growing.

As a Catholic, I could relate. Our religion is full of rules with right and wrong choices. Giving up on marriage was not a choice in my mind. I deemed rules as the compass to staying in God's good graces and struggled with those who broke them. However, I was also a realist who knew there were two sides to every story, leaving some exceptions to the rules—just no exceptions for me. I was taking no chances where God was concerned.

"Why do you think she cheated?" I inquired.

"I was married to my construction company and never realized how lonely she felt. I reckon I had a role in her pulling away."

He paused, bowing his head just enough for his hat to mask his distressed eyes.

"I just never thought she would give up on us for a rebel like him."

He took a deep breath to compose himself and switched gears.

Fixing his bold blue eyes on mine, he said, "Enough of my sorry story...what about you?"

My chest relaxed glad to escape the heavy dialog,

"What you see is what you get. Like I said, I'm an open book. I married my best friend from high school. We have three kids...a boy and two girls. My husband was like the brother I never had growing up. I think my parents like him more than me," I said chuckling, while continuing to crumple my drink napkin. "Patrick and I have been best friends for so long the line eventually became blurred...getting together after college. My husband's a good guy...a little uptight, but a good guy."

"He doesn't sound uptight if he lets you loose in Texas to dance with strange men."

Chad gave me a skeptical look.

"Well, I guess I should say uptight about everything BUT me."

I smiled at the thought of Patrick's goodness, but quickly deflated at the thought of his inability to express his feelings for me.

I blurted my thoughts.

"All through college Patrick's buddies would call him to ask permission to date me, and he never denied a one of 'em. I chalked it up to the fact that either he knew he had nothing to worry about since my reputation as a tease proceeded me, or he was hung up on his upbringing not being good enough for me. The funny thing is...most days, now, I don't feel I can live up to *his* expectations. I remember when we were teenagers washing his car. He would come behind me and rewash the area I had just done. Not much has changed. He's got a thing for perfection."

"No wonder he chose you," Chad teased.

His quick charm flushed my cheeks.

"Ha ha! You're good," I spouted, trying to compose myself from his flattery.

"Like I was saying...Patrick has a particular way of doing things. He's so busy trying to get things just right that he never relaxes long enough for a little spontaneity or adventure. Don't get me wrong...his OCD can be a good thing. He's successful and an incredibly hard worker. He even cleans and takes care of the house and kids much better than I do. He probably should have been the stay-at-home parent, and I should be using my finance degree from Notre Dame...but I HATE numbers."

My guilt snuck in at the thought of my inability to function as wife and mother without feeling a little less than.

Chad's eyes bore into my emptiness, yet I didn't flinch. His presence was calming.

I was not alone.

My insides began to quake at my revelation of how alone I had felt my entire life—until this moment.

Needing to deflect my irrational emotions, I thought of Patrick's goodness. He was my rock, never wavering when I leaned on him. He just couldn't give back. I accepted his limitations knowing how buttoned up he had to be to protect himself from the unpredictability of his father. I just didn't realize what I had given up in the process—being pursued as someone's great love, his priority, not just a conquest or ego boost. I may be Patrick's great love, but he was incapable of opening his heart to me.

Chad pulled me from my thought.

"Notre Dame, huh?"

"I told you I was an innocent flirt...a good 'ole Catholic girl."

"Innocent?" Chad questioned with a laugh and *that* heart melting smile of his.

"Yea...innocent!"

I pointed my finger at him.

"So don't get any ideas. I'm getting on a plane in a few hours."

"You're tough!" he harassed, while putting his hands in the air and shaking his head. "No worries, Kristy, I heard you loud and clear the first time, and, for some reason, I'm still here...against my better judgment."

Ohhh that grin!

"Hey! Thanks a lot!" I fired back, as I nudged his side.

"You know what I mean."

Chad's conciliatory tone made me blush again.

"No, I don't. Do tell."

I was fishing.

"There is something 'bout you, Kristy..."

He stopped in my eyes and caught his breath before he continued, "...like I've known you a lifetime."

His grin was intoxicating, and I froze as he leaned toward me. My heart stopped, thinking he was going to kiss me.

CHAPTER 8

I Could Get Used To You

Chad offered me his hand.

"Dance with me," he insisted.

"Here?"

My nerves leaked through my voice.

He didn't answer—just took charge. His hand scooped around my back pulling me into a tight embrace, while his hips swayed mine to the imaginary music. The moment mirrored my forgotten dream, and I didn't want to wake up.

The next thing I knew, the place was empty except for a lone man sitting at the end of the bar talking to the bartender. The chairs were on top of the tables. Closing time had come and gone, and so had my senses.

I found myself in the same predicament as earlier. I didn't want to let this cowboy loose. My heart was doing acrobatics—ones I deemed impossible. I needed to dig deeper into how this magician was getting my heart to perform these tricks. There had to be a catch—there always is. I needed more time to pull the curtain back and reveal the secrets behind his magic.

The electricity in the room was reminiscent of *The Notebook*, and not the kind you write in. In that movie, the main character, Allie, was conflicted by two loves—the "good guy," Lon, who loved her and whom her family approved of, and the passionate man, Noah, who was full of heart and struggles. After all my years of dating anyone and everyone who asked, I never discovered even one man who could reach the inner depths of me like Noah did with Allie. I married my "Lon," fully convinced a real life Noah was an unrealistic dream.

Could this cowboy be him?

Passion I had only dreamed about was percolating into my heart. This stranger had breached the inner depths of my soul—a soul I didn't even know existed within me.

Why wasn't my logic prevailing? These feelings were impossible...or were they?

We walked past the pool toward Danielle's apartment. The full moon reflecting off the water created a glow on our path. The night air was cool by Texas' standards, but not for this Northern Michigan girl. I kicked off my bronze boots, seizing the moment to prolong our evening, and waded into the pool. I made my way to the warmer water of the whirlpool, while Chad followed my lead by removing his boots and cuffing the bottom of his jeans. He sat down on the edge of the bricks that surrounded the rippling water I was wading through and submerged his feet.

"Tell me more about your upbringing," I inquired, while trying to distract myself from the racing heartbeat and sweaty palms that still loomed from our music-less dance.

"Not much more to tell. My two younger brothers are a pain, but I love 'em. They were always fixin' to keep up with me...even following me off to college. I can't complain though. They never missed one of my games. Hoops occupied my life and kept me out of trouble."

"You are TROUBLE!" I teased, splashing water in his direction.

Basketball too?

My heart couldn't take many more coincidences tugging on it. His responses kept jumping off the pages of my childhood diary.

I tried to keep him on his toes and me grounded.

"Is that where you met your wife?"

"Ex-wife," he corrected with a wrinkled brow. "And yes. We met there."

I dug deeper into a subject my mind disapproved of to counter-act his increasing grip on my heart.

"So, how'd your family take the whole divorce thing?"

"As well as any Catholic family would...not well. My mom took it the hardest. She was fond of Jo...the only daughter-in-law she had... and sad for our boys. She eventually realized I had no choice in the matter. Jo had checked out."

Chad's head hung a bit lower as I sat down beside him.

"My dad kept his opinion to himself, and I reckon my two brothers were in as much shock as I was," he added. "The whole family took it hard. This is not how I expected my life to end up, and I wouldn't wish it on my worst enemy."

Disappointment and defeat filled his eyes, and my heart sank at the concept of divorce. To ease his pain, I reached over squeezing the top of his hand which was propped on the bricks surround-ing the whirlpool. I felt my temperature rise and tried to distract myself with the fact Chad had only brothers—a wish of mine. The parallels with my childhood fantasy were getting ridiculous. He couldn't be the one I dreamt of.

Could he? No. Strong girls don't break their vows, strong girls don't give into feelings, and strong girls are not vulnerable to their hormones.

My mind kept my body in check for the time being. I needed the subject to change before my guilt hijacked the moment for which my heart yearned.

"You have been interrogating me all night. I believe it's my turn."

Chad's words were playful yet direct.

"I'm not done expelling the myth of you."

I splashed more water his direction hoping to extinguish the heat, but Chad gave a matter-of-fact rebuttal.

"I'm not a myth. I am what I am."

His eyes attached to mine, and my cheeks flushed.

"I can't wrap my mind around you," I blurted.

"Why do you have to? It is what it is."

His confident voice reassured my fluttering heart.

I didn't know what to do with this laid back Texan.

"How can you be so calm about all *this*?"

I shook my hands toward him and waived them around between us. He shrugged his well-defined shoulders and smiled.

"I just am. So, now quit avoiding the subject of you."

"OK...OK," I said as I put my hands up in defense. "I'll talk."

CHAPTER 9

Deep In The Night

The moon hung over the whirlpool like a spotlight, revealing the random swirling patterns of the bubbling waters, symbolic of my insides. His eyes followed me with a look of genuine interest, as he prodded for more information about my identity. I wasn't fond of the shift in the interrogation process and sensed Chad could read every emotion invading my heart.

What is happening to me?

Chad hunched forward, resting his elbows on his knees, while his bare feet remained submerged. His powerful calves peaked above the waterline. I sensed I might be in trouble if he revealed the rest of his calves with another cuff of his jeans. As I glanced upward, his smoky blue eyes met mine, drawing me in like a mesmerizing melody.

Stop, Kristy. Stop the inappropriate thoughts.

I'm not sure which was a worse vice, the bulging calves or inviting eyes. I stood and began pacing back and forth on the whirlpools's wrap around seat, trying not to let my dress get wet.

I could get past his mouth-watering exterior traits, but his ability to play my inner heart strings was a skill I thought no human possessed. My normal open-book mentality didn't seem quite the same knowing of his x-ray vision. I wasn't used to being viewed through eyes like his. I tried to focus on black and white facts, and not the unfamiliar turbulence within me.

Caving to his inquiries, I leaked information like ooze from a cracked egg.

"My upbringing was text book...nothing extraordinary. I'm an only child from a middle class family in a classic Michigan small town, opposite Detroit. Quiet was not in our vocabulary, despite being a house of only three. My father was a college educated salesman...my mother a homemaker. She left college to marry my father in Germany where he was stationed after being drafted during the Vietnam era...not his favorite time. He isn't much of a risk taker and neither am I, except if you count taking his life in his own hands when arguing with my mother. Mild mannered is not in the family vocab, as bickering is a way of life. Have you ever seen the television shows *Everybody Loves Raymond* or *Seinfeld*?"

"Of course," Chad replied.

His deep blue eyes never left mine.

"Well...my parent's relationship made Ray Romano's and George Castanza's parents' relationships look easy. Each day of my childhood I wondered if today would be the day they announced their divorce, yet divorce never came. We're Catholic...or at least we went through the motions of being Catholic."

"I understand," Chad interjected with fervor.

"Catholic rules have been my road map to God's good graces. I definitely wanted to be in God's favor...and my parent's as well. If all were focused on my 'good girl' accomplishments, I could keep the peace within my home and with God. It was a simple life in my eyes...our family endured no real hardships or major tragedies. I never went without and was an ambitious, social girl with big hopes and big dreams...appearing to have *it* all together...whatever *it* was. But I longed for the day I could escape my small town. Sometimes I wondered why I wanted out. Life there seemed easy...grades, basketball and boys summed up my accomplishments."

"Boys, huh?" he prodded.

Feeling back in control, I plopped myself down next to him on the cool bricks.

"Your dress!"

Before I knew what was happening, Chad reached over the edge of the whirlpool, grazing my bare leg with his hand and lifted part of my dress from the water.

I started to giggle.

So much for control.

I hoped to deflect from my clumsiness.

"Once a flirt, always a flirt," I teased, batting my long eyelashes which now lacked the day's mascara.

"Somehow I don't believe damsel in distress is your tactic."

"Maybe not," I responded, trying to distract from the wet of my dress. "But would you believe I was voted most likely to be President AND most likely to be on the dating game?"

"Brains and beauty. Hmmm...that explains everything," he joked.

"Ha, ha...very funny," I added with a smirk.

"So graceful wasn't part of the resumé?"

"My resumé was just fine, thank you."

Hoping to redirect my stirring emotions, I recited black and white facts.

"I did miss the coveted Valedictorian spot and had to settle for Salutatorian, despite my 4.0. An English teacher gave me a grade I thought was unfair, while giving the introvert I was tied with an A. He told me I was a horrible writer and only got good grades because I had everyone snowed with my 'goodie, goodie' act. I hated that teacher, but Patrick loved the guy."

A bit of disgust snuck into my voice.

"The irony was that I wasn't acting," I continued. "I was a priss in every sense of the word."

I waived my finger and shook my head at him for dramatic effect or, possibly, to convince myself of what I was about to say.

"As I told you...you picked the wrong one to go home with."

"No, I didn't," he assured, with his calm accent and that smile of his.

With a nod, he directed me back to my story without flinching. "Now go on."

"Like I said...rules have been my compass. Most weekends you could find my classmates huddled around a bonfire in the backwoods down some two-track with Busch Lights in hand."

I chuckled recalling a memory from our two-stepping.

"Sounds like that country song from earlier tonight," I joked.

"I knew my country music would grow on you," he replied with a chuckle.

A tingling sensation traveled down my spine as I recalled how the strange, twangy music stirred foreign feelings in me, but my mind pretended to ignore his comment.

"When I did show up to the party in the middle of nowhere, everyone knew I wouldn't be drinking...more than likely my motive was to catch the attention of a hot guy. That wasn't against my rules...but drinking was. Plus, I wasn't going to jeopardize my true love, basketball, by getting drunk," I explained.

"You played basketball?"

He looked stunned—which was understandable since I'm only 5'4".

"Yep! I was brought up to Varsity during my freshman year by a coach who believed in little 'ole me. He sparked a chord within me and made me believe I could play despite my size. I had a scholarship to play at a small college, which probably had more to do with my good grades than my passion to play, but instead decided to accept the challenge of venturing off to South Bend, Indiana."

"I'm starting to understand why your head keeps spinning."

Chad caressed the back of my hand easing my anxiety, and I felt as if he connected to what I was feeling about all the coincidences.

"Remember, I didn't put out either," I jabbed, trying to break the grasp he had on my desires.

"Right," he murmured.

"I believed boyfriends were only sticking around in hopes of being the one to crack my vault, but I enjoyed the attention. I didn't care about being labeled a 'tease' or a 'goodie goodie,' because that made me stand out from the rest of the hormonally confused. I was simply passing time until I found the man of my dreams."

My words stung my tongue.

Was he sitting right here in front of me?

Ignoring the virtual pain, I kept up momentum.

"My goal...simple...stay in God's good graces, and He would deliver my heart's desires. Well..at least that's what I believed."

He lifted my sagging chin and looked into me.

"And now?"

"Now..." I sighed. "I don't know. I thought I had all my heart's desires until YOU crashed into my life."

We just sat there gazing into one another's eyes, enjoying the peace of the moonlit night. Silence wasn't my friend, but, tonight, I sank into it like a soft featherbed, never wanting to be awakened.

My chest was heavy. I couldn't breathe.

CHAPTER 10

Out Last Night

The sun was rising as I drove Danielle's unfamiliar car down a strange, empty street. I didn't recognize this person I'd become overnight. My heart was bleeding, spilling over. I was overwrought with emotions unknown to me. I was trying to keep my hand steady on the wheel and my rational mind intact.

It could not be him. He was not supposed to exist.

How could he?

Yet there he was in the passenger seat, staring at me. I tried to remain in control even though my heart was exposed. His soothing Southern voice directed me through the streets of Houston. I could not avoid feeling his eyes pierce right into my soul, never wavering. He knew me to the depth of my being, and I knew him too.

How was this possible?

My mind raced with so many more questions, yet I was speechless.

The drive felt like eternity. However, I did not want it to end.

If I could only keep driving, never stop, and never let him leave.

He returned us to the parking lot of the bar that changed the course of my existence. My heart sank deep within the walls of my chest. It couldn't be over—not yet. I had so many questions. I had to make sense of the last 12 hours, but there was no solution. My heart raced, my mind was weak, and I had no idea how to cope. He smiled his wide, mesmerizing grin as he reached for my hand. Squeezing it tightly with both of his hands, he stared into my blurred blue eyes.

For the first time in my life, words were not necessary. We were both feeling it, whatever *it* was. I couldn't go—not now.

What was that drifting down my cheek?

Chad reached up and gently wiped my tear, his hand lingering. As he opened his door, he never lost eye contact.

How could I let him go?

The enormity of the moment engulfed me. There has to be a logical explanation. I pleaded with my brain—there has to be! For the first time in my 35 years, logic could not explain what I was feeling. As I pulled the car away, my sobs erupted like an inactive volcano that was deemed dormant. My hands pounded violently against the steering wheel. I looked in the mirror. He was still staring.

Why? Why was this happening?

Tears flowed down my cheeks and pooled in my lap. My mind was spinning. Yet, I was eerily peaceful. I had no idea how to go back. Somehow, I returned to Danielle's apartment. My weary hand opened the door to find Danielle and Chloe staring at me.

"Well?" Chloe inquired, morning coffee in hand and a bewildered smirk on her face.

She knew this guy had thrown me for a loop.

I stared back with pleading eyes.

Danielle piped in with her gotcha attitude.

"How was he?"

She didn't really know me at all. Despite the fact that I had flown all this way to make her transition to Texas easier—less lonely—I was the one feeling lonely and lost. How could I muster up enough energy to pack my bags and get on a plane? I couldn't. Not just yet—not now.

I threw myself on the open pull-out couch in the small living room where the girls were lounging. They waited for my lips to move. My mind was roaming, hoping to bump into something familiar, something concrete. The stable world I had known had vanished. My flight was three hours away.

How could I leave feeling like this?

Maybe, I didn't have to.

"Wow! That must have been some night!" Danielle probed again.

"Are you OK?" Chloe asked, now looking concerned. "I've never seen you at a loss for words before."

Sleep deprived and confused, I finally spoke.

"No. No! I...I...I'm not OK. I can't leave! I just can't! I need one more day...just one more day."

An annoying dampness had crept back into my eyes. Tears couldn't be happening—not now, not ever.

I don't cry!

"So something did happen!? Spill it, Kristy!" Danielle pried with her sheepish grin, pouncing eagerly to push me off my moral high ground.

"Nothing happened! I just can't get on that plane."

My mind began turning with plausible reasons to stay an extra day. I turned to Chloe in anguish.

"Please!" I begged. "We have to miss our plane. I need more time. I have to figure this out. There has to be an explanation. I just...need...more...time. Can't we go tomorrow?"

"I'm not missing our plane," Chloe responded in a clipped, mothering tone. "We have to go home. There is no reason to stay.

We've been gone for four days, and it is time to go home. You need to go home."

In that moment, I hated her. I had been there for her time and time again. I always bent over backwards to do what she wanted. This time I needed her. I needed her to stay with me.

"I have never asked you for anything, and I am asking you now... please miss the flight with me," I pleaded. "I HAVE to prove to myself he is not *him*!"

By this time, Chloe was already up and moving around the apartment—popping ibuprofen, shoving stuff in her suitcase, running the shower, distracted.

Danielle, our giddy spectator, was enjoying the role reversal between Chloe and me. My eyes darted to her for back-up. However, Danielle was far too entertained by my relentless pleas to come to my aid. My whining and badgering continued solo.

Chloe finally spoke. However, she had a stern tone that I had never heard pass from her lips.

"One day isn't going to change things, and I am not willing to put up with the wrath of my husband calling me 'irresponsible' if I missed the flight. Plus, I miss the kids and God knows he can't get 'em ready for school in the morning like Patrick does. He's on call tonight. We have to go. Get up and pack! We're going!"

I couldn't envision what burned my tongue next.

"Can't we just tell him it was cancelled and find a later flight?"

She stopped bustling and looked at me.

"Who are you..."

I interrupted her as an idea came to me like a bolt of lightning in a storm.

"Today is daylight savings! We moved the clocks ahead an hour last night. He can't fault you for that," I pursuaded. "This is the one day of the year where this will work! What are the odds of this? See? We were *meant* to stay. It is so logical."

Her expression was lifeless, so I continued with even more vigor.

"He will understand that we drank too much, forgot to change the clocks and missed our flight by an hour. You KNOW me! I don't scheme. I don't plot. I AM the 'good girl!' I stick my neck out for everyone else all the time. I keep myself in check. I'm the rational one. I don't break the rules, EVER! But I am asking you now... pleading with you...do this for me. Don't you see how important this is?"

She had already shut me out. She was not budging. We were getting on the plane.

CHAPTER 11

My Wish

I was slumped, moving with heavy steps, pouting—pissed!

As we maneuvered through security, Chloe worked to boost my dragging spirit.

"I'm ready to be home. Reality doesn't seem that bad after a weekend away. Plus, I'm excited about your idea. So what's our first step to getting our chapter of CHADD off the ground?"

I was silent. My gut was rotting, and no bait she dangled was appetizing. The passion I felt on the flight down for starting a new chapter of CHADD had been snuffed out by the existence of a living, breathing Chad. The irony of his name smacked me.

"You'll have to give me all the info the national organization sent you," Chloe urged. "After all our ideas over the years, this is the first one that intrigues us both. This is exactly what our lives need...a purpose outside of wife and mother. What's your plan this week?"

Chloe kept prodding. It was as if she had turned into me.

Listening to *her* try to goad *me* into conversation was odd. My pursed lips were not going to dislodge. Up ahead—my solace. There were empty chairs at the gate opposite ours. I sat, created my own little cage and gazed at the plank I would soon be forced to walk. The gate read "Delayed," which simply postponed my demise. I shot Chloe one last desperate look.

Tormented by these impossible feelings, I pondered calling him. I wanted to hear his tender and assuring Southern accent one last time.

Would feeling his voice be the medicine I needed to abolish the clots now surrounding my heart or would it stop my blood flow altogether?

I froze in my thought of home.

As the terminal awakened with grumblings, I felt a wind from people briskly moving about. This was it. I wearily lifted my head towards the gate and saw "Cancelled!" My eyes burst open wide and my failing heart experienced the shock of life-saving paddles on my chest as the blood flow returned to my arteries.

I was alive! Was this fate?

Almost impossible for me to absorb, an ice storm in the Midwest, which first delayed our flight, worsened to include gale winds, plummeting temperatures and a blizzard of snow. This crazy combination of circumstances ultimately caused our flight and all other flights to Chicage to be grounded. Even if flights were to resume later that night, I knew our "puddle-jumper" across Lake Michigan would never be able to fly into the westward moving storm.

Could this be a "sign" Chad was really the man in my dreams?

Wind returned to my sail, and my exploration into this new mesh of emotions continued. Chloe could spend her time at the airport waiting for flights to resume, but I wasn't wasting another minute. I had been given a precious gift—time.

I was like a giddy school girl rejoicing in her triumph over her older sister in the spelling bee. There was no way to wipe the smile off my face—at least not for the next 24 hours. I convinced the ticket agent to book me on a flight for the next day and called *him.*

"Be careful what you wish for...cuz you won't believe what just happened," I said.

After my brief call with Chad, Chloe and I hailed a cab and climbed inside.

"You don't have to gloat," she said with a mystified smile and a shake of her head. "But I'm glad you're back to your bubbly self."

The reality of what just happened was almost too much to comprehend, but, at this point, *everything* about the past 24 hours was surreal.

As we drove back to Danielle's executive apartment, my mind sobered. I was not boarding a plane back to my scripted life. I was staying here, able to explore the myth of Chad being *him*—the one from my childhood dreams.

My feelings couldn't be real. Could they?

Terror overwhelmed me as if I stood at the front of the roller coaster line and was forced to climb aboard. I hate roller coasters. I never ride them. But what choice did I have? My wish came true, and it was time to set fear aside. Control was out of my hands.

If the flight back to cold Michigan had taken off, I would have never looked back at my encounter with Chad. I would have chalked it up to my mind playing tricks with my heart and accepted that my feelings for Chad were not real, only fantasy. I would have clung to the logic that love at first sight is merely infatuation, not *real* love. My black and white image of love would have overruled my heart, and I would have convinced myself that passionate love dies over time.

Who needs passion anyway?

I married a wonderful and devoted man, but I've always lived a life without passion. I convinced myself that a friendship nurtured over time is *real* love, despite my yearning for passion of the heart. Logical love was the only type of love I had ever felt—at least before Chad. My feelings for *him* were foreign to me, yet undeniable. These were feelings I had dreamt about and watched played out in movies like *The Notebook* but never experienced.

Patrick was my husband, a covenant I did not take lightly. Yet my heart contradicted my thoughts. I couldn't think about home— not yet—blocking it out of my mind to focus on the gift I had been given. I had another day in Texas to explore the foreign feeling paralyzing my heart. I prayed for answers. Maybe Chad was the answer.

Chad climbed out of his truck. I snickered to myself. Of course he had a truck—it's Texas! He was wearing khaki shorts and a slim-fitting, light blue, button-down shirt that hung untucked around his slender waist. His attire was a far cry from the jeans, boots and cowboy hat he had worn the night before. Despite his huge smile that entranced me on the dance floor, I couldn't help but focus on his amazing calves.

Strangely enough, I have a thing for calves, and Chad's were even more supersonic in the daylight when not hidden beneath the cuff of his jeans like the night prior. Calves were at the top of my list of favorite features in the perfect mate, and his were sculpted like a perfectly inverted heart. Trying to ignore the ever growing list of coincidences that were making my heart do a foreign dance, my mind darted to the non-superficial traits on my list for protection as I was sure Chad wouldn't be able to conquer all of those.

Could he?

Startling me from my trance, his strong arms lifted me in a bear hug and spun me around.

"Hey, baby!"

He spoke with his signature Southern drawl and wide grin.

"Couldn't stay away, could ya?"

I didn't answer him. My head was still spinning. I'm not quite sure if the cause was his amazing calves, the rush of twirling around or just the fact I was in his arms. It had been only a few hours since

I said my forever goodbye, ready to stand my moral high ground and return to the life I chose with my best friend. Yet here I was in his presence once again with the same rush of emotions.

My mind replayed Chad's words from the night before, realizing how prophetic his statement was.

He had said,"your leaving is not the end of us, but a preview of the good to come in our lives."

I started to feel maybe he was right.

As we arrived at the restaurant, I noticed the floor to ceiling windows which made it like a giant aquarium. Chad opened the door for me, an unfamiliar gesture I appreciated. Looking at him instead of where I was walking, I tripped, and Chad grabbed my hand.

"Falling for me already?" he joked. "I guess you are easier than I thought."

I dropped his hand and slugged his shoulder in playful protest.

"Don't bet on it!" I sounded.

I led him to a eight-person circular table in the corner of the restaurant where Chloe, Danielle and some of her co-workers from the other night were already seated. I felt comfort in knowing their presense would serve as a buffer between my pounding heart and Chad's presence. Here, I was safe. I told myself none of God's covenants were being broken. A group dinner wasn't a sin. My yearning heart—maybe—but not if I didn't act on it, and, if history was any indication, I *wouldn't* act on it. I had built my life on my righteousness, and, if I strayed, *who* would that make me? A flirt maybe, but not a cheat!

Despite my interrogation throughout the evening, Chad's perfect resumé remained unblemished. I wasn't ready for our time to end and needed to debunk the myth with more intimate questioning. We retreated back to Danielle's apartment—alone—while the rest of our dinner companions visited another bar. I was caught in a gray area and didn't want to think about right verses wrong. I was finally "feeling," and I didn't want it to end. I needed to cherish every moment of time I had left in Texas. I wasn't going to squander one moment together.

"You really have never seen snow?"

I resorted to lighter topics back in Danielle's apartment.

"Nope...never."

"Do you want to?"

My lighthearted voice masked my motive. I was curious if he had entertained the thought of coming to Northern Michigan, the place holding me hostage.

"Only if it involves you, baby."

He smiled with his irresistible charm, squeezed my arm and continued, "I'll go anywhere if it means another day with you. Even a blizzard...I think."

His mouth made a crooked grin I longed to kiss.

"You don't know what you're getting yourself into, Mr. Texas," I said in my flirty tone with my eyes wide and lashes fluttering.

My heart was ready to sprint places I deemed sinful, but I didn't care. I waited my whole life for this "feeling" that I had only seen in movies. I craved a taste of the forbidden apple.

Hadn't this 'good girl' earned it?

Danielle and Chloe returned to the apartment and found Chad and I nestled on the couch, half asleep, but still talking. Danielle immediately disappeared into her bedroom. Chloe updated us on the rest of their evening, while standing in the kitchen mixing a drink.

After a few minutes, Danielle emerged with a bag.

"I don't want to spoil your quiet, but a few of my friends are headed over and who knows how long they'll stay. So why don't you take my bedroom."

She glanced our way smiling as she continued talking.

"I'll sleep on the couch tonight. I have to leave early for work anyway...so, remember, you'll have to get a taxi to the airport in the morning," she said. "Or have Chad take you both."

She raised her eyebrows in my direction. Her actions were oblivious to Chad who had stood up from the couch and walked toward the bathroom.

I knew my move into the bedroom didn't make me look good to my friends, but I didn't care. I wanted to be alone with him for as long as possible. This was probably the last of our time together, unless Patrick left me or died. Neither scenario was appealing.

My nervous chatter continued as I sat on top of the bed propped up against a mound of pillows. Chad wrapped his strong arms around me and pulled me into his chest. I melted under his spell.

"I shouldn't be feeling this way," he said.

His guilt sneaked into the moment.

"That makes two of us. But I don't care! I've waited a lifetime to feel this way. You've awakened something in me, and I don't want it to end," I confessed.

His eyes fixed on mine. I longed for his lips to press against mine. My pulse quickened, but he restrained. He didn't want to be "that guy"—the same guy who stole his wife.

We sat in silence entranced by each other's eyes—lost. I found a peacefulness I had never known, while wrapped in his arms. My cheek settled comfortably into his chest like *the* missing puzzle piece. Chad and I fit, and he wasn't afraid to tell me so. I had never known any man so expressive and so respectful. His quiet confidence about us being "united for a reason" and "in time we would understand why" was baffling to me. My mind doubted him, yet my heart wanted to believe. I needed to believe.

He whispered, "I just know, baby," at the right moment which eased my doubts. He enveloped me in his arms and held me, expecting nothing in return. I felt protected for the first time in my life by this stranger.

Or was he not a stranger after all? Only God had known my heart. Could this be His doing?

Chad felt like the answer to all my desires, including the ones I'd never spoken out loud. He defied logic, and my mind was as overwhelmed as my heart. Yet there he was, staring at me—his smoky eyes burning right into my soul. I could not deny his existence. I searched to find a flaw because my heart could not handle prolonging this childish dream.

"Love at first sight" was no longer a cliché to me. I understood how the heart could take over the mind. My judgment of others was thrown out the window. Even though I believed no intimacy unless married, my mind wanted to surrender to the yearning of my heart. If I had experienced these feelings before marriage, I don't know how I would have stayed a virgin until my wedding night. All of my life, I had followed God's covenants so righteously to earn a front-row spot in heaven. I based my worth on my strength, yet the biggest challenge had been missing—the feeling of true, heart-stopping, can't get enough—LOVE.

This was the feeling Chad ignited, a feeling I wanted to explore to the depths of me. I held my breath, exhaled and brought my lips to his—losing myself. His warmth melted into me. Our emotional connection converged on a whole new level. Time stopped.

"I feel it too, Kristy, but I know you'll hate yourself in the morning...and me. I can't bear that."

His eyes looked heavy and conflicted with stress.

"I can't do what was done to me. That's not who I am," he added.

I was finally willing to give all of me to a man without strings attached, and he was strong enough to refuse my body in an effort to connect with my soul. He didn't want to taint any future we may have. Proving to me, Chad must be the man in my dreams.

I didn't want to hold myself back. I knew Chad was right, but I didn't care. I wanted to feel, even if there were consequences.

CHAPTER 12

Don't

"So May...huh, baby?"

Chad's question startled me from the quiet of the morning and the comfort of being nuzzled safe in his chest.

"Yep, May," I replied with a hint of a smile, while matted blonde locks impaired my vision.

"Which weekend is your 5K?"

Chad was exploring the carrot I had previously dangled.

"I'm not exactly sure, but it's been Mother's Day weekend the past two years."

My insides were tingling at the thought of this dream not ending.

"You realize I don't know if I'll be able to stay away from you knowing you're at a hotel alone in a strange city," he added.

His face locked on mine.

"Oh, really?" I asked, trying to hide my giddy demeanor.

"Baby, looks like it might be year number three where you don't run," he teased.

"Don't tempt me. I told you I hate running. but I have to do it this year. I promised myself no more excuses of cold weather and hangovers. I need to prove I can do it even if Chloe chickens out."

"Then, maybe, just maybe, you'll have a secret fan on the sidelines watching...and wishing," he teased.

His eyes penetrated to depths of me, far beneath where I had ever been.

"Wishing what?"

My tone was sassy to hide the desire oozing from my heart.

"I think you know," he insisted with a smirk.

The tires rhythmically hummed along the expressway as we made our way to the airport. My mind dug deep into its archives, searching for where along my journey toward my "Happily Ever After" I gave up on a romantic, passionate love existing for me.

Why did I give up on finding the "him" I longed for? Had I settled by marrying Patrick?

Chad's touch distracted me. From the driver's seat Chad had reached across the center console and placed his hand on top of mine. He turned up the country station and started singing the lyrics, while caressing my finger.

"Baby, Baby...Don't. Don't just say you're leaving. Why don't you just stay a little bit longer..."

I couldn't help but smile, despite the bleeding within my heart. Chad was singing to me, another wish from my dreams, making me feel like the most important person alive. I don't think my heart could take much more. I interrupted my gushing.

"I see you're trying to woo me with someone else's words now."

"Billy Currington's to be exact," he said with a coy chuckle. "I can't help it if I get to you. It's not my fault the most appropriate country song comes on the radio just as you're about to leave me. I don't want you to leave...not now...not ever...but I know you have to, baby."

In that moment, his eyes spoke things his lips never could.

Dampness seeped into my eyes where it did not belong. I broke his gaze and peered out the window. What I saw was as breathtaking as what I was feeling. The field as we entered the airport was a magnificent blue hue, unlike anything I had ever seen.

"What's that?" I asked.

"Isn't it amazing? I love this time of year when the brown of the winter starts to fade and a new horizon blooms. That's Texas' state flower...bluebonnet. And it smells as sweet as it looks...like someone else I know."

He gazed my direction with a mischievous smile. His look pierced my heart like a jolt of electrical current.

"I must say...it's beautiful, but I'm ready to get out of Texas and see my kids," Chloe chimed in.

Her voice startled me. I almost forgot she was in the backseat. I'm glad my safety net had me harnessed to reality.

As Chad pulled the car to the curb, I wasn't ready to leave these feelings. I dreamt my whole life of feeling this free. I had to let it go just as quickly as I had found it—whatever "it" was. As he came around to open my door for me like the consummate Southern gentleman he was, he took my hand and pulled me to my feet in a tight embrace, neither of us wanting to let go.

Chad whispered in my ear with his irresistible Southern drawl.

"I feel it too, baby."

He lightly brushed my cheek with the back of his fingers, looked into my soul and kissed me. Tears started to fall onto his fingers, and he spoke softly with glassy eyes.

"Don't."

Chad breathed life into my dead heart and stirred something so deep within me. The life I had once known was shattered. I had no idea where to go from here. I was lost. I felt like someone picked up the snow globe containing my unblemished, white picket fence life and shook it violently. The scene inside would never look the same.

I would never be the same.

CHAPTER 13

Undo It

On the plane bound for home, my heart felt defeated and my mind shattered.

Why am I "feeling" these feelings now? This isn't fair! It's too late! I have a life, a husband, three kids. This is crazy! God, why Chad? Why now?

My watery eyes turned icy, and my heart hardened. Anger engulfed my spirit.

How could a loving God do this to me?

I pleaded with Him. I follow your commandments, I obey the Sacraments, I was a "good girl" and *this* is the reward I get?

Where had I gone wrong? Why did I stop believing in a passionate existence?

My list of Prince Charming attributes flashed before my eyes, just the way it had been scribbled into my diary during my adolescence years.

My Prince Charming (My hero)

Sincere smile
Loves to dance
Catholic
Athletic (Basketball a must)
Amazing calves
Eyes that talk
Sings his emotions to me (even if out of tune)
No sisters, two brothers (This only child does not want to compete with girls)
Strong to protect me from harm
Pursues me with his whole heart and soul
Puts my feelings before himself
An open, honest and playful best friend
Can just BE (Peaceful Soul)

Why had I lost faith in my dreams becoming reality?

I rehashed the comparisons between the list of Chad's attributes, the requirements of my childhood Prince Charming and the man I married. My goal was to debunk Chad from the fantasy list so these *feelings* cease, and I could go back to my secure life with Patrick.

Chad couldn't be real, and, even if he was, I'd have to forget him.

With hopes of resorting to my traditional black and white reasoning to reaffirm my marriage, I tried to undo my irrational feelings for a mere stranger. My mind drifted to Patrick and high school.

I continued to flirt with jocks and plan my perfect life after high school, while Patrick moved to the next phase in his life—college. I missed seeing my best friend every day, and Patrick wasn't one for talking on the phone. He was only an hour or so away from our hometown attending a state school, but, to me, he might as well have been living in Alaska. On every holiday and school break, Patrick would show up at my house, including a few random occasions when he seemed most interested in seeking life advice from my daddy. I never fully understood their connection since my daddy was a salesman and couldn't answer a question straight if his life depended on it. But my daddy was fun to be around, always the life of the party—just like Patrick.

Patrick's parents only lived a few miles away, but he would often stay with us in the guest room during those visits. He never said why, and I didn't care since Patrick's presence was like a snake charmer who prevented the venomous bites of my parent's bickering. A few years later I would come to find out that he was actually avoiding conflict in his own home when his parents divorced after 26 years of marriage just before Patrick graduated college. Patrick wasn't one to express feelings, but his visits confirmed he was fond of my family and always would be a part of it—even if he didn't verbalize his emotions like chatty me.

Sometime during my last year of high school, the phone rang. It was Patrick. I hadn't seen him for many months since he left for his second year at Central Michigan University.

"Hey, Kris! How you been?" he asked.

It was a surprise to hear his voice, but we slipped right back into our usual rhythm.

"Hey, you! What a surprise to hear from Mr. College," I joked. "I'm really glad you actually found time to call me."

My humbled tone came out like a grateful servant shocked to have been acknowledged by her important employer.

"I always have time for you. How's your year going? I'm sure you're tearing it up on the court."

He was so supportive of everything I did, even basketball, regardless of it not being a game he was interested in.

"So far so good. Thanks for asking. So, to what do I owe this pleasure? You need chick advice already?" I prodded.

"You're so funny I forgot to laugh," Patrick shot back. "Maybe I shouldn't ask you what I was going to."

He was baiting me, and we both knew this dance.

"OK, OK...tell me...what's up?" I asked with piqued curiosity.

He knew I couldn't stand not to be in the know.

"Never mind. You wouldn't want to a go college fraternity dance anyway. You're probably too busy with high school stuff," Patrick teased.

Now, he was the one laughing.

"What?! Of course I want to go, but I need details!" I demanded.

"I've been inducted as TKE president, and there's this dance."

"Oh...so I'm your secret weapon," I joked, snorting ever so slightly. "Can't you do better than me, Mr. College Man?"

"Yeah...probably," he said in his witty sarcastic tone. "But I don't want to worry about some silly date the first night I'm in charge. So you'll come?"

"Of course!" I said obligingly, as though I was doing *him* a great favor.

But, I was secretly smiling. Patrick hadn't forgotten me, and I was going to a college party!

When I arrived in Mount Pleasant, I didn't expect what I found. Patrick had blossomed. He was bolder, more confident. He was no longer the shy, skinny, "boy next door." He had matured into a muscular, 6'1", broad-shouldered, college stud, and his newfound role as fraternity president helped morph him into a witty, popular, driven guy with plenty of interested female admirers. The insecurities of his modest upbringing had been shoved to the back burner. He had evolved into the type of man I always dreamed of, minus the cocky and sarcastic attitude accompanying his physical transformation.

I was surprised how his changes made me pause. Had our desires flip-flopped?

I found myself hoping to find out if his kissing had improved, but no lip-locking opportunities presented themselves at the party. Patrick was too busy being the "Big Man On Campus." I was simply his arm candy—nothing more, nothing less.

While our dating relationship never bloomed, Patrick continued to.

CHAPTER 14

Small Town USA

Headed home, I stared out the airplane window. The cottony clouds seemed in harmony with one another, almost Heaven-like. Maybe they knew something I didn't. I pondered why Patrick never once expressed his love or desire for a commitment during our summers together after high school.

Why wasn't I good enough for "Mr. Big Man On Campus?"

My reflections continued, as I tried to sort out my tainted white picket fence life.

While attending the University of Notre Dame, my list of boyfriends grew longer. Some would visit me in my hometown, and there would be Patrick—the brother I never had, and the son my parents wanted—hanging out with us. No one ever discouraged Patrick from hanging around, and he never missed any important family gatherings. During my junior year at Notre Dame, I brought home my then boyfriend and a few other friends for Thanksgiving. As we were getting ready to sit down to eat, Patrick walked in with a miniature Norfolk Pine, fully-decorated Christmas tree.

"It's about time you got here, Patrick! We were missing you!" my mother shouted.

She gave him a big bear hug, while he was still holding the tiny tree. Patrick wasn't much of a hugger, despite my mother's attempts to break him of his formality for years. After her overbearing squeeze, he handed her the tree. He was always so thoughtful to my parents. Unphased by the beeps from the expired oven timer, my mother continued to dote on Patrick. She set the Christmas tree on the counter, front and center in our large kitchen window—a place of honor for Mother, but not me. That location had been tainted by Patrick's "it" conversation a few years back. The same pit returned to my stomach as I recalled staring blankly out that window during his confession.

"Aren't you going to get up? Patrick's here," my mother shouted into the dining room, while hugging him once more before tending to the timer.

I excused myself from our guests to say hello, but I wasn't about to compete with my mother for Patrick's attention. We already fought like sisters over the attention of my daddy.

"So, who's the flavor of the month?" Patrick joked just quiet enough for my guests not to hear.

Did he just say that? What does he care?

It's not like he's ever shown any interest in pursuing me for his own since I was thirteen. Girlfriend is a foreign word to him. At least I have long-term relationships. Patrick on the other hand, dates but never commits. I know his limitations. Maybe someday he'll get his act together.

I punched him on the arm and said, "Nice to see you, too."

Patrick was my best friend and always would be. Boyfriends knew it, accepted it and couldn't help but like him.

One would think that among all the smart, eligible bachelors on Notre Dame's campus, my Prince Charming would be there somewhere. I did my best to find him, dating everyone who asked me out. I even had a few long-term relationships, but, in the back of my mind, I knew each was not *him*. I was saving myself for my one *true* love and was just passing the time until he presented himself. I knew he must exist because every movie and each song described that intimate connection I longed to have. But I had never felt anything remotely close to that "movie feeling" or been so lost in someone's eyes that I could not mentally or physically control myself.

I was always in control.

Sometimes in my dorm room, I would stare at the ceiling and dream of a changed, more open Patrick rescuing me from my solitude. My mind would secretly drift to a place where Patrick had escaped his protected heart just enough to meet my passionate side. I knew his boundaries, but the odds were more in his favor than any other Notre Dame guy I dated thus far. Patrick had proven trustworthy, noble and the closest I had come to a real prince. 'Domers' were proving NOT to be marriage material for me, no matter how much I wanted them to be. Each guy would simply pass the time until either I got bored or they got tired of waiting.

I kept searching.

Patrick would routinely jab, "Your daddy sent you to Notre Dame for that MRS degree. What's the hold up? You've had enough of 'em parading around here. Can't you make up your mind?"

What was the hold up?

It wasn't for a lack of trying. I just never felt the connection I dreamed about, which was possibly the real reason I never gave in fully to my hormones and upheld the Catholic rules. I had been a "good girl," waiting for him.

Why couldn't I find him?

Boyfriends, yes. Passion, no.

I wanted true intimacy—someone to love me to the depth of his soul—a soul I hoped to experience to the depths of mine. I began to think perhaps passion was a lie, or I just hadn't earned it. Either way, for me it didn't exist.

I must have decided the first of the two must be more accurate, concluding that passionate love must be a fantasy written for books and played out in movies but not a long lasting love upon which that forever was built on. Just look at my parents! They fight like cats and dogs, but are still together after 30 years and never an ounce of passion between them—that I've seen. Passion—being skeptical that it even exists—must eventually die. Otherwise, why would there be so many divorces?

Based on this logic, I convinced myself passion would be a bonus, not a necessity, and loyalty must be the key to my "Happily Ever After." After searching for my Prince Charming for what felt like a lifetime, I convinced myself he would never surface because he probably wasn't real.

What I did know at the time was that boyishly handsome Patrick—my best friend and permanent fixture in my life—was the best part of me. I wished he would pursue me like the passionate man in my dreams, but skepticism had corroded those dreams hatched from a little girl's unrealistic heart.

Despite all of this, Patrick remained my confidant. During summer vacations from college, we would be influenced by the comfort of the warm night air and the sparkling stars glistening like silver confetti on the lake's glassy surface. The romantic summer nights on Brooks Lake masked our minds, and Patrick and I would fall victim to our hormones. We would find ourselves kissing and settling into each other's arms. I finally found out that college had improved his technique. If only he had the courage to commit his heart, then maybe we could move past these childish games—although I hadn't met any man who could, so I settled for flirtatious attention.

During the day, we hung out on the boat with friends who were clueless to our evening pastime. Patrick and I would make private gestures across the boat to one another, winking and laughing about our evening activities. This was our secret—no strings and no depth. It was simply sneaky summer fun to fill my emotional cup. In those moments, my heart would wander somewhere deep into a place I rarely trusted. I wanted Patrick to be *him*, my one.

My fluttering insides would secretly hope Patrick would express his undying love towards me and prove to be my Prince Charming, yet there were so many obstacles to that reality. His passion and emotions were vaulted tighter than my virginity.

CHAPTER 15

Then

Why was I having all of these flashbacks? Was I about to breathe my last breath or something?

My mind took me to one weekend during college when I blew off studying for mid-terms and jumped in my white sports car and cruised four hours north to Central Michigan to visit Patrick.

Ignoring the discrepancies between Patrick and my version of Prince Charming, I took a risk on the hopes of my heart. Maybe he was softening.

Patrick asked me to come celebrate his last weekend before his graduation. I'll never forget his words, as my heart vibrated a little with the melancholy of his voice over the phone.

"It just wouldn't be the same without you, Kris...for my last hurrah. Tell me you'll come."

Patrick needed me, and, in that moment, I felt special being his choice. I had given him a pass on the issue of remaining a virgin until marriage after having realized long ago that most boys don't possess the inner strength necessary to save themselves for *true* love. Their physical desires usually overpower their brains. If only he wasn't so polite and controlled, then he might be able to unleash his passionate side to converge with my throw-me-up-against-the-wall secret fantasy. I continued to pray that Patrick would eventually unlock his heart and meet my Prince Charming job description.

A girl could dream.

I brought him a bottle of champagne and a sentimental card, hoping to add a tinge of romance to the weekend. No such luck.

Patrick hugged me at the door, threw the bottle into the refrigerator without even opening the attached card, and whisked me into the back of a crammed Mustang with three of his roommates. I sat on half Patrick's lap and half on Jon's, Patrick's roommate with an attractive, bodybuilder's physique but a womanizing personality. We had socialized with Jon on numerous occassions over the last few summers, and each time he had new arm candy that, I'm sure, he consumed and tossed out. Nevertheless, I enjoyed Jon's attention, while Patrick remained oblivious.

It was only 9 o'clock when we got to the small town bar, but the small, dirt parking lot was already jammed packed. So the driver made his own spot on the grass. Patrick's swagger and gorgeous green eyes turned girls' heads before we even made it inside. He knew the bouncer, who motioned us passed the long line and waived our cover charges—must be a perk of being fraternity president.

Patrick had some difficulty weaving through the crowd. He was stopped by high fives, hugs from beautiful girls, or a "Hey, man. What's up?"

Jon got tired of waiting on Patrick. Grabbing my hand, he led me through the dense crowd toward the bar. Jon bought me drinks, stole a few dances and entertained me with verbal banter. Patrick continued to socialize with his "fans," checking in with me every now and then to make sure I was having fun. It wasn't the fun I had anticipated, but at least he left me with my own eye candy.

While in mid-conversation with Jon, Patrick spun my barstool around to face him.

"Hey, Kris. I want you to meet Chris."

I expected to see a fraternity brother standing there, but, instead, I came face-to-face with an attractive, long-legged blonde with a cute, girl-next-door face that could rival Meg Ryan's in her heyday. She was arm in arm with Patrick, and she was using my nickname.

Really?

Chris was the one and only girl who captured Patrick's attention for longer than a month or two. He met Chris his freshman year and dated her off and on throughout his four years at school. He never fully committed to her though, or her to him—I could never get him to give me the full story as to why not. I just knew she struck a chord in him.

Why was Patrick introducing me to her? Please tell me this is not the reason I drove four hours and blew off studying.

"Hi!" I responded, hoping the alcohol coursing through my bloodstream would keep my envy monster happy, relaxed and in-check.

Chris released her grip on Patrick and pounced on me with her arms wide open. She gave me a huge hug, knocking me off balance. I had to brace myself on the bar in order to stop from falling off my barstool onto the sticky floor below.

"When Patrick told me you were here, I just had to meet you! I have heard so much about you all these years, and, finally, I have a face to go with the name."

She squeezed me again.

"You are as gorgeous as Pat said you were."

Her perfect smile and sweet demeanor was sickening. I was doubtful Patrick had described me to her in that way. He always kept his cards close to his vest and his emotions in check. I was positive she was only being nice to me to get closer to him. He was a hard one to catch, and I wasn't about to help bait her hook.

Chris continued her rambling.

"I still can't believe it has taken me this long to finally meet you. Patrick hasn't stopped talking about you for the past four years. Please come and have a drink with us. We are celebrating my 21st birthday, and any friend of Patrick's is a friend of mine."

"Well, I...uh..."

I was looking for Patrick to save me, but, to no avail, as Jon had him distracted.

What could it hurt? Only my ego!

I wished she wasn't so attractive. Her pining eyes glanced at Patrick, and I didn't like how her baby blues sparkled for him. I wondered why he hadn't been riding on her train for longer than a one-way commute. Time to stick with my daddy's old saying—friends close, enemies closer!

"Sure. Why not?" I answered.

In her excitement, Chris squeezed me again, locked her arm in mine and pulled me off the barstool. My touchy-feely personality must have been hibernating, because all I wanted to do was punch her in her perma-grin of gleeming, white teeth and smear the gloss off her pouty, red lips.

Her giddy voice broke my tension,

"Gosh...I can't believe you're here," she said. "We have so much to talk about."

"Maybe we do," slipped off my tongue instead of staying tucked between my ears where my thoughts belonged.

But maybe she would provide some dirt on Patrick's love life and her intentions with my best friend.

Arm in arm, Chris led me through the crowd of half-drunk students much in the same way I imagined she coaxed Patrick across the room to meet me. Along the way, she dispensed a deadly cocktail of knock-out looks and effervescent personality which made even me wonder how Patrick had avoided getting hooked on her elixir.

"I have had a crush on that boy forever," Chris admitted. "But it seems no one can live up to you."

I tried to ignore what she was saying, but the band had stopped playing, the crowd hushed and her statement echoed around the room like a sneeze in an empty arena—or at least that's how I heard it in my head.

Part of me wanted to hear more, and I knew her 21st birthday celebration had relaxed her state of mind and loosened her lips. I hesitated, taking a deep breath, before deciding my course of action.

"What do you mean?" I asked coyly.

"Girl...you've put some kind of spell on that boy," Chris slurred. "Patrick talks about you all the time. He insists you're just friends, but a girl knows when she isn't the one a guy's thinking about. He's a broken record...saying he's too busy with classes and the TKEs to have a serious girlfriend."

She grabbed me and looked me square in the face.

"We all know that's just an excuse," she added, as she stumbled over a chair. "You are the one occupying his heart."

Could she be right?

That thought vanished when Patrick escorted the overindulged birthday girl into his room, while I found myself on his couch.

CHAPTER 16

Sideways

The white noise from the plane's engines hummed. Chloe had slipped into a peaceful slumber, but my stomach was still in knots. The flight attendant asked if I wanted anything to drink, and I could only shake my head in response. She released the brake on the cart and moved on. If only moving forward was that simple for me. My head fell against the window as the brown landscape of Texas disappeared below. Continuing to breathe the stale air, my mind spun with thoughts of Chad, who seemed to check off every element of my Prince Charming, and Patrick, the *good* man I married.

As a little girl, I continually fantasized about a one and only *true* love. Fairytales my mother read me reinforced a romance that was destined to be. I believed! With each passing year, his personality and physical traits evolved into the perfect résumé. Our imaginary relationship became more and more real in my mind. I knew him better than I knew myself. He was my destiny.

My lack of faith in my dreams becoming reality brought me to this crossroads—the life I chose versus a life I dreamed of.

Where along my journey toward "Happily Ever After" did I give up on finding my one passionate love, my Prince?

I retraced my steps.

Shy, I wasn't. My search for him was relentless. My hopes of my Prince Charming's existence deteriorated with each uninspired date and empty kiss. I started thinking maybe a soul mate full of passion was only a scam concocted by romance novelists to keep hope alive.

I recalled the phrase my daddy used to say over and over.

"Kristy, it's just as easy to fall in love with a rich one as it is a poor one."

Maybe my daddy was right. Love was a choice, not a feeling. Since I had no man declaring his undying love for me, I focused on a path I could control—a life with financial security. Even though I was more passionate about people than numbers, I discarded the psychology track and pursued a finance degree from the University of Notre Dame—more future income potential, or so I thought. The only problem was, I was bored to tears by numbers and deferred to another one of my daddy's sayings for back-up on my decision.

"If you understand money, no man will ever get one-up on you."

His point was well made. I just hated the detail work, even though the math came with ease. My determination to succeed and stay the course was at the heart of my existence but not my *actual* heart. I believed there was no turning back on my decision—except for a brief moment after confronting the Sheriff about 'the incident' when I became capable of anything, including hearing my heart's desire for a change in majors.

Dreading having to make such an important decision alone, I traveled home unannounced for advice on the route I should travel—numbers or people? Instead of being greeted by my usual boisterous and opinionated parents, I received nothing.

"Whatever you want to do, honey. Take a break...change majors...whatever you think."

My parents were never hands off, let alone treat my emotional state with white gloves. Their reactions, or lack thereof, made me even more uneasy about trusting my own feelings. I buttoned back up and did what I did best, overcome a challenge. My identity was shaped by achievements. Nothing would stand in the way of the logical path—financial security—not even the hope of my Prince Charming rescuing me on his white horse. Nose firmly to the grindstone, I pushed through to earn a bachelor's degree in Business Administration with a concentration in Finance. I would never be vulnerable to a man where money was concerned—or any other area for that matter, if I had my preference.

After graduation, I had an opportunity to follow my then boyfriend, valedictorian of the Notre Dame Business School, to Denver where a branch of the Federal Reserve offered me a job. Since I always told myself I would never follow a man without a ring, the safest option was to go home and keep control—even if the job offered financial security. He didn't ignite the sparks I craved but was probably the closest I would get to my dreams of the white picket fence. Despite the white flag being waved by my lonely heart, something in me clung to the hope of finding the man of my childhood fantasies.

With no room in my life for doubt, I accepted a job in the commercial loan department of a large bank in Grand Rapids, an hour from my hometown.

I headed home for Easter break to tell my parents I would be moving back after graduation. With the windows down to let the spring air into my new car—an early graduation gift from my parents—I embraced the thought of starting a new chapter of my life.

Maybe there I would find my prince since college proved unsuccessful, but hope was fleeting.

Since my family wasn't expecting me, I took a detour to Patrick's Grand Rapids apartment to tell him of the job offer. He was my only connection in Grand Rapids, and I was relieved to have a friend in my new city for support. Patrick lived there for the past year and held the title of Director of Sales and Marketing for a manufacturer of trade show displays. He had followed in the footsteps of his mentor, my father, the consummate salesman. It was a decision his father did not appear to approve of. Patrick's father, a self-proclaimed "entrepreneur," owned his own business. He never praised Patrick for his successes, but, instead, forced his views on him about how he could be living better. I think Patrick never felt good enough in his father's eyes, even though he would never say those exact words. When his father would give me an overabundance of praise, Patrick's expressions told me everything I needed to know.

Thankful to see Patrick's car in front of his apartment, I rushed inside. When the door opened, Patrick's jaw hit the floor.

"Surprise!" I spouted with a wide smile.

The rest of my words came out in one stream of thought.

"I've decided not to follow Mr. Notre Dame to Denver...and instead you're stuck with me...because I'm accepting the job here. Lucky you!"

Patrick was not fazed by my exuberant declaration.

"Well...I guess that means you're tagging along with me and the boys tonight to celebrate your rebellion against your daddy's MRS degree plan!" he responded, without skipping a beat.

He raised his beer in my honor, and I jumped into his open arms almost spilling his beverage.

Patrick's arms felt like home. I missed him more than I had realized.

We joined his best friend, Brian—the same Brian from our childhood—and some of their other buddies downtown. Instead of their usual Irish Pub, the boys took me to a cellar bar. The music had a distinctive beat, more suitable for dancing than talking— an odd choice for these rhythm-lacking boys. I guess their hormones dictated the choice, since some prime estrogen was flowing through the bar's veins.

Patrick's sarcastic shell broke for the evening, along with his need to work the room like a politician. He never left my side, except to refill my drink or when I decided to dance. His behavior was out of character, embodying a new role—bodyguard. I wasn't sure why since I had hung out with most of his friends a time or two before and even dated a few. Patrick never protected me before from his friends.

Why now the sudden urge to step up?

"I'm gonna hit the bathroom and grab us a refill," Patrick announced, scooting out of the high booth and leaving Brian and I alone.

Brian didn't waste his opportunity to move over and hug me.

"Boy, we missed you. It's good to have you back. And from the looks of things, he's glad you're back too."

Brian nodded his head toward the wooden bar where Patrick stood.

Brian had been Patrick's best friend since second grade and was my first crush. I knew him well before Patrick. Our parents were friends. Brian has always been a straightforward guy who embraces emotion, unlike Patrick. I smiled at the compliment.

"Thanks, Bri. It's good to be back."

I probed for more.

"And what do you mean by the 'looks of things?'"

"Patrick's face," he said with a chuckle. "Plus, he hasn't left your side all night. When are you going to get a clue?"

His smug look irritated me.

"We're all just friends," I said, dismissing his accusation.

"Come on, Kristy. Wake up! Patrick has been fielding phone calls for years from our friends wanting his approval before they asked you out. Everyone knows how he feels about you."

"I've never known him to reject a request," I rebuked. "Not even during a summer where we were hooking up out of his convenience. He's been more than willing to pass me along to whichever of his friends asked and was never quick to claim me as his own."

Brian set his beer down. His face grew serious in spite of his few drinks.

"That's 'cause he's the proverbial 'nice guy' and didn't want to hold you back."

I had no words and just stared at him waiting for the "but."

"Tonight's different. He's different. I know he's relieved you're not moving to Denver with what's-his-name. I even heard him tell Mike you were off limits."

I rolled my eyes, trying to absorb his comments.

"Well...that's a first!" I blurted with a sarcastic tone.

Inside, I was oozing happiness, hoping Patrick evolved in favor of my dreams. I tried not to get my hopes up. Disappointment always follows a vulnerable heart.

When we returned to his apartment after our great night out, Patrick slipped back into his old summer habits and made his move just as I started to fall asleep on the couch.

"Hey! Whatcha doin'?" I yelled, raising my shoulder to block his advance.

It was a reaction even harsher than I anticipated. I could feel his body tense. His expression froze. I tried to soften myself.

"As fun as kissing can be," I said, recalling in my mind his improved technique over the past few summers. "It leads to nothing but hard feelings. You are my best friend and the only real friend I have in Grand Rapids. I don't want to mess that up by hooking up.

You're stuck with me, like it or not! I'm not going to be your place holder just until you find a 'real' girlfriend."

Our summer routine of secret hook-ups was over. I was done with his friends with benefits game. It was time we both grew up. I wanted a prince who wanted to save me, not one needing to be saved. His needs could no longer trump mine.

Testing his intentions, I continued to spell out my terms.

"I'm done playing our childish games. So, if you're serious about us, you're going to have to take me out on real dates...like a grown-up...without the guys...and without kissing all over me. Otherwise, friends will have to do!"

This was more of a punishment to me than it was him. The truth was, I liked kissing and kissed any chance I could—without crossing the proverbial line, of course. I knew time was running short to find my prince and didn't want to waste what was left being Patrick's crutch.

He stepped up to my challenge, even with the stipulations. For two months, he courted me. I use the old-fashioned term, because that is exactly what he did—flowers, dinners, chick flicks, and no kissing. Well, at least for a few weeks before I relented on my terms.

The words of Chris, Patrick's toothy piece of tail from college, replayed in my mind.

Was I the one capturing his heart or just filling his void?

CHAPTER 17

Love Story

Adjusting the small pillow, I peered out the window relieved the white I was seeing was not snow covered land but clouds. We were still in the sky, but reality was drawing near. I kept trying to erase the new feelings brought on by Chad—his touch, his words, his passion.

Stop! I'm a married woman! Why would I meet this man now? I have a good life!

My mind wandered to the amazing day Patrick asked me to marry him.

Vivid.

Patrick planted the seed months before our engagement.

"I have no intentions of getting married anytime soon," he explained. "I have to figure out my career first. I don't want to be working for this small town manufacturer forever."

I believed his words. Marriage wasn't on his mind and not in our near future.

About a month or so later, Patrick invited me to escort him to a mid-week business dinner with the owner of his company, a few other executives and their wives. The dinner was to celebrate a big account Patrick landed. It was a big deal for his career, and I felt honored to be his date.

The restaurant was a converted mansion perched on a hill in the heart of Grand Rapids. It was the same fancy place Patrick took me on my seventeenth birthday, one of our only romantic dates.

He had a rose and a heartfelt card waiting in the front seat of his coveted Mustang when he picked me up. I thought maybe he wanted to take our friendship to the next level, until I saw my daddy try to slip him some cash as he shook Patrick's hand goodbye. I didn't want to know his motives and focused on the excitement of going out to somewhere elegant. While at the expensive dinner, we watched a marriage proposal unfold at the table next to us. The whole place erupted with applause for the couple.

"I would never want a bunch of strangers gawking at me on what's supposed to be the most romantic day of my life," I told Patrick.

He knew how I felt about restaurants and engagements.

More than six years had passed since that summer date, and now we were headed to the same old mansion but, this time, as grown-ups. The prestigious iron gate surrounding the large estate of the restaurant was exactly as I remembered it, except this time crimson, gold and orange leaves created a colorful canopy for our entrance. Once inside, the maître d' informed us we were the first to arrive and our party called to say they were running late due to traffic.

Patrick and I were seated at a large round table in a cozy private room of the mansion with cherry walls and a high ceiling full of decorative moldings and beams. The waiter brought us drinks and said appetizers were on the way compliments of our late guests. Patrick was nervously rubbing the seam of his well-pressed cuff, so

I thought maybe a tale from earlier in the day might distract from his anxiously awaiting for the executives to arrive. I was a little uncomfortable telling Patrick what crossed my mind, while sitting in my cubical at work earlier in the day, but I knew he could benefit from a comical story.

I began explaining how, for a brief moment, I thought he was up to something when I called his work and the V.P. picked up the wrong line. He struck up a small conversation of pleasantries, since he knew me from living in our small hometown. He hadn't remembered tonight's dinner and thanked me for reminding him.

"My wife's gonna kill me!" he exclaimed. "I was thinking it was next week."

Maybe—just maybe—a thought popped into my head. Was the dinner a scheme so Patrick could return to the spot of our first date for a marriage proposal? As quickly as the thought came to me, I wiped it from my brain knowing Patrick knew *not* to propose in a restaurant. I had never been shy about my opinions including my negative thoughts on public proposals. In that moment, I realized how much Patrick meant to me and was feeling a bit vulnerable at the thought of my hoping for a proposal. But I knew it wasn't coming tonight—if ever.

I fumbled my way through the story, embarrassed at the thought of marriage crossing my mind after he told me only a month or so ago that he wasn't ready. I emphasized how I knew better than to think he would ever pick a restaurant for such a big moment. While I was mid-story, the white-gloved waiter appeared, set a shiny, silver covered plate in front of me and lifted the lid. On the plate was a black, velvet box. I turned back to Patrick perplexed to find him down on one knee next to the table. I had lost control of the conversation and was thrown off kilter.

"Will you marry..." were the only words able to escape his lips before I burst into tears and fell off my chair collapsing into his arms.

My words were coming to life in this surreal moment. While he was still on one knee, I buried my face into his muscular chest for support. I was a pile of mush, incapable of controlling my emotions. His actions caught me completely off guard. Time froze with my sobbing. My heart was overwhelmed. I was flabbergasted by his secretly planned proposal—one of the few times I cried in the last 15 years.

"Is that a yes?" Patrick sputtered from his moist lips.

God only knows how long I sobbed in his arms before I could answer. To him, it probably felt like an eternity.

"Of course!" I garbled through the tears.

I just couldn't stop crying. I'm not talking about tender, gently rolling drips down my cheeks cry either. I mean ugly cry, the kind where disgusting, blubbering sounds honk out of your lungs.

"Are you even going to look at the ring?" he asked, likely trying to shift my focus to help me regain control my emotions.

Raising my head, I noticed his crisp white shirt had big black smudges where my face was buried.

I should have worn waterproof mascara.

"Ah! The ring!" I said with excitement.

I failed to even open the box, having been so enamored with Patrick's surprising romantic gesture.

He designed the ring himself, pairing a new diamond with a family diamond he received from my maternal grandmother. His thoughtfulness was irresistible. Patrick planned the whole evening to catch me off guard. The executives were never coming. The whole dinner was a ruse. He figured the restaurant would throw off any suspicions of his plan, and being seated in a private room negated my no restaurant proposal request.

I had underestimated his affection. I could not believe it.

To make the evening even more special, Patrick arranged for a limo to drive us from the restaurant to my parent's house so we could tell them my answer. Earlier in the day, he drove the hour to my parent's house just to ask my daddy for my hand in marriage—just like I always imagined my future husband doing.

Patrick thought of everything. In that moment, I knew he loved me and would do anything for me. Although Patrick wasn't emotionally wired like the man I hoped I'd marry, he was at least trying—even if his feelings couldn't always be attached to words. I trusted him with my whole heart and soul. He had transformed into someone better than I could have ever imagined him becoming. And he wanted to marry me. I was finally his priority. His pursuit of me proved superior to any mythical passion I had concocted in my childhood fantasies, and I would choose reality over an unproven fantasy any day of the week.

CHAPTER 18

I Want My Life Back

"Please return to your seats. We are beginning our descent into Traverse City," the flight attendant announced.

Traverse City—The words sent chills through my spine. A place that was once my dream destination, with its Caribbean-hued waters and beautiful beaches, had become my shackle.

How was I going to face Patrick?

I couldn't breathe. Patrick was not *him*, not the one I had dreamed about since I was a little girl. Yes, I loved Patrick—more than I thought I could ever love another. His surprise proposal had penetrated my heart, and I believed we were destined to be with one another till death do us part. He had been my best friend since adolescence and my trusted confidant, but he hadn't evoked my desires from within. No one did—until Texas, until Chad.

My heart ached.

I created a perfect man in my head, knowing he could never really exist. I knew if I found half of him I would be lucky. I was *more* than lucky with Patrick and wasn't prepared for my Prince

Charming fantasy to ever come to life. Chad's existence, and the feelings he provoked within me, caught me off guard and knocked this structured, control freak off balance.

I should have believed the whispers of my heart could come true. Instead, I married my best friend and wasn't patient enough for the one that would ignite passion and fulfill my dreams. My faith hadn't been strong enough to believe, so now I was paying the price. My punishment? A passionless marriage. I was going home to a man who was not the prince I envisioned in my dreams. My best friend? Sure. But not the man that could reach the inner depths of my numb soul.

I couldn't grasp why this stranger could.

"You'll be fine," Chloe said with a this-to-shall-pass look.

I had seen this look from her before. After divulging too much emotion about her unmet needs from her own husband, she would button-up and move forward like we had been discussing the weather—an uncontrollable topic. Maybe my emotional outbursts were hitting too close to home with the loneliness she felt in her own marriage.

"I'll talk to you tomorrow about how we get started with CHADD," she added.

Chloe tried to keep me on the path of reality, while I wanted to retreat back to thoughts of a living, breathing Chad.

As I opened the door of Chloe's SUV, white flakes blew into my face like a flour storm. My picture perfect house looked different through the blowing snow, and I knew it would never be the same.

I stomped the snow off my cowboy boots and entered the front door of what was my supposed paradise with the high ceilings, large windows and a sparkling view of the blue water outside. Even the familiar smell of the burning wood from the two-story field-stone fireplace that I personally designed could not relax my tension. My eyes now saw the house for what it was—a substitute for my empty heart, void of the one thing it desired—intimacy. That was the delicious, gooey filling missing inside our perfect-looking truffle.

I had been distracting myself with all these material things in order to fill a void I wasn't aware existed—until Chad. Everything changed in the past two days, and I wanted to erase my memory of Texas and re-box my heart. I knew my feelings for Chad were illogical. Love at first sight is *not* real love. I told myself a best friend is what makes a long lasting marriage. I hoped being home would prove my bond with Patrick was stronger than any two-day lark. I prayed logic would prevail and my awakened core would stop aching.

As two of my three children came running to greet me, Patrick and I locked gaze from across the room. His eyes radiated a sparkling green that was warm and familiar. I longed for him to take me in his strong arms, lift me up, spin me around and express his undying love for me, begging me to never leave again. But that didn't happen. I got a half hug and a quick peck on the lips— nothing had changed. The reality of the life I was sentenced with slapped me hard in the face. My heart was numb in this house, and Chad was the only one with the prescription to cure it.

"Hi! Welcome home," Patrick said.

As the children hugged my legs, Patrick was distracted by unaligned dining room chairs. His need to straighten them trumped my return.

"Thanks!" I replied, as I moved toward our bedroom with my arms full of luggage and trying my best to hold back the dampness that had clouded my eyes these past two days.

The house was no longer picture perfect. My black and white approach to mapping out a planned life was a lie. Security was not the solution for my "Happily Ever After." My true heart had been freed by Chad, a mere stranger who defied my logic. The thoughts were more than my soul could bear in that moment, so I quickly escaped to the bathroom, collapsed on the cold tile and tried to hold back the tears with my hands.

A ding from the phone in my coat pocket signaled another heart wrenching text from Chad.

I was trapped.

Divorce wasn't an option. I believed that was only for the weak or the abused, not for someone who had a good life. The consummate rule follower in me, who prided herself in righteous accomplishments, was now a slave to them. I was a sinner, a hypocrite! I was stuck in this life with nowhere to escape.

Who is this girl?

My once vivacious and tenacious self was forced into hiding, consumed by shame. I longed to escape to a world with Chad—the only place I felt alive. I believed my heart found its missing piece, but my body was trapped in the life I created.

Each day moved in slow motion. My life in Traverse City continued, but it was as if I wasn't there. I didn't answer calls from friends. I didn't show up at social luncheons. I stopped volunteering at our children's school. I was a shell of a woman, wife and mother.

Each passing day, I withdrew more and more into my own head. I knew society admired those who emerged triumphant from tragedies to make something of their lives—just look at Oprah. I was not one of those people, nor was I a person born of privilege. I was in the middle—a good life, with something missing.

My nice lifestyle had masked my unhappiness.

The thought stung.

I was unhappy, and not an unhappy I could share with my friends. I had buried my unfulfilled emptiness deep within the walls of my protected heart. Sharing my feelings would be like the size 2 friend saying "I feel fat" to her size 12 friend.

Who can sympathize with that?

I was drowning in a good life.

Shame on me!

Patrick was so good.

Shame on me!

I found "passion" in Texas, but at what price?

I feel so disconnected.

How can I go back to the way things were before Texas?

Everything I knew to be true about myself and my life had been turned upside down. Every waking moment was consumed with thoughts of when I could talk to Chad and hear his voice. Our rigorous texting just wasn't enough to get me through my days. My heart was having a boxing match with my head, and both were exhausted. The "good girl" in me needed to press forward in my current life despite the pain, but the awakened woman in me wanted to feel alive and important as only Chad had made me feel.

I reached out to Chloe for support but she had been MIA since we got back. She decided to rent a condo on the nearby ski slopes for a next week or so and was commuting the thirty minute drive to take her children to and from school. Robert was too busy saving people's lives to join them in the spontaneity. I also didn't ask to join Chloe on her escape to the slopes, since I wouldn't be much of a companion with all the crazy feelings invading my head. Besides, I hated being cold. I needed to figure out my predicament at home, becasue nobody was going to save me from my mess but me. I struggled to hold on to some form of normalcy. I was desperate to avoid the knockout punch of a failed marriage or a disconnection from Chad.

I continued my daily exercise routine.

Just keep moving!

Working out was a way to exhaust my body and run from my fatigued mind. The gym became a regular part of my mindless daily routine after baby number three which helped me lose 50 pounds of lingering baby weight. Despite my curves, I was thinner now than when I got married, and I was learning to like my physique. Yet, I couldn't afford to lose control of my body the way I had lost control of everything else in my life. My workout partner, Sarah, was another reason for my not staying in bed all day, every day. I had an obligation to her and didn't want to add her to the list of disappointed people in my life.

CHAPTER 19

Whatever It Is

Thank God for Sarah. She and I worked out together most mornings the past few years. I wasn't too fond of her when we first met. I thought she was too into her work to be bothered by more friends. Our connection happened quite by accident, as we often found ourselves frequenting the same gym at the same time. After dropping our children off at the same school, we would both head to an out-of-the-way gym that offered fewer social distractions and more focused participants. Sarah had two boys, and her oldest was the same age as Brooke, my middle child. She was one of the few people I knew there. We would usually engage in light, noninvasive conversations until one day when we decided to split the investment in a personal trainer.

Sarah was an attractive blonde a few years younger than me. She was easy to be around and, fortunately, too consumed with work and kids to worry about assessing me. She sold tanning bed franchises and other business opportunities, and she was addicted to her Blackberry. Sarah spent most days fielding email leads and making sales calls. She never missed an opportunity to make a deal, even on a treadmill. In spite of our differences—Sarah, an independent, and me, a conservative—we could discuss anything. I did not feel the need to convince her of my point of view. It was probably impossible anyway.

We respected each other, and I was at ease with her. I told her of my growing desire to find purpose and passion in my life, and how my bubbly self was not fully content in my chosen life. I spoke of my current crisis only in hypothetical terms to avoid my real issues. Sarah would listen without judgment and would not pry for specifics, making her easier to be around than my other friends. She appeared to have no expectations from our relationship, easing any pressure to live up to a "good friend" label.

After Texas, I grew quieter and less feisty in our discussions —maybe depressed was a better description. I dropped hints that my marriage felt more like a business arrangement, lacked passion and never really had any to begin with. I prayed the heaviness of my changing tone would be too much for her preoccupied mind to handle, and this sinning hypocrite could stay in bed where I belonged instead of being accountable to this daily workout routine.

I wasn't worthy of her time.

No matter how much I worked out and tried to relieve internal pressures by talking through smoke and mirrors, hopelessness hung over me like a black cloud. My discussions with Chad were moments of relief, but the weight I was feeling from my immoral thoughts simply pulled me into a deeper abyss. I turned to country music to comfort my fractured heart.

I didn't deserve a white picket fence.

My distant attitude provoked more questions from Patrick. I dismissed his concerns with excuses of exhaustion from raising three active kids. He might have bought my excuses, except for the fact I wasn't drawing comfort from him, my best friend. Instead, I was avoiding him. I was spending more quiet time with my children.

Since quiet was not in my vocabulary, my withdrawal was probably raising red flags.

I noticed Patrick's car radio was tuned to country instead of his typical Top 40. Maybe he was listening to country music for some insight into my sudden change and withdrawn attitude. I knew Patrick had to know the truth about what happened in Texas. Telling him would be the right thing to do—just not yet.

I had to try and wrap my mind around my heart first.

CHAPTER 20

Don't Think I Can't Love You

If I could have only run away from my shattered reality. But, I couldn't. Any diversion was welcomed, so Tae Kwon Do became my evening solace. It occupied my children for a few hours, while creating another convenient excuse to be away from the house and reach Chad.

How could one man cause me to question everything about my life?

I desperately needed interaction with Chad to expel the myth and set my heart free from his hold. Patrick would understand. He always understands. He knows I'm a flirt, and he has never freaked out when others have made advances. He trusted me. He had no reason not to since he knew the good, bad and ugly of my life—including 'the incident' with the Sheriff. That is, until Texas happened, and I failed in my promises to both him and God.

Maybe this time would be different and Patrick would show some emotion. I wanted him to fight for me. I needed him to be my protector. Instead, I had become his, protecting him from his insecurities about not being good enough. I knew Patrick's spirit was burdened from his father's constant rejections—first by his harsh critiques, then with his disappearance. Patrick didn't deserve that pain. However, I sometimes wondered if I was more of an ego boost for him, rather than the love of his life.

Patrick's favorite line was, "Kristy and I are like *Lady and the Tramp.*"

Maybe his insecurities about my upbringing and Notre Dame education in comparison to his own family life and schooling were restricting his ability to express emotion or be vulnerable. He prided himself in doing the right things, leaving me to wonder if his romantic gestures were more about looking the part for others than feeling the part for himself. Unless he was angry, Patrick did not share his feelings. I accepted this limitation when we married, but that was before I knew all I was missing.

"What's wrong with you? You haven't been yourself since you got back from Texas," Patrick said, as he nudged himself over to my side of the bed.

Believing his questions were leading to ulterior motives, I acted cold and withdrawn. I didn't want him to touch me. I felt that would be wrong since I was struggling to understand my feelings for Chad. I could feel a single tear run down my face as I laid there facing away from him, pretending to be asleep.

My heart was broken.

I was supposed to be saving myself for the man in my childhood dreams. I was weak, not the strong girl I portrayed.

Had I betrayed Chad by giving up on my dreams of finding my Prince Charming and marrying Patrick?

All of me had been tainted. I was no longer in God's favor. I had feelings for a man who was not my husband.

How was I going to deal with breaking a commandment?

I had built my identity on a right and wrong way of living and the shame of feelings overwhelmed my ability to move. Patrick kept trying to coax a response from a lost me.

Patrick's advances were soon silenced by his snoring. I needed to escape.

Trying not to make the stairs creak, I proceed to the second floor where the children were sleeping. Brooke's bed was normally foreign territory, but, tonight, it was a place of solace and comfort.

Despite her independent nature, she was a daddy's girl at bedtime. This was suitable for me, as I wasn't the type of mom who would cuddle for hours or lay at night, while they slept.

I focused on all the things I should be doing and couldn't relax. I knew Patrick needed the house to be neat and orderly or his anxiety would skyrocket, and I would have to deal with his agitated state. Keeping things tidy was the least I could do for him, even if I didn't do it as well as Mr. OCD.

Patrick seemed better around the house, including nurturing the kids at bedtime. My parenting role had been a simple kiss good night and a prayer. Sometimes, I would muster enough energy to read a book or sing a lullaby, then Patrick would handle the rest.

The quiet of night was never my strong suit, except tonight. I was comforted by Brooke's steady breathing. As she slept, I stroked her long blonde locks and snuggled next to her. Even with her as my beautiful distraction, I was unable to block out the overwhelming thoughts of my dismantled family.

At some point, exhaustion must have caught up with me.

I woke to Brooke shaking me, shouting, "Mommy, mommy...I can't believe you're here! You never cuddle with me like this. I like my new mommy!"

I squeezed her.

"What do you mean *new* mommy?" I asked.

"The one that came back from Texas," she replied as she bounced out of bed to get ready for school.

Later, in the quiet of the house, I could no longer suppress Brooke's words. Her statement seeped into my heart, and I dropped the basket full of clothes, fell to my knees and began to sob.

Why had it taken me so long to "feel?"

I refused to believe that Chad was the sole reason my world had crumbled. But what other explanation was there for my vulnerable heart?

I wanted to be a loving wife and nurturing mommy—a woman full of love, compassion and understanding. That's what my children needed, not the hardened mother of my past who had been focused on order and rules. I had changed, so our home had to change.

I had scripted my whole life. I played out the picture-perfect family. Patrick and I were emotionless actors handcuffed to the script, just going through the paces. Execution of my plan, personal ambition and outward appearances had controlled our existence and our identities for so long. Where was the spontaneity and passion for living? Where was the fun?

In Texas, I had been awakened to new possibilities.

I wanted to live, to feel, to laugh, to love with passion! I deserved that, and my children deserved that! Even Patrick deserved that.

Life as we knew it had to change. But how?

Patrick loved me, and I loved him, but we couldn't enjoy the little things in life anymore with so many expectations outlined for us and our children.

Why couldn't I look into Patrick's eyes and feel?

Patrick was a good and loyal man! What was wrong with me? Why couldn't I feel passion when I already had a true companion and trusted partner?

I had no answers. I was a sham.

CHAPTER 21

Sweet Thing

During the next few weeks, I avoided Patrick as much as any wife could avoid her husband. Errands became a priority. I started running again, and I hated running! Any excuse I could find to get out of the house was a good one. I knew Patrick would know something was wrong if I gave him an opportunity to be near me. After all, we had been married for twelve years and best friends for over twenty.

I dodged as many social functions as possible. Yet, no excuse could get me out of St. Patrick's Day celebrations. I was Irish and a "Domer," making it almost a sin not to partake in the day's festivities.

Where was the luck of the Irish when I needed it?

It was my first social appearance in weeks, and, to make matters worse, it was Chad's birthday. If I couldn't pull off a happy charade, then I'd wrap myself in Chad's warmth.

I thought of the green dress I wore for our first encounter, and shame draped over me.

Yet, I longed to feel "that" way again.

Patrick was on the other side of the bar, among the sea of green. I sat in a booth drinking a beer with two of my girlfriends. I was detached. All I thought about was when and how I was going to excuse myself so I could call Chad. I hoped hearing his voice would give me the strength I needed to get through the rest of the day.

I watched Patrick laughing and enjoying himself, wishing he made me feel the way Chad had. My hopes fleeted, as I knew he was too reserved and buttoned up to ever let his real emotions show.

Patrick looked gorgeous in his green, fitted t-shirt which showed the definition of his broad muscular shoulders and enhanced his emerald eyes. If only those beautiful eyes could dance with mine the way Chad's did.

Why couldn't Patrick be the one to stir my inner most passion?

Tonight I tried to drink my happy back. The band played an Irish jig, and then switched to more contemporary songs. Two of the other wives I had been sitting with scooted out of the booth to hit the dance floor. I followed them, hoping a little boost of adrenaline would lift my spirits. The heavy bass drowned out my pounding heart which ached for Chad. Just as I settled into the groove of the music, I was startled by a hand on my shoulder. It was Patrick bringing me a beer—so thoughtful. He had apparently consumed enough liquid courage to feel comfortable joining in with a bit of controlled bouncing and weaving.

Why wasn't I be like the other wives who felt it sweet when their rhythmically challenged husbands danced to please them?

I could see in their eyes the adoration the other wives had for their spouses. I couldn't think of any other moment when Patrick danced for me. God knows he doesn't like to dance, so I should have been touched by his gesture. Instead, his performance made my stomach turn.

Or was that my guilt?

Either way, I had to escape. As soon as the song ended, I made a beeline for the back door to call Chad.

"Happy Birthday!" I blurted into the phone

The warm, fuzzy feelings returned.

"Hi, baby. It's so good to hear your voice. I thought you were going to a St. Patrick's Day party. How'd you manage to sneak away?" Chad asked with his thick Southern drawl I missed so much.

"The pub is crazy crowded, so I snuck out to the alley," I explained.

"How you doin'?"

His voice changed after sensing my inner turmoil.

"I've been worried about you all day," he added.

"I'm conscious," I said. "Being at this St. Patty's Day thing is rough, though. I don't know how to fall back into my life with these feeling I have for you holding me hostage."

"I know. I hate this too. But, you have a life and kids, and I can't be the cause of you giving up on that...on them. There will be a time for us. Just not now. Stay focused. I don't want your kids to go through what mine are. My heart's not going anywhere, believe me."

Although his tone was calm and reassuring, my emotions were stuck in crazy "Kristy-land."

"My heart's in knots. My mind won't quit spinning. I'm not this girl!" I insisted, as I held back tears. "How can you be so peaceful about all this?"

"I just am," Chad said before pausing for what felt like a lifetime.

I could almost feel each breath on my ear through the phone, remembering the last time we laid together and how it felt to melt into his arms a little more with each quiet exhale.

"I feel it too, baby," he added, as if he knew what I was thinking. "You are an answer to my prayers. It's enough to know you exist."

"You still listenin' to country?" he asked.

"Like you have to ask?" I scoffed playfully, as if to scold him for having any doubt.

He had changed the subject, so I didn't have time to fully absorb the sentiment of his last remark.

He began playing "I Will" by Jimmy Wayne in my ear. The words of the song, "So you're the one I've waited on,...the one I've been dreaming of..." put my heart in a chokehold.

The lyrics later reference a devotion so deep and true that the guy would sacrifice everything for the woman he loved.

Chad wanted me to be happy and certainly didn't want to feel responsible for the weight that hung on my heart like an anchor.

"I'm not good with words, but that song says everything I feel for you. So listen for it and, when it comes on, have no doubts about my level of commitment to you, even if we can't be together."

I dreamed of this moment, however corny that may sound. Chad's selflessness toward me was hard to swallow. I hadn't given him anything—no ongoing physical affair, nothing but my mess of a life. Yet, he felt our deep connection hundreds of miles away. It was all too much to process.

"Oh!" I blurted. "I almost forgot to tell you! You won't believe this! Can you handle another 'sign?'" I asked, with tears welling up in my eyes and not pausing even long enough for him to answer. "You know how I said the only thing tying me here was this house? Well, a realtor knocked on our door and said she had a buyer that might be interested in buying our house for an obscene price...and it's not even for sale! Can you believe it...in this economy? What are the odds? I can't take much more."

Why didn't I just wait to find him? Everything would have been so much simpler.

I scolded myself and continued to talk.

"I've created such a mess. Don't get me wrong. I love my kids, but Patrick is so much better with them than I am. They love their daddy so much. Patrick's the one who gives them their baths and tucks them in at night. In that regard, he's great. He even takes care of the house better than I do. How can I be so selfish? He deserves so much more than I can give him. He is my best friend, and I don't want that to change, but he deserves a woman that makes him feel the way I do when I'm with you. I can't give him that. I never could. The house is the only thing that binds us financially. Maybe this is a 'sign' that I shouldn't stay with him when I don't feel what I should. Without the house, it's a 50/50 split of cash."

I caught myself burdening him with all the details of the debate I'd been having in my own head for the last few weeks.

"There I go rambling about my husband...again. Sorry," I said, sincerely.

"No, no...He's a part of your life. I'm glad you can express yourself," Chad chimed in. "That's just one of the things I love about you...your openness. I've never had that in a relationship before."

Chad knew how to calm my nerves and force me to breathe.

"You're too good to me. Why didn't we find each other sooner?" I questioned.

I was still mad at God.

"I don't want to go back in there and pretend to be someone I'm not."

"I know, baby. I know," he recognized, sympathetically.

Had Patrick even realized I had left the bar? Very likely not, which was part of our problem. Chad would have noticed my absence!

It was common for Patrick and me to separate at a party and reconvene later to compare stories. We were secure in our relationship, so detachment hadn't been a concern before. But, once I met Chad, I quickly realized the adoration every wife *should* feel for her husband just wasn't there when I looked at Patrick. Chad opened my heart to something new—a feeling of being wanted for more than just a bedroom activity or an ego boost.

My separation from Patrick that night was necessary for my survival. I knew he would see right through my poor happy act. He trusted me, and I had ruined everything. Patrick didn't deserve this treatment. He deserved better.

Maybe I did too.

Needing to find some sense of happiness among the wreckage I called my life, I downed a shot, grabbed a strong drink and hit the dance floor again. I wanted to feel alive any way I could, especially if I couldn't have Chad. Drowning my sorrows in alcohol allowed me to forget my predicament, even if only for the night. I was determined to make the most of my situation, without abandoning all common sense and fleeing to Texas.

I was trapped in my marriage and shackled to predictability. This was the life I chose, and I wasn't a quitter. I needed to accept that this was as good as my life was ever going to get—sinful memories and a few stolen moments of forbidden love—and find a way to make it work.

I knew I had until March before the cell bill would arrive, and hoped that maybe Patrick wouldn't notice the calls down south, so I could continue my dialog with Chad. Either way, I decided I needed to do the right thing and come clean.

How was I going to tell Patrick that his wife was a fraud?

I decided to prolong that conversation just a bit longer. I wasn't ready to give up my fantasy.

CHAPTER 22

Let Me Down Easy

Time was of no concern. I was a pile of mush, incapable of performing most daily activities, so simply sitting alone in my car was much appreciated.

I had ditched my daily workout with Sarah to have breakfast with Chloe, at her request. Maybe she needed me or maybe she sensed I needed her. Either way, I didn't have to pretend and put on a smile. When she wasn't at the restaurant as planned, I called her. She said she had gotten sidetracked and would be late.

Tears kept pooling in my eyes. With time to kill and needing a distraction from the rainstorm about to let loose from my eyes, I headed back out to my SUV to make a call. It was too early to bother Chad in Texas due to the time difference, so I called my mother. I prayed she had the wisdom I needed to make my pain stop.

I remembered her telling me numerous times over the years about how she had to choose between marrying two men—my father, the responsible salesman, and another guy.

Sound familiar?

"Mom, tell me the truth. Are you glad you chose daddy?"

"Where is this coming from?" she questioned in a tone that was already defensive.

"You've always complained about the lack of affection daddy gives you, and you two fight like cats and dogs at times."

My voice cracked, and I gulped. I needed to know the answer to my question, but the thought of asking it a second time made me nervous.

"I need to know...Have you ever regretted choosing daddy over the other guy?"

"No. I've never regretted it," my mother said sternly. "I have a good life. I have a very good life."

Her words sounded scripted, almost rehearsed, so I wasn't sure I believed her answer.

"But are you happy?" I pleaded.

"Every marriage has its ups and downs," she insisted. "Nobody's perfect. I wouldn't be any better off with the other guy. I have a good life...and you have an even better one with Patrick!"

But, I didn't want to settle for *good*. I wanted *happy*—and not the happiness you feel when you have a "good life," the happiness you feel when a dream finally comes true.

I think my mom forgot about her dreams, but I still wanted mine—those I thought were impossible before my trip to Texas.

I desperately wanted my feelings for Chad to be erased and logic to prevail. I knew I had to tell Patrick about Chad before he found out on his own, especially if I ever wanted to salvage my "good girl" identity and preserve my family.

I prayed I could prove Chad wasn't the man in my dreams. Maybe then Patrick could forgive me.

My thoughts were interrupted as I saw Chloe walking toward the diner. I quickly wrapped up the conversation with my mom, who didn't want to understand my situation anyway, and I headed back inside. Chloe was settling into a booth in the far corner of the spacious room. Most of the tables were vacant, except for a couple on the far wall. A few older gentlemen sipped coffee at the bar, while conversing with a middle-aged, brunette waitress who seemed to be entertaining them.

Despite the expansive size of the room, I felt like the dark stained, cherry wood walls were closing in on me, or maybe that was just my deflated state of mind. Either way, the place didn't deliver a cheery vibe.

I thought breakfast rooms were supposed to be bright and happy to awaken the soul for the possibilities of a new day.

Disappointed, I plopped down into the booth across the table from Chloe with such force that it caused a sound of faux flatulence to echo off the walls of the nearly empty eatery.

So much for grace.

"What's going on?" I asked, wondering why she looked so distraught.

Had I underestimated her indifference to my crisis? Maybe the "ickiness" of my moral dilemma had pushed her to the ski slopes—an activity she knew I didn't enjoy and wouldn't ask to be a part of.

"Are you disappointed in me too?" I asked, biting nervously at my lip.

"What?" Chloe responded, looking up from her trance.

Her eyes were swollen and her makeup non-existent. Things were worse than I thought.

Chloe began to ramble, which was usually my role. Her train of thought bounced around like the marble in a pinball machine. She touched on her time away at the ski resort, our trip to Texas, her conflicting thoughts about her future, her unhappiness, her frustrations, her marriage and her divorce.

Divorce?

Chloe had filed for divorce! I felt like I was in a fog, as she took the conversation in a direction I never expected it to go. I thought

I was the one in crisis. I was the one with the dilemma. I was supposed to be the one with the conflicted heart.

Where was this coming from?

Chloe was done with lonely nights, missed dinners and playing second fiddle to her husband's career. She had checked out of her marriage, and I didn't even know she was thinking of cancelling her reservation.

"Why now?" I asked. "I thought you were working on expressing your needs."

"I'm done trying to get through to him. He isn't listening, and I'm tired of talking."

"You can't be done. This is crazy! Go to counseling. Do something," I pleaded. " You can't just drop this on Robert."

She got defensive.

"I didn't! This isn't all of a sudden. We have all tried for years to get through to him. He just jokes about it."

"That's 'cuz he didn't think you're really unhappy. I didn't even think you were this unhappy, Chloe."

"Then none of you have been listening to me," she countered. "I've said enough. He hasn't heard me, and I can't do it anymore."

Her voice sounded defeated. I was defeated. Despair overwhelmed me. I sensed—no, I knew—her decision was final.

How had we both gotten here?

We had *good* husbands and *nice* lives, yet we were choosing to destroy them. I didn't see any of this coming—not Chad, not my feelings, not her feelings and definitely not her actions. This was a total mess—completely out of control.

Selfishly, I was mad that she filed for divorce in the middle of *my* crisis. I needed her, and now I had to find the strength to go on—alone. Her divorce was much worse than anything I was going through. I couldn't go down the divorce road now, even if I deemed it necessary.

What would people say?

Our marriages were falling apart, and I had to find the strength to continue on with mine at least until Chloe unraveled her mess.

Tears welled up in our eyes, but nothing came out. There was a new emptiness shared between us.

How could I make it all go away?

Now, *she* needed *me*.

CHAPTER 23

The Truth

"Baby, what are we becoming? It feels just like we're always running, rolling through the motions every day..."

Country music played as I toweled off in my bathroom. Each word by Luke Bryan stung with each phrase intensifying the pain.

"What happened to that girl I used to know? I just want us back to the way we were before..."

I couldn't look at myself in the mirror and turned to gaze out the big picture window that provided breathtaking views of the white caps outside. In spite of the 20 degree temperature, rays from the sun danced on the waves, and, for a brief moment, I was at peace. The kids were at school, Patrick was at work, and there were no expectations of me—at least not for the next four hours.

I put on my favorite jeans, which now fit loose on my shrinking frame, and I searched for a shirt in my closet.

"Whatcha doing?"

Patrick startled me as he rounded the corner into the bathroom.

"Gettin' dressed," I replied, while covering myself with a black v-neck t-shirt.

I wondered if I had deleted Chad's last text message from my open phone on the counter near where Patrick was standing.

"What are you doing home?" I asked, cracking an awkward smile.

"Can't I be home?"

His sarcasm irritated me.

"Sure. It's just earlier than normal."

"What's going on with you, Kris? You haven't been yourself since your trip to Texas. I know this divorce talk with Chloe and Robert is messing with your head, but enough's enough! You've got to stop moping around, avoiding me and everyone else. Something's got to change!"

His face was distressed, and his tone was angry.

"I'm not avoiding you," I replied, lying.

He threw his hands up in frustration and bolted out of the bathroom—his usual response to conflict. With the kids gone, I decided now was the time to prepare him for what was coming.

I finished dressing and marched a virtual plank to his office. He sulked in his leather office chair with the sun shining through the sky light like a Hollywood spotlight focused on his emerald eyes. I sat on the floor near his feet, because I felt inferior beneath the vaulted ceiling and cherry bookcases lining his office walls.

"This whole divorce thing with Chloe and Robert has got me thinking about us."

I paused, taking a deep breath.

Here goes.

"I love you. I do. But, we're missing something. I think back on our honeymoon. It was you and me at a couples-only resort in St. Lucia where we spent the entire time hanging around with other couples who couldn't keep their hands off each other. We listened to them tell stories of passionate escapades on moonlit beaches and in private pools. Where was our passion? Where were our sparks? I want that in my life. Don't you?"

I awaited his response with bated breath.

"We had plenty of fun! What the hell do you mean?"

His voice more defensive and even louder than before.

I hesitated to continue, knowing what I was about to say next would be very difficult for him to hear.

My twelve year silence on this matter had been unfair to both of us. I protected his insecurities at the expense of my own desires, growing my resentment about not having my dreams of a passionate connection fulfilled. Perhaps if I would have shared with him my feelings about what I wanted from a relationship in the beginning, maybe he could have found a way to lower the walls protecting his heart. But, I knew better. I accepted his limitations and didn't like rocking his security boat. He had already endured so much as a result of his father's constant rejections.

His father always kept him on edge with his volatile moods, including the day Patrick called him about our engagement. Instead of congratulating him on one of the happiest days of his life, his father exploded. He told him he should just change his last name to mine since he would never come to a wedding of such a selfish son. The whole conversation was about his father trying to extort guilt about how Patrick wasn't good enough—not good enough to be his son, my husband or a salesman, despite the fact Patrick was already more successful than his father had ever been. That day was the only time I can remember ever seeing Patrick cry. I understood why his emotions were so bottled up, but I couldn't protect him at my own expense any longer.

It was time for the truth of our marriage to be revealed.

"Remember when we saw the movie *The Notebook*?" I asked, taking a different approach to ease the tension.

"How could I forget?" he answered with a softened voice.

"We walked out of the theatre, and you had such an amazing smile believing you were my Noah and I was your Allie. I felt how much you loved me in that moment. Remember that?"

While twisting the fibers of the carpet, I gazed up at him with tears starting to flow down my flushed checks. I choked out the words that followed.

"Only you saw us that way."

Trying to gulp the lump out of my throat before delivering the damaging blow, I continued.

"I saw you as the other guy...the good guy she loved...the one her family loved. But, not the one who instilled passion and reached the inner depths of her soul. I never met my Noah, despite all those years of trying. I believed he didn't exist."

He sat there blank, handcuffed to my words. I continued.

"We are great together. You're my best friend. We tell each other everything, but something is missing. We are more like great business partners working to achieve each goal we set."

I was barely audible through my sobs yet continued to pour salt on his wounds.

"I love you more like a brother...than how a wife should love her husband. You deserve better than that!"

"We are not Chloe and Robert!" he snapped.

His face reddened and the twinkle faded from his green eyes.

"I know their break-up has been hard on you. It's been difficult for me, too. But, we are not them! Is that why you have been listening to country music? Are you trying to find answers in those songs? Is that why you now say pop music is empty?"

Patrick wasn't really asking anymore. He was yelling.

"What the hell happened in Texas to the two of you? You both came back messed up in the head! Is Danielle having so much fun out there away from her family that you want the same freedom?"

His sarcasm spewed, wall erected—his anger now a runaway train.

It was all too much for him to process, and he appeared to be searching his mental Rolodex for a plausible reason for my detachment. His armor rose to shield himself from his vulnerable feelings, when he didn't have solutions to bring to the table. Anger prevailed over his boy-next-door persona.

His rage spiraled. Nothing I said would break the force field. This was why I never told him the negatives. He was so busy trying to be a noble man that the tiniest finger poke would set off alarms. He would protect himself, even though I hadn't been the enemy—until now.

I tried to refocus and continue our conversation in a rational manner.

"It's not about them. It's about us."

Nothing. It was too late. He had stopped hearing me.

There was much more truth to be told—but just not yet.

It was time to pick up the kids.

CHAPTER 24

Who Are You
When I'm Not Looking?

Chloe sat in the living room chair adjacent to me. We were watching the previews before *The Notebook* on DVD and discussing Chad when Patrick walked in the door. I thought he was gone tonight for work.

I couldn't look at him, my predicament plaguing me.

"What are you doing home?" I blurted.

"Is that a problem?!" he snapped back before disappearing into the bedroom.

I increased my volume as if I had picked up a megaphone.

"No. Chloe and I were just about to watch a movie."

My response fell on deaf ears—or he was just ignoring me.

A few minutes later, he emerged from the bedroom changed from his suit into a pair of dark jeans and a tailored shirt that accentuated his v-shaped physique.

"Where you going?" I inquired.

"Out!"

His curt tone caught me off guard.

"Out where?" I asked.

"Just out!" he snipped.

Impatience resonated through his voice.

Since I didn't have enough energy to fight, I didn't resist. Part of me was glad he was leaving. That way, I didn't have to feel more guilt.

We heard the back door slam.

After a moment of uncomfortable silence, I spewed my frustrations to Chloe. She was like a sponge, absorbing my dirty mess. In the middle of my rant, her phone rang. She answered and quickly shushed me. Something more pressing had obviously come up. She didn't tell me what, but it prompted her quick exit.

No problem.

A little time alone would do me some good, but watching *The Notebook* alone probably wasn't the best idea. I had forgotten that during Noah's first encounter with Allie, fairly early in the story, he asked her to dance and she told him "No"—just like I had done to Chad.

Why were there so many parallels between my life and my favorite fictional love story?

After the movie, I couldn't sleep—so I called Chad and talked for a bit, which only further complicated my thinking.

Much like Allie experienced in the film, having to make a very difficult decision had my heart *and* my head bouncing back and forth between Patrick and Chad like two games of ping pong being played on the same table simultaneously.

On one hand, I had Chad, who held nothing back and wasn't afraid to open up about how he felt about me. He liked the things I liked, he said all the things I needed to hear—and those calves. On the other hand, there was Patrick. He was an amazing father, hard worker, reliable provider and my best friend since forever but refused to allow himself to be emotionally vulnerable.

What to do?

It was well past one o'clock in the morning, and still no Patrick. He hadn't even responded to a single one of my earlier calls or texts.

My frustration festered.

Instead of talking about his feelings or my feelings, he just disappeared, which was exactly how he coped with any situations that made him feel left open to criticism or scrutiny—with avoidance or rage. Both reactions pushed me away.

His best friend, Ralph, probably knew something about where Patrick was, but he also failed to respond to my texts.

Why didn't Patrick care enough about me to let me know he was OK?

He was likely drowning his emotions in liquor—the same song and dance he would do any time we fought. But, this time was different. This time, he didn't come home. That was out of character for him, and that was the main reason my worry meter kept rising.

What if something happened to him on his drive home?

I dismissed the thought. He was far too responsible not to call for a ride. But, after a few more hours of tossing and turning, I called Ralph's home phone. His wife, Mandy, answered.

"Hell-o?"

"Mandy, it's Kristy. I'm so sorry to be calling so late, but is Ralph there? It's past four, and I haven't heard from Patrick all night. You know that's not like him."

"Don't worry, Kristy. He's here, passed out on the couch."

"What?!"

There was no capping my frustration at this point.

"I've been calling him all night, and he didn't even bother to tell me he was safe."

Mandy defended him.

"Don't be mad. They probably got carried away. You know how those two are together."

I hung up.

I was sick of it—all of it. I no longer wanted my life or any of the characters in it.

After dropping the children off at school the next morning, I drove to the gym, oblivious of the slick road conditions. As I attempted to turn a sharp corner into the gym's parking lot, my car failed to turn and hydroplaned toward a large oak tree. I gripped the wheel tight as everything started to move in slow motion.

If I stepped on the gas, the collision would likely end my misery.

I didn't flinch, and the vehicle came to a screeching halt just shy of impact. Two force fields saved my life that day. The first protected the tree from me, and the second kept my foot from punching the accelerator.

I was alive but still living my nightmare.

With no luck of escaping my predicament, I proceeded into the gym and joined Sarah on the treadmills before our session with our trainer. Sarah was chatting into her earpiece and typing away on her blackberry without missing a step. She gave me a quick acknowledgement with her index finger and resumed her business dealings. I was off the hook for conversation—at least for the time being.

Hoping that a little self-inflicted torture would help distract from my weary state of mind, I upped the speed on the treadmill. I was lost in the pain until Sarah's voice snapped me back to reality.

"So, is it true?" Sarah asked.

I think I turned fifty shades of white and wanted to throw up.

Did it show? Could she see through the guilt paralyzing my life?

"You know Chloe better than anyone, and it seems like her filing for divorce came out of nowhere."

I exhaled. Thank goodness. Sarah was not talking about me.

"Unfortunately, yeah. I don't know what to make of it. We came back from Texas, and, only a few weeks later, she's filed for divorce without even telling me first."

No matter how much we complained about our husbands' lack of passion, divorce had never come up in any conversation.

I held back tears and escaped to my own thoughts.

My life was falling apart, and my best friend, Chloe, filed for divorce without even talking with me about it. This was not the life either of us planned for. We talked about couples trips and retirement spots, not divorce proceedings. No respectable Catholic girl would divorce her husband, especially not with a *good* life and *nice* husband.

What could have caused her to take such drastic actions?

I thought I was the one with the moral dilemma in Texas, not her. I had no idea where her head was. She knew every gut-wrenching detail about Chad and my marriage, yet she keeps a life changing decision like this to herself. I thought we could talk about anything.

Disappointment blanketed me. Chloe didn't trust me enough to tell me she was even considering divorce, let alone filing for one. Not until everything was set in motion does she bother to tell me.

Had I not been a good enough friend to her? Had I been so self-involved that I missed her despair?

I thought we were working through our marriages not giving up on them. I knew she could be emotionally reserved, but I couldn't help but still feel inadequate as her friend. She needed me, and I had been preoccupied with my issues. I should have helped talk her off the proverbial ledge, even if I was a pile of rubble myself.

Had my meeting Chad changed her heart?

Wait! It was my heart that backed me into a corner, not hers. I knew she had felt alone in her marriage, but I thought she had started to communicate more with her husband about her desires to have him home more. I believed she could find love with Mr.

Surgeon once she opened up about her needs and returned to what they once had. I saw their potential and assumed she did too. I was so lost in my own black hole that I hadn't realized Chloe was in one too. I was too late. Chloe had given up hope of finding the light. I prayed for God's intervention to light my path before Sarah realized the truth of my pathetic state.

"That's terrible she's getting divorced," Sarah said. "Now, it makes sense why you've been so distant and withdrawn these past few weeks. People have asked me what's up with you, since no one has seen you out. You've been MIA on the social scene for awhile now."

As Sarah talked, I realized that Chloe's unfortunate situation had become my unintended alibi. My mind flashed to Patrick.

Did he think my withdrawn attitude since Texas was a by-product of Chloe's surprise announcement?

Chloe and Robert were two of our dearest friends, and Patrick had taken the news of Chloe's filing pretty hard. Recently, Robert had been calling Patrick more often and arranging get-togethers.

I thought maybe Robert was taking to heart our years of advice about living more and working less. Instead, he must have been confiding in Patrick about his situation with Chloe. I'm not sure how much talking Patrick had done in return, but, regardless, their frequent bonding was odd for both regimented men. It now made more sense why he was giving me so much space since I returned. Maybe he knew about the divorce before me.

The tornado of emotions made me dizzy. My head was a pressure cooker needing to let out the steam. I had the urge to tell Sarah the truth. I was a fraud, a phony—not at all the strong, confident woman I portrayed. I wasn't to be admired or valued. I was a failure to myself, my friends and my God. If I showed her my true colors, I'd be able get off the treadmill for good. No one needs a tainted friend like me.

Maybe my time to surrender had come.

CHAPTER 25

Miss Me Baby

"Kristy, the grass isn't always greener on the other side," my mother said with a matter of fact tone.

My mom was in full meddling mode today. Thankfully, Patrick was busy with work out of town—a relief to me. My mom, however, knew something was up. She became worried after adding Patrick's random calls and our earlier discussion.

I couldn't hide my feelings any longer.

Through the phone I could 'see' my mother pacing back and forth as we spoke.

"It's bar talk, Kristy. Don't put all your pennies in one basket," she advised. "Have fun, but don't throw your life away!"

"You don't understand!" I insisted. "I've never felt like this before. He's different. I'm different!"

"Come on, honey! You're being irrational," she concluded.

She wasn't hearing me again. She wanted to control the situation, not validate my feelings.

I was too beaten down to debate her logic. I knew how crazy I sounded to be feeling what I was feeling for a mere stranger. The problem was Chad didn't feel like a stranger. It felt like I had known him my whole life. There were too many "signs" to be simple coincidences. Logic couldn't battle the emotions that had resurrected the Prince Charming I had outlined in my youth.

"You are going to break Patrick," mother warned. "He can't know about the continuous calls."

"I've gotta tell him the truth. I don't keep secrets. I can't keep secrets!" I yelled.

"Don't do anything hasty! I'd hate for you to throw your life away based on one weekend. Think about this, Kristy."

"I have! This is all I've thought about morning, noon and night. I want more than what you settled for," I shouted, with tears streaming down my face.

I wanted to suck my words back in. I wasn't playing fair. But I didn't want a life full of arguments and no passion. I had been caught in the middle of my parents' fights my entire life, and I didn't want their conflicts to be mine.

"Kristy, your father has always been good to me. If we didn't argue we would both explode. That's just how we communicate."

Her voice had lost its fever.

"I don't regret my choice to marry your father, and you shouldn't regret yours to marry Patrick either. He's an amazing man who loves you. Give things time. Things do get better. Don't pour salt in this wound. Please just get one of those prepaid cell phones until you can figure yourself out."

Maybe my mother was right. Maybe I just needed time for the flames with Chad to extinguish before I burned down my marriage. Patrick's anger over my "*Notebook* revelation" was rough enough. I heeded her advice and bought a prepaid, untraceable cell phone to lessen the blow. I figured Patrick didn't have to know all the gory details of how much Chad and I had been talking. It was bad enough I was talking to another man—period. Patrick didn't deserve more pain from the details. I prayed for a solution, all the while knowing a miracle wasn't possible. I had been simply treading water until the final wave of destruction emerged.

Needing a physical release, I continued playing on a ladies volleyball team one evening a week. These women were not in my normal social circles. They knew me only as the loudmouthed Kristy who chattered play-by-play like a sports announcer. Yelling helped me mask my emotional pain, and, for a couple hours, I didn't have to think of my failures as wife, mother and friend. My goal was to exert my limited energy to finish the game so I could have a long conversation with Chad before going home. Scraps were better than nothing.

Chad had more time to talk in the evenings than during the day when I was more available. Thus, volleyball nights were coveted like Tae Kwon Do nights—except tonight. Chad and his boys were headed to a rodeo. Tonight, I would again be alone in my mess. Chloe had been the one person with whom I could talk personal issues through, but she was preoccupied with her own problems. Sarah was a good listener, but I'm sure she didn't need a weepy friend with *real* problems. Our friendship was one of convenience, so I'm sure she wouldn't want me inconveniencing her during the busy evening hours with my boo-hoo problems.

Just the thought of going home to my lie made me queasy.

I loaded my beaten body and trampled spirit into my cold SUV before noticing the light blinking on my phone that shows me when I have a text message waiting. My heart fluttered.

The message from Chad read: Hope you played great! Miss me, baby.

My hopeless romantic side couldn't be suppressed. I knew what I wanted, but I couldn't figure out how to have a soulful connection without breaking the rules that had guided me my entire life. Despite the miles between us, Chad connected to my inner needs. I longed to have someone want me for me, without needing something in return. I stayed in my car listening to country music long enough to know that, by the time I got home, Patrick should be asleep. I didn't need another sarcastic confrontation or, even worse, a skirt chase.

The first song on was a tune by Chris Cagle. "Miss Me Baby" belted from the speaker—another "sign" of my undeniable connection to Chad—as the words from his earlier text message seemingly came to life.

"And every time you feel his touch...I pray to God it's not enough...and that I've touched your heart so deep...girl you can't shake me...'cause I love you, yes I need you..."

I read his text again.

"Miss me, baby."

I sobbed into my gloves.

The most I had received from Patrick in regards to music or emotion was the time he tossed a Hootie and the Blowfish *Cracked Rear View* CD at me as he pulled out of my parent's driveway when heading back to college. After analyzing the tracks, I struggled to figure out Patrick's motives. I hoped he was trying to express his feelings for me through the popular track "Only Want To Be With You" and not "Let Her Cry" or "Goodbye." I never pressed him for an explanation. I was just happy he made the gesture—even if his intensions were vague.

In comparison, Chad's attentiveness and romantic gestures were almost more than I could handle. I didn't feel worthy. I wanted to stop having feelings for this complete stranger who had vigorously shaken my snow globe and changed my world forever. I pleaded with God to help me forget him. I needed to forget him.

I couldn't forget him.

Once home, I stumbled through the dark house. It wasn't like Patrick to forget to leave the lights on. Our bedroom was dark, except for the small light over the glass shower that illuminated my path to the bathroom.

There stood Patrick.

It was well after 11 o'clock, and I hadn't noticed he wasn't in bed.

"Oh! You startled me. What are you still doing awake?" I inquired against my better judgment.

"Is there something you want to tell me?"

His voice was uncomfortably calm.

The moment of truth had arrived. The time had come to spill the beans and shatter our lives forever.

I lowered my head in shame.

What happened next perplexed me. Patrick reached out and embraced me. I couldn't hold back the tears. My wails echoed in the silence of the night.

"Tell me what happened in Texas."

He was in control, calm.

I unloaded on him—about Chad, how we met, what happened, what didn't, the "signs" I didn't believe in but were now undeniable, how I had feelings that I didn't know how to put a stop to—all of it.

We didn't sleep, and Patrick didn't yell. The night was pure agony. I was torturing his heart and mine. I was sorry. This was a place I never expected to be.

Where was our marriage to go from here?

Patrick, I and the kids were to be board a plane in only a few hours. All five of us were flying to Florida to spend spring break at my parent's house.

When the sun rose, we were still hashing things out.

"You called my mother last night?" I asked.

I was the one now showing anger, fearful she may have told him she already knew about Chad.

"How could you do that?" I barked, before realizing maybe it was good he called her. She always had his best interest at heart, including her suggestion of the prepaid cell phone. Patrick didn't deserve more torment from me.

"I didn't know what else to do after I discovered Ralph's suspicions were right! He told me he thought you were acting strange on St. Patrick's Day. Then, the night I disappeared, I ended up on his front steps with a bottle of whiskey. I don't even drink whiskey. I was messed up...wondering what was going on with you...with us. Ralph was convinced there was someone else in your life after seeing your social media post about watching *The Notebook* just after you delivered your low blow in my office. The phone bill said it all, but I needed to know more. That's why I called your mother. I want to understand you."

"I don't know if I even understand me."

I couldn't look at his disappointed face.

"At least we will have time in Florida to try. Your mother can take the kids off our hands so we can work this out. I want us to work this out. I love you."

How could he love me after all I told him? He shouldn't love me! I'm not worth it. I'm a fraud!

"Please tell me you want to work this out," he asked.

CHAPTER 26

Here Comes Goodbye

The evening replayed in my mind as we drove to the airport in silence. I kept asking myself the same question over and over to drown out the deafening silence—even the children were being silent.

How could he still love me?

No life preservers anywhere. Patrick knew. He knew everything about Chad.

Why didn't he react? Not even when the life we built was on the line did he fight for me! Why was he so calm?

I wished for a passionate fight, an impassioned plea, but instead I got a rational man, fully in control of his emotions, and an "I love you," which only reinforced my predicament.

Patrick loved me but not how I wanted or NEEDED to be loved.

Wasn't the truth supposed to set you free?

I sunk deeper into my hole.

Part of me hoped that, upon learning about Chad, Patrick would swoop me up in his arms, share with me his darkest fears and take back my heart by professing unbridled expressions of love and affection. But, since that didn't happen, I knew I would never be free from my sin.

I stood on the curb at the terminal holding Ally's hand and watching Patrick disassemble the luggage puzzle he had expertly crafted that morning. He always had a particular way of doing things, and I didn't dare to offer my help for fear of damaging his ego more than I already had.

The terminal was bustling. I was not. I'm not sure how I survived the first leg of our flight to Orlando. I disembarked like a zombie.

Patrick and I agreed that Chad should be told all secrets were now out in the open. As he wrangled the children into a quiet corner to watch a video and wait for our next flight, I found a private spot to make "the call."

My hand was trembling as I dialed his number. I prayed he would answer so I could get this over with, but I was nervous to hear his voice again.

"Hey, baby," Chad answered promptly.

My heart sank.

"Hi. I don't have much time to talk. I'm actually at the airport headed to Florida with the family."

I paused for a beat before explaining the reason for my unexpected call.

"I told Patrick everything last night."

"Oh," was his initial response.

I could hear him take a long deep breath in and then exhale.

"You OK?" he asked.

While his question showed concern for my well-being, the tone of his voice noticeably changed in a way I wasn't used to hearing. It was if he knew where the conversation was headed.

"I'm just tired," I said.

And that was true in so many ways.

I huddled down tight into a corner behind a kiosk in an attempt to hide from my own shame. From there, I could see Patrick on the other side of the terminal, and, judging by his body language, he was trying his darndest to not look over in my direction. I sensed his anxiousness as he waited for me to return.

"I had promised Patrick I wouldn't contact you during our vacation, but I didn't want you to worry when you didn't hear from me. So, I asked him if it was OK if I gave you a quick call to let you know..."

"What?" Chad interrupted. "Why would he agree to let you call me?"

"I told you before...he's a good guy. He gets me."

Now the hard part.

"I've waited thirty-five years to feel the way I do with you, and I'm not ready to give that up yet..."

I glanced around the other side of the kiosk to see our children watching their movie.

"...but I have to try. I owe Patrick that. I owe our kids that."

"You're right. You do."

Did I hear that correctly?

I was surprised Chad agreed with my decision without debate and took my news so well.

"You know how I feel about you. And, if you told him everything, your husband does too. So, I just don't get why he'd let you talk to me. I would never allow that," he assured.

"Because he's not just my husband. He's my best friend, and I can't imagine him not being a part of my life. I just need time with him. I do love him."

I could feel my eyes misting over. I didn't want to say goodbye to Chad, but I didn't want to destroy Patrick and the family we've worked so hard to build either.

"Thank you for being so understanding," I added with all the sincerity I could muster.

"Remember, baby. I'm not going anywhere. You do what's best for your family. Don't worry about us. Someday we'll both understand the reason for all this, and we'll be together."

His words were soothing.

"How do you know? How can you be so sure?" I asked, tearfully begging for reassurance and knowing this might be the last time we speak.

"I just do. Believe..."

And, with that, we hung up our phones. The simplicity and certainty of his final words brought me peace. In some way—though unexplainable—I did believe him.

Why would God allow Chad to enter my life, let me feel and then punish me?

I had been a "good girl" following His rules—maybe I hadn't been faithful enough, patient enough. I wanted an explanation for all this.

It wasn't fair. It wasn't fair to any of us.

My steps were heavy as I returned to the row of gray, vinyl chairs where Patrick stood waiting. A sea of emptiness surrounded him, despite the chaos still bustling about in other parts of the terminal.

I felt as if I was walking into the eye of the hurricane.

"Well?" Patrick asked, waiting for a play-by-play of the conversation.

His voice was more nurturing than normal and not as tense as I expected.

"I told Chad that everything is all out in the open now, and I wouldn't be talking to him, while we are in Florida."

I paused for a moment to glance at the kids and then looked back into Patrick's green eyes.

"But, that's all I can commit to right now. I'm sorry."

I could tell by the blank look on his face, it wasn't what he was expecting to hear. Only minutes ago, I was telling Chad I had to *try* to make thing work with Patrick, giving him and the kids my full attention, and during my fifty paces back across the terminal to our seats, I'd already changed my plans.

"I'm really sorry," I told Patrick as I fought back tears. "I don't want to hurt you. I don't know who I am anymore. I'm feeling all these things I have never felt before and don't know how to make them stop. I want to...but I can't."

My explanation was hollow. He deserved more. Nothing short of saying it was all a bad dream would fix the mess I'd made, but there had been enough charades. I hated what I was doing to Patrick and my family, but no longer could I deny my feelings.

CHAPTER 27

Why

My mind was blank. My body motionless. My spirit was gone. I didn't deserve to be a part of the beautiful scene unfolding before my eyes. I sat frozen, watching my joyful children rush from the rental car to hug their grandparents. The tropical landscape framed their enthusiastic embrace. I still hoped this change in scenery from the white abyss of home to sunshine and palm trees would overpower the gray that currently filled my heart.

Why was this happening to me?

Patrick glanced back trying to coax me out of the vehicle before he followed the children. I gathered my strength and opened the door like an intruder entering someone else's life. The warm breeze rushed against my coldness and the scent from the nearby orange groove overpowered me. Maybe the fresh air would do me some good.

Why can't I feel? What is wrong with me?

My mom kept the children busy, and, since she already knew my dirty laundry, I didn't have to explain every change in my demeanor. She hadn't told daddy anything, despite his intense questioning about our despondent attitudes, but she urged me to "enlighten him" soon.

I'm sure she liked having one up on him for a change. I liked not being their referee. Notwithstanding, the focus was now on Patrick and me.

I knew my parents would probably be in Patrick's corner. They adored him. He was like a son to them, even before we married.

When Patrick left for college, my parents invited David, an exchange student from Sweden, to live with us for a year.

What parents allow a seventeen-year-old boy to move into their house with their sixteen-year-old daughter under the same roof? Were they mourning the loss of their pseudo son?

David was not close to a replica of Patrick—in looks or personality. He was into the arts, mainly theatre and acting, and very gray with his thinking. We had nothing in common. He didn't fill the shoes of a brotherly confidant like Patrick did—until later when we became adults and began to appreciate our differences instead of competing for attention. Who knows why David got stuck in my "podunk" town with our chaos except maybe to bring equilibrium to our home? At least my mother had David, while Patrick was away.

When I left for college, no one moved in. The empty nest was working to my mother's advantage this time. In a letter she sent my first year, she described how my daddy was stuck to the couch missing me, but the good news was he was treating her like a queen! Though she didn't say it directly, I knew she was happy to be rid of the princess in the house. Daddy's little girl was no longer in the picture, and my mother was finally getting the attention she deserved. I knew whose side my mother would choose if Patrick and I split, even if she wouldn't admit to choosing him. My daddy was another story. He was wishy-washy with opinions, never picking sides unless the topic was me verses my mother. This time was different. I had never disappointed him, and he would have every right to side with Patrick.

I was the problem.

Once alone with my daddy, I gathered enough courage to share some of the details of my failure through watering eyes. He was not good with deep discussions and his inability to look at me reinforced his discomfort. I expected a lecture that included how the grass isn't always greener on the other side—his favorite quote when rationalizing why he never divorced my mother despite years of bickering.

To my surprise he hugged me and said, "Whatever happens we love you both and will always be here for you BOTH."

What?

I wasn't cast out like I deserved, but shown mercy—at least for the time being. I hadn't jumped off the deep end...yet.

Each morning I escaped for a long walk with myself. My steps were slower as my brain worked overtime trying to contemplate an exit out of my mess without causing more pain—an impossible task. I tried to listen to the country music, but that breached the walls of my heart. Isolation is what I deserved—a complete silence. I wasn't worthy of this life or any other. The rules were broken. I couldn't turn back the clock.

I'm doomed.

My spirit was withdrawn in spite of Patrick doing everything right—tending to the kids, giving me space, staying calm (not even a glimmer of rage). He even held me at night, while I cried myself to sleep. His touch comforted me like a pair of old blue jeans. But it didn't stimulate intimacy since I had discovered a new *fabric* in Texas and my favorite jeans would never fit the same, no matter how much I wanted.

Despite knowing the truths of my heart, Patrick tried to be the husband I wanted. He planned date nights almost every evening, while at my parent's house. He seemed like a fish out of water with his affectionate gestures—trying to hold my hand, touch me or hug me—anything to be close. His new-found warmth felt forced. His behavior seemed more like a desperate effort to save our marriage by being someone he wasn't. I appreciated his attempt, but it failed to connect.

I feel dead inside.

No matter how much I wanted to make us work, I couldn't force my heart to feel...especially at night.

I awoke to find Patrick pressed against my backside. I tried to pretend I was sleeping—unsuccessfully. I tried to tell him I'm not in the mood—ineffectively.

My body tensed as anger boiled.

Why am I so angry?

I felt like an object for pleasure, not a partner in passion.

But my feelings didn't matter. My feelings *never* mattered. His needs trumped mine. I needed to play the role. He deserved a "good wife."

The sun rose day after day without lightening my heart.

Was I prolonging the inevitable?

If Patrick and I never had this type of intimate connection before, how could we find it now? I didn't have an answer, nor did I see options.

I was *not* ready to give up the one person that had touched my heart, but I had to be strong. With every ounce of my being, I ignored the hidden prepaid cell phone. I had to do the right thing—quit Chad. I owed Patrick that much. I agreed to see a marriage counselor when we returned to Michigan.

I survived the vacation, but knew Patrick couldn't survive another call to Chad. If I was going to be committed to working on my marriage, I needed to cut the last string tying me to Chad without furthering damaging Patrick. I pulled out the prepaid cell phone and made the call.

"If I'm going to work on my marriage, I can't have you as a distraction or crutch," I said through sniffles.

"I know, baby, I know. Like I said, you need to keep focusing on your family no matter how hard it gets. We may not be able to be together, but we will always be connected—right?"

His words soothed my fears of being alone, yet I could barely muster out a "right."

"Promise me...you are safe?"

Composing myself, I said, "I told you Patrick has been amazing through all this. He loves me and would never hurt me. I'm hurting him, and it has to stop. I promise. I'll be fine...It's my heart that won't."

My desperation to be the "good girl" I used to be in God's eyes fueled my secret goodbye. Patrick knew my sins, but telling him about the final phone call would feel like slowly ripping a Band-Aid from a not yet healed wound. Chad was now out of the question as an outlet if I wanted to recapture my "good girl" persona. I couldn't turn to Chloe. She was consumed with her own crisis. She and I were a train wreck, adding fuel to each other's destructive fires. Danielle was across the country and had her own challenges. Sarah was Sarah, my faithful workout partner who hadn't signed up to listen to the confessions of a sinner. Any day I knew I would share too much with Sarah and lose my last social connection.

All of them were among the torn pieces of my ill-constructed blueprint to "Happily Ever After." I was lost.

CHAPTER 28

Solitary Thinking

My journal was a reliable friend listening passively as I chronicled the pain of my once valued masterpiece of a life. I skipped specific thoughts about Chad in case Patrick read my words. He didn't deserve more suffering. I quit Chad the way a smoker quits cold turkey and never has another puff. But that didn't mean the *vice* wasn't constantly in my dreams.

I missed Chad.

After a month of no contact, I decided to vent those feelings in daily letters to him. Since Chad was the one to bust my heart free from its confinement, I wanted him to know my journey of self-exploration, even if I never saw or spoke to him again. I didn't believe writing to him was breaking any rules. To me, it was more like putting an unlit cigarette to your lips and remembering how it felt without reliving the experience. I needed to be the strong girl I had prided myself to be for 35 years. My newly discovered emotions weren't going to hijack a life I worked so hard to fabricate.

I evoked memories of how much I loved Patrick before Chad changed the landscape. I remembered how I signed each little note or birthday card to Patrick with "Forever and Always." I couldn't taint those memories, so the salutation I used when signing the letters to Chad was "Forever in my Heart," which was more appropriate for a man I may never, or should never, see again.

Yet, writing letters didn't stop my longing to hear his voice, to feel my heart beating again. I reassured myself I must stay true to my word and work on my marriage with no interference (even if my mind escaped to him in my moments of silence or through words expressed in my one-way letters). Patrick and I couldn't move forward if I had Chad as my crutch, and a divorce didn't fit into my vision of "Happily Ever After."

If divorce became inevitable, then I needed a logical reason to justify or at least forgive the behavior...Chloe's, Chad's and possibly mine.

Clinging to the memory of Chad, I remembered cornering him on breaking his Catholic vows.

"If you loved her so much, why didn't you fight for her?"

My skeptical mind continued to question his convictions, trying to uncover any weakness I could in his resumé.

"Of course, I fought for her," he said. "I fought for her for months, even seeing a counselor by myself when she wouldn't go. You name it, I did it."

"So, why did you give up on your marriage?"

"I did not give up. I woke up!"

When would I wake up?

I wanted my own *aha-moment* so my nightmare would end. Would my words ever be as matter-of-fact as Chad's were on the subject of divorce? I was torn between my irrational feelings for Chad and my Catholic rules bonding me to Patrick.

I prayed for God to show me the way.

I wasn't sure how much more pain I could endure without feeling the right answers. My cautious release of sins to Sarah during workouts hadn't awakened me to reality or her to the reality of me.

The nightmare grew as more individuals gawked at my shaken snow globe.

Linda, the next captive audience member, was a polished, middle aged, marriage counselor with not enough time in a day. I realized my husband had gone to great lengths to ensure we met with the person considered the best marriage therapist in Traverse City. She accepted couples on a referral basis only, and Patrick pulled strings in his medical sales world to get us on her calendar upon our return from Florida, without divulging himself as one half of the couple client. He had a knack for getting information without people realizing his motives.

With her good looks and professional demeanor, Linda reminded me of the therapist on *The Sopranos*, and I'm sure she'd quickly uncover the fraud sitting in her office.

We were in front of Linda for the second time this week, for the third week in a row. She requested we read "The 5 Love Languages" by Gary Chapman. This book was a prime of example of what we didn't need—self-help. Chapman's solution did not fit *our* problem.

Patrick and I knew each other's love language and could be the poster couple for living out his principles. While reading the book and comparing notes, we laughed at our identical answers. It was welcomed amusement in a house void of happy, except for moments provoked by the kids. The book helped us understand our children rather than address our passionless problem. It was no match for our long history of open communication. Our behaviors fueled our marriage like a reliable sedan, nothing passionate or sexy about either. I had no idea how Linda was going to help. I just wanted her to fix us.

"You say you talk about everything, but do you really? Why didn't you tell him how you wanted to be kissed?" Linda probed.

Patrick just stared.

"If I told him the truth, it would hurt. He would only focus on his perceived failure, not my needs. His insecurities about not being good enough already hinder his ability to express emotions. He knows he is a perfectionist and can't handle screwing up."

I could not stop.

"He is noble and wants to do the right thing. Yet when he thinks he can't, he resorts to sarcasm or explodes at me, while being 'Mr. Nice Guy' to everyone else. I knew his emotional limits and accepted them when we married. I love him for who he is. But now I have these feelings for a stranger that are not logical and that's messing with my whole world. Patrick and I are great together. He's my best friend."

This was brutal.

I paused to breathe, and then continued.

"The problem is I don't 'feel' for him how I should and it's not fair to either of us."

"I must say you two are the most honest couple I have ever dealt with. You don't hold much back, do you?"

To Linda's rhetorical question Patrick replied methodically, "No."

Then, he continued.

"In fact we got almost a perfect score on our Catholic marriage compatibility test and were accused of cheating because our compatibility appeared TOO good. Of the two questions we answered differently we misunderstood the question and our answers did in fact match. The priest and the moderators didn't know what to do with us."

His voice lightened with the description of the test confirming we were meant for each other.

Of course, he would resort to the test...black and white. It's right there.

Then again, who was I to throw stones at this way of thinking?

I had also been proud of our results. We built a good life based on our black and white road map...until Chad's existence threw a wrench in the works.

A wrench that would twist, pull and revive my heart to the existence of this roadblock, forcing me to doubt my life's choices.

CHAPTER 29

Strange

Patrick, Linda and I formed a "Bermuda" triangle. Bermuda serves as an appropriate adjective, in this case, since there were no answers coming from any direction to explain our missing hearts.

I stared at the wall above Linda's head with Patrick on my right in a stiff-armed chair that matched the one holding me upright. Uncomfortable, I began to unload my baggage as if I were giving a speech in our couples therapy.

"Communication isn't our problem. We agree on almost everything. Patrick's lack of emotion, other than anger and sarcasm, hinders us from an intimate connection. This is our problem. It's the broken record that keeps playing through our marriage and is the instigator for all arguments. I question Patrick on his way of doing things and his automatic reaction is combative. He thinks I am critiquing him instead of hearing what I want. He focuses on how he can fix what he was doing wrong, not what I am saying. I need him to express HIS feelings, not just adjust them to suit me."

I picked up momentum.

"Linda, sometimes you want a latte and sometimes a café mocha. That doesn't mean one of them is wrong...just different... Patrick can't grasp this concept. I quit saying which I wanted to avoid provoking his feelings of inadequacy that lead to his explosion and me shoving my wants on the proverbial back burner. I didn't marry him to change him. I knew his limits and loved him anyway."

I paused to catch my breath then kept going in spite of the pit in my stomach. Patrick sat motionless, almost detached, as I talked some more.

"Linda, it's not like we are trying to rekindle something we had lost through life and kids. We never had 'it' to begin with. A friendship, yes...a passionate connection, no. What are we supposed to do with that?," I asked.

I knew she didn't have an answer. None of us did.

Linda tried to stir hope through her somber expression.

"I hear what you are saying, but feel we are missing something. Your connection seems stronger than any couple I've seen. Maybe something from 'the incident' with the Sheriff is holding you back from feeling the true emotion you want with Patrick."

"I told you I dealt with that, and did everything you're *supposed* to do....acknowledge the act, confront the perp, and forgive him."

I paused, making eye contact with both of them to reinforce my conviction.

"This is NOT the issue here."

My words were confident believing every word I uttered.

"Linda, I knew on my wedding day we didn't have the sparks I wanted, but I thought that didn't matter."

I turned to Patrick.

"This is so unfair. I'm so sorry."

His full armor intact, Patrick sat stoically.

Tears engulfed me. I knew I would be tainting our wedding day if I continued, but they needed to understand. I fought through the emotion and proceeded to describe the day—just seven months after our "picture perfect" engagement.

The fresh smell of the gardenias filled the room as my bouquet was unboxed. My body tensed and anger swept over me as I berated the flowers being unveiled.

My mother tried to calm me, saying, "Honey, the bouquet is beautiful. The florist designed it exactly how you described. What's wrong with it?"

I couldn't answer her.

I escaped to the tiny wooden bathroom. The walls were closing in. As I looked at the bride in the mirror, I knew the flowers hadn't given me the feelings I wanted. Sadness swept over me. From Patrick, would I ever experience the wild, heated passionate love I craved? He is so reserved and controlled. Yet passion is what I need. Verbal expressions of emotions are not Patrick's forté. I knew his limits and insecurities. He just wasn't that type of guy.

My traditional white wedding dress was a consolation prize. In it, I would have to mourn the loss of my fantasy—the passionate man in my dreams. He would forever be lost. I had willingly given up on *him* and the fiery expressions of love I would never know. My best friend and confidant would be my husband, 'til death do us part, and we would have an amazing life together with the same values, aspirations and trust. I loved him more than I had ever loved another, which was the only meaningful love I understood at the time. My hope for storybook romance would forever be buried in my dreams. Reality gripped hard on my heart. I had to focus on pursuing my white picket fence life without him, and focus on reality.

In that tiny bathroom, I said goodbye to the man of my childhood dreams and welcomed instead this amazing man, Patrick, into my toned down fairytale. I was blessed to have this honorable man by my side for the rest of my life. I loved him with all of my exposed heart—never expecting a deeper love could exist in this world. Beneath the stained glass windows and large columns, I let go of the "fantasy" to say "I do" to my best friend.

I intended to never look back.

"Do you see what I'm saying?" I asked, before taking an exhausted breath. "If we didn't have passion when we married, how are we going to find it now? We aren't some non-communicating, lost couple, in need of a 5 step fix-it plan. Nothing's broken. It's just not complete. We are doing all the right steps, just at an arm's length, no intimate connection into a fluid dance. But now I understand what 'that' feels like and I want 'that' in my life."

I stopped.

Linda's face cringed. We both sensed Patrick's pain despite his stoic exterior.

"I understand, Kristy. Maybe we need to move in another direction. Patrick, you've remained unmoved as Kristy poured out difficult feelings."

"What do you want me to do? Get angry? Isn't that the problem she's complaining about?" Patrick used the tone he knew I loathed.

"Emotion isn't limited to anger. Anger is the byproduct when feelings are bottled up and need an escape. I believe your ability to control your emotions is what makes you a successful salesman. For example, if you took rejection to heart, then you would never sell anything. Anger, frustration and hurt would paralyze every action. On the flip side, being so in control may limit your ability to express yourself with Kristy."

"I tell Kristy everything. I don't know what else she wants. I tell her my feelings, but that's not enough. I don't possess this depth she wants."

There was defeat in his voice.

Linda brushed a dark brown strand of hair away from her eyes to focus on Patrick's.

"Have you told her how you feel about all she's been telling you?"

Patrick looked down.

"What's there to say? Of course I don't like what I'm hearing, but I can't change how she feels. I just have to try harder to show her how much I love her and be what she needs."

Her tone softened.

"Don't you think you have a right to get angry with her?"

"Yes, but what good does that do? I want to fix things, not ruin them," he snapped.

Patrick was stepping up to a challenge I didn't realize I had presented. Why couldn't emotion be behind his efforts instead of his need to do the right thing? I had given him plenty of opportunities to step up during the last twelve years of our marriage and take down the barricades protecting his heart.

I interjected my thoughts.

"How 'bout showing me something? Yell. Cry. Throw something, anything to show me you care! You haven't shown an ounce of jealousy or passion in protecting me over the years. You were the first one I told about 'the incident' and no response...Nothing! I didn't tell anyone else for years after your flat reaction. Then when we were first married, I told you about my superior asking me to get a room in the airport hotel during our layover, while trying to kiss me...no reaction then either, just a pat on the back for doing a good job handling myself. Then, I told you about waking up to your customer, your so-called friend, groping me and you did nothing!"

"That's not fair. I was young and didn't know what to do about the Sheriff. And as far as the scumbag in the airport, I believed you when you said you handled him. For months you didn't tell me about what happened on the couch with Matt. Then, when you did, you said not to intervene because you didn't want to hurt my career. You are a strong, capable woman, and I didn't think you needed protecting. I had no reason to be jealous because I trusted you!"

Of course he would justify his responses—or lack thereof. Patrick's heart was barricaded, and he didn't know how to free it. My heart was dehydrated and craved Chad, the immoral drink potentially capable of quenching my thirst.

What Linda interjected next made me believe she agreed with what I had been trying to ignore.

"I feel I have done all I can do for the two of you until you have a better understanding of yourselves."

She continued.

"You hired me to advocate for your marriage, and I can't do that and counsel you individually. You both need someone to advocate for your individual needs. With your permission, I would like to refer each of you to your own therapist to work on personal issues that may be getting in the way of your emotional connection to each other."

She was unloading us after only three weeks. Our marriage was doomed!

CHAPTER 30

People Are Crazy

Linda found me a "personal advocate"—i.e. Psychologist with a PhD. Neil was a Catholic who had divorced his high school sweetheart after ten plus years of marriage (no kids) and remarried the passionate "love of his life."

This is who Linda hand-picked to help me salvage my marriage? Really? Patrick and I were doomed.

Neil was slender, not too tall, with a little balding spot and a warm smile. His office was a small converted house in the peaceful, historic part of Traverse City where towering, ancient oaks line the streets. It seemed fitting that his office was adjacent to the abandoned State Mental Asylum built in 1885, a perfect location for a horror film with its barred windows and dilapidated brick exterior. The multi-building campus had slowly begun a trendy refurbishment to house posh restaurants, stylish boutiques and airy lofts.

I was praying for the same revival.

Despite my lethargy, I was still a chatterbox, so getting comfortable with Neil wasn't a problem. I described my moral dilemma of logical thoughts (Patrick) versus irrational feelings (Chad).

During my ramble Neil interrupted.

"Do you go to the Catholic Church around the corner?"

"Yes," I answered, curious how he knew.

"Well, I've seen you there with your family and I wanted to make sure this wasn't going to be a problem running into me outside of the office," he responded.

"Oh...I don't think it's a problem."

My mind was rifling through its archives to see if I recalled his face. Nope. Our church was the size of a small town—odd he would notice *me*. I guess that was a compliment. However, I knew that this image would be shattered once he saw my insides. This was inevitable being the open book I am, and why I avoided friends since Texas for fear of spilling my sins.

Even though I knew Neil couldn't help my fate, I couldn't get enough of seeing him. With Neil, I was safe to be me despite, or maybe because of, paying for his time. The irony—I hadn't followed a dream of becoming a psychologist to help people because I figured I wouldn't make any money. Now, I'm paying a fortune to one—another financial casualty of not following my heart and my happiness.

In Neil's office, I didn't need to pretend I had it all together. I could hang all my icky self on the line, even if it continued to rain. I prayed Neil would have the magic recipe for the sun to shine—hope was fleeting.

"Tell me more about your marriage."

Neil asked questions like a close friend, full of compassion.

"Like I said, Patrick's a good guy. He's always been my rock and confidant. I can't imagine life without him. Everything was fine until Chad walked off the pages of my dreams and unleashed feelings I never knew I had. Yet, I know my feelings are not logical for this man I spent barely two days with..."

I paused. My aching heart needed a breather.

"A fire has been lit inside. No matter how hard I try, I can't extinguish it. I have been exposed to the heat and now understand what Patrick and I have been missing all these years."

"Tell me about your feelings for Patrick when you were first married?"

"When we were growing up with our secret on again off again flings, I would say to my friends if only he could be more expressive then we could have a real future. When I would give up on the idea of him changing to be what I needed in a potential husband, Patrick would surprise me by exceeding my expectations. I never shared my wishes, but only watched as he matured and grew. He was shy about his feelings but surprised me with small romantic gestures. The tough, sarcastic, frat boy would take me to a chick flick or drop a rose off at my apartment. Even after twelve years of marriage he randomly brings home flowers. They might be from the grocery store, but I appreciate his efforts..."

A smile crept up my cheeks, and then drooped.

"I just don't feel passion behind his actions. He's doing them only because it's the right thing to do."

"Did you ever think he may be nervous?" Neil asked.

"I KNOW he's nervous. He's always uptight and in control. It's hard to pull off passion if you're planning instead of feeling the moment. I appreciate all he does for me. He gives me the best of him. Even our engagement was well thought out..."

I shared the story of the dinner, surprise proposal and limo ride.

"Neil, I believed Patrick was my forever love. I dismissed the passionate piece I craved as fantasy, not reality. I never imagined someone such as Chad could crash into my structured existence and shatter who I thought I was. My life no longer makes sense."

Don't cry.

"I know I love Patrick. For a wedding gift to him, I wrote in a daily journal after our engagement. Until our wedding, each day for 160, I started with the phrase 'I love that you...' and finished it with some little thing Patrick did that day to make me love him more. It was a labor of love. I never wanted him to forget why I chose him. The journal was meant to be a beautiful reminder of our love and a gift for both of us in the years to come. Sadly, he left the journal in the honeymoon suite in St. Lucia without ever reading my words. The hotel never found it, and my daily thoughts and feelings were lost forever."

I adjusted myself in the chair.

"Patrick struggled to understand the journal's importance. He can't connect with the inner depths of me. I am alone in my heart. I know he loves me, but any intimate connection is just not there."

I looked down in shame and glanced up at Neil.

"I didn't know it wasn't there until now...until Chad."

CHAPTER 31

I Told You So

The cramped quarters of Neil's office was made more so because of a cluttered desk pushed against the wall. This allowed his office chair to float in the middle of the room. A black leather couch hugged the parallel wall—on which I would NOT sit. Each time I chose a stiff armchair closest to the door. A window on the opposite wall provided a backdrop to Neil. Sometimes the filtered light coming through would bounce off the back of his head.

Was that a halo?

I prayed it was because I needed all the help I could get to escape my self-made mess and earn a place in heaven.

"Neil, after all these years do you *really* still have passion in your marriage?"

This concept went against my rational thoughts.

"Yes. Yes we do."

Neil's answer was quick and heartfelt.

I believed him. I never expected our discussions to be so conversational. Both Neil and Linda must have realized I didn't need a shrink, an attorney maybe, but not them. I was just passing time until Patrick could figure himself out with the help of his own therapist and realize he didn't need me to validate his existence or calm his anxieties.

If only Patrick was seeing his therapist as much as I was seeing Neil, then maybe he could move forward. I wouldn't push. Patrick was an amazing man who couldn't see his own worth. I wasn't sure I could continue to be his cheerleader at the expense of my starving heart, but perhaps I had to try.

I kept seeing Neil.

His words were not always welcome because they often led to places of failure and broken rules.

On one of my visits, Neil leaned back and put down his pen.

"If it's OK with you, I'd like to get in touch with Linda and Patrick's therapist to discuss how we can better help you both."

"Sure, I have no secrets," I said with a sigh. "But, if passion exists, and Patrick and I don't have it, how are we ever going to find it?"

I was backed into a corner with no good exit strategies.

Neil sat upright, took a breath and looked me straight in the eyes.

"I don't know if you are."

"You're no help."

I sank deeper into the chair.

"I thought I had it figured out. If my parents could be married this long without PDA (Public Displays of Affection), then they must know something I don't. Marriage is forever in God's eyes. I wanted the formula for that success. So, I fixed what I didn't like about my parent's marriage and married a man I enjoyed being with. Patrick is my best friend. I believed we didn't need so-called passion to be successful, but Chad ruined that! I know my feelings for a man I don't even know are irrational, but I can't stop them. I'm so confused!"

"Kristy, this seems more like a marriage issue. Why do you think Linda sent you to me?" Neil asked.

"I'm not sure...maybe 'the incident' with the Sheriff has loose ends. But Linda agreed I handled it in text book fashion. I know Patrick needs to work on his opening up and letting down his walls so he can address his real feelings. He is trying so hard to be perfect for me. My raw words in our sessions with Linda weren't helpful to breaking down those walls."

Neil paused. An uncomfortable stillness enveloped us. I was ready to fill in the void, but Neil beat me with his own agenda.

"What if one of the neighbor girls you are so fond of came to you and told you a coach touched them? What would you tell them?"

I was annoyed. Where was he going with this?

I stared out the window at the gray sky.

This was stupid.

"Humor me, Kristy. Visualize one of them standing at your kitchen island one night after babysitting, and instead of telling you about her day she tells you about a coach touching her."

My pulse escalated. Anxious for the conversation to change I answered, knowing what Neil wanted.

"I would tell her it wasn't her fault."

Neil prodded further.

"What if she said she should have done something to stop him?"

Taking a deep breath before humoring him, I replied, "I would say she couldn't have stopped him. He was the adult, not her."

I whispered to myself, "...but it's not the same thing."

Here it comes. Neil's head tilted with quizzical puppy dog eyes.

His *shrink* tactics weren't going to work. I knew myself too well, and what I saw was no longer pretty. My mind knew the difference between them and me, and nothing Neil could say would change what I knew to be true.

"What do you mean, not the same?"

"I'm not them. I'm me, the strong girl who does whatever I put my mind to," I insisted, voice trailing. "And I didn't stop him. What does that make me?"

"You were just a girl. He was a grown man."

Neil stared into me.

I was pathetic.

"Let's try this, Kristy. Close your eyes. Now take a deep breath. Visualize yourself alone at the rest stop after 'the incident.' See yourself again as that young girl looking into the mirror."

This was pointless, but I did it.

"See yourself as you are now, a thirty-five year old woman... standing behind your younger self. Both of you are looking in the mirror. Would you tell her it was her fault?"

Neil's question stung.

I let out a tearful shudder as my whole body gave way to the pain.

Why hadn't I been stronger?

I was drowning in guilt.

CHAPTER 32

How 'Bout You Don't

Our home was at a standstill—frozen in a black abyss with no light in sight.

The white noise of the television had been absent since April. Patrick and I were forced to be in the uncomfortable silence of each other trying to *feel*. Each night after the kids were tucked in, we would sit in the corner of the sectional staring at each other, hand in hand, lost in our own thoughts, praying for a miracle. Patrick ignored his usual nightly work. I ignored everything else.

I was at his mercy.

Patrick refused to entertain an unsolicited offer from a stranger to purchase the house we built together. He wasn't ready to give up. I didn't push.

His bedroom pursuits had ceased, replaced by forced gestures of kindness mimicking our kiss-less courting just after college. Patrick tried to be the man I wanted and focused on my needs. He never yelled or showed his anger—but I sat on pins and needles waiting for his fuse to light. He was amazing amidst all my ugliness.

He couldn't hold his emotions in forever, could he?

Our home was eerily peaceful except for the crackling fire in the fieldstone fireplace. Its smell brought familiarity to the room. Patrick's warm hand comforted my aching soul—absent was my desire for more. The question in my head was repetitious.

Why could I not feel for Patrick the way I felt for this stranger?

Nightly, I kept holding Patrick's hand, silently praying for him to give me the feelings I craved.

Patrick broke the silence.

"How long we going to keep doing this?"

"I don't know!" I snapped. "I want to feel for you the way I should!"

My eye faucet began to leak.

"Tell me what to do to fix this," Patrick said with a sigh.

Since my blunt outburst, he was like a punctured tire—slowly leaking air.

My exhausted soul knew there was no cure for what ailed us. I prayed for a miracle as I locked on his aching green eyes...speechless. Our marriage was wilting and there was no water in sight.

A loud bark reverberating through the house made us jump to our feet. It sounded like a dog, but we had no dog.

Patrick was on the move toward where the sound originated when the noise stopped. He froze in front of the glass-paned French doors of his cherry walled office when the barking began again. Two more barks and then it stopped. I heard what sounded like a giggle. Patrick disappeared through the French doors into his office before the sound blasted louder. A strangely familiar noise accompanied the barking—uncontainable belly laughs from Patrick.

I rushed into his dark office. Patrick was huddled around the glass cage where one small spotlight illuminated the anoles the kids brought back from Florida. We weren't the type of family to have pets. However, considering our weakened states of mind down there we couldn't muster the energy to refuse the request.

"What's the problem? Lizards don't make noise."

Patrick could hardly speak through his laughter.

"It's the tree frogs!" he sputtered.

"What?"

"Along with the anole lizards, the kids must of smuggled tree frogs—BARKING tree frogs!" He couldn't contain himself as the frogs resumed woofing.

I joined his laughter. These tiny amphibians and their barking turned out to be a gift as their exuberant sounds cut our tension. After more than a month in our home they decided to bark to-night—if only they had spoken out weeks ago.

I realized I missed our playful laughter.

Sunday morning and the excitement from the prior night had been replaced by the overwhelming knot in my stomach. I wanted to pull the covers over my head, but Patrick forced my lost soul out of bed for church. I didn't see the point. My God had failed me, and I him. Yet, week after week, Patrick insisted we go as a family.

Life had become torture...a torture I deserved. Catholic mass was no exception. Even though this ritual had gotten me nowhere, I couldn't further disappoint Patrick. While I struggled to get ready, the children selected their best unmatched outfits, while Patrick did what he could with the girls' snarled hair. The once picture perfect family now appeared as it was—disheveled.

We always sat near the front of the old-style Cathedral, with its tall ceilings and stained glass windows, hoping the kids would be quieter if they could see what was happening. (Plus I sensed Patrick hoped God could reach me easier at the front of the line). For me, our location highlighted the hypocrite I had become. I couldn't survive the hour without a waterfall escaping my eyes. My *scarlet letter* may not be in view, but I knew it was there, and so did God. My façade may be concealed from my peers in the pews behind, but Neil knew the truth no matter where he sat. He was a reminder I couldn't evade my sin and deserved the wrath of God. I masked my tears from the children, but Patrick knew. He reached for my hand, squeezed, and wouldn't let go. He was a good man.

Why could I not feel the passion for Patrick that I craved so much?

I didn't deserve him. In time Patrick would realize I wasn't worth the trouble. But for now, I had to keep up perfect family charade, while praying for a miracle for Patrick's sake, for my sake.

As our disheveled family climbed into the SUV, I broke. Going through daily routines was not returning my heart to its comfortable ways, nor erasing my overwhelming feelings for a stranger. Despair wracked my body, and physical pain stung my extremities. I detached from Patrick and the children. I was lost.

The unthinkable became real...

Everyone would be better off if I didn't exist!

My dark bubble burst as powerful words belted from the car radio.

"Save me, I'm lost, oh Lord. I've been waiting for you. I'll pay any cost. Save me from being confused. Show me what I'm looking for."

I had to escape. I had to run.

"Patrick, if you don't mind, I'm going to run home from here."

My tone was polite.

"What?"

He looked confused.

"It's Sunday."

"I know, but I have the 5K in a week or so and I want to be sure I'm ready."

"A 5K is only 3.1 miles. And you're in great shape, just like every other year you go and don't run."

His snarky tone was back.

"Yes, I know," I sniped. "This year is different. I am running, with or without Chloe."

186

"I'm still not thrilled about you going anywhere with HER after the last trip."

His voice was calm, but his face grew crimson. It was time to exit before we argued in the church parking lot.

I grabbed my gym bag, still in the car from Friday's workout, said goodbye to the kids and went inside the church to change...

I never looked back.

CHAPTER 33

If You're Going Through Hell, Keep on Going

I sprinted from the church. I didn't belong there—I was an undeserving hypocrite. Trying to avoid my truth, I focused on the crunch of shoes hitting the pavement. My pulse quickened.

What was I really running from? Faster, Faster!

My heart pounded against the wall of my chest...begging to escape. I wanted out. The intensity of feeling trapped the tears in my eyes. I remembered....

Every painstaking moment dredged up in vivid detail.

The Sheriff who shattered my trust and stole the girl I once knew...

I loved the Sheriff like a second father, and looked up to him. His strong jaw, glassy blue eyes, and silver hair complemented his charismatic personality. This combo kept getting him reelected, and on the divorced list three times. He was a trusted family friend and a valued member of my parents' social circle. He went out of his way to help in any and all family situations. He tag teamed with my father to stay with me during my emergency appendectomy until my mother returned from an out-of-state trip. He helped my daddy and me throw my mother a surprise birthday party. He also sponsored a drug prevention performing group to which I belonged.

If something ever happened to my father, the Sheriff would be at the top of my list. My mother deserved someone to dote on her, and he doted on us. His generosity and warm spirit made everyone feel special.

I felt special too…until the day he stole a part of me.

In late February of my senior year, my mom dropped me at his home well before dawn. Twenty or so students and chaperones were caravanning ten hours to Tennessee for a National Drug Prevention Youth Leadership Conference. The Sheriff was to look after me during the four-day conference.

"It's too early in the morning to be awake. Rest your head on my lap and get some zzz's. It's going to be a long drive."

The Sheriff had a way of easing my anxiety, and I felt at ease with him at the wheel of the unmarked police car. I laid my head on his lap, my body in a fetal position. Darkness cradled me as we drove. I drifted off.

I awoke to his hand on my stomach and his fingers nestled inside my waistband. He was caressing my bare skin and drifting south. I froze. Time stopped. I prayed I was still sleeping. I wasn't.

I didn't breathe. But he did. Each breath became heavier, each breath faster. His moist, exhaled air fell on my closed eyelashes. He placed his other hand over my mine.

How was he driving? I wished we would crash.

His hand lifted mine like a limp, motionless puppet on a string. He placed it on the rough exterior of his stiff jeans, and then freed his privates. I didn't move. My hand was dead.

He forced a back and forth movement of my hand—faster and faster.

Please make this stop.

His breath quickened. My head felt his thigh tighten. He pulled his hand from inside my jeans. His body shook. I heard his hand thump the steering wheel as my limp body swayed from the swerving of the car.

He released my now damp hand. I didn't move. He placed it back on my hip. I was paralyzed, only able to hear the inhale and exhale of his slowing breathing.

Time froze.

When the car finally stopped, I popped up from my fetal position and looked out the passenger window. Light had come, and we were at a rest area.

No one in the caravan had extra room in their vehicle and, despite my desperate pleas, nobody was willing to trade spots and abandon their friends. I was stuck in the middle of God-knows-where with no way to escape. I remained quiet the rest of the trip and huddled next to the window to get as far away from the Sheriff as possible—which wasn't far enough.

Once we arrived, I tried to tell a friend about what had happened but was interrupted by the Sheriff turning the corner. He spotted me. I couldn't find words. I was a wreck. I was like a conch shell on the beach—lovely on the outside, but the living, breathing, creature occupying the inside was gone.

The Sheriff approached with a sickening smile and waved his hand for me to follow.

"Let's go. I have a big announcement and I need you there."

His voice gave me goose bumps.

I froze, but then my starry-eyed friend moved in step just behind the admired law officer. I followed like a solider heading to battle without a weapon.

Everyone sat expectantly as the blue-eyed Sheriff announced the Governor had agreed to speak at our commencement—a huge honor for a small high school in the middle of nowhere. As Senior Class President and Salutatorian, I was responsible for securing the main speaker. The well-connected Sheriff and family friend aided my task. The cost, however, was far more than I had ever imagined. He paraded me in front of the group, hugged me tightly and gave me full credit. The crowd cheered.

I couldn't escape.

CHAPTER 34

How I Got To Be This Way

My panting was heavy.

Running away from something or running toward something? I didn't really know.

I stopped to hold my chest. My heart was pounding, my breathing heavy and labored.

I'm done with 'the incident.' It's over. Move on. Stop rehashing, Kristy. Keep running.

So I did...I settled into a nicely paced jog, the view of the calm bay over my shoulder. My mind wandered to the days after 'the incident.'

I convinced myself the situation was 'not-that-bad.' Others had dealt with worse. My life was blessed with many gifts.

Who was I to complain?

I put on a face, bottled up my disgust and dealt with the Sheriff. The community loved him, and if I changed my behavior toward him, people would ask questions. Stay under the radar was my mantra. Graduation was in three months—I could handle 3 months.

The "American Dream" was at my fingertips. In a few months college would be a distant safe haven. I needed that—a place with no connection to him. I left town never telling anyone, not even my mother, my confidant. My parents didn't need the pain of knowing they trusted a monster.

However, the summer after my first year, I had to face him. The Sheriff was getting married, and my parents expected me to attend. Excuses and pleas fell on deaf ears. My parents didn't understand the clues.

Why would they?

This was my battle, not theirs. I endured three months of him already. I figured I could endure one more day.

I was wrong. The "ickiness" weighed on my conscience.

I hadn't escaped.

His reappearance suffocated me. The fun, confident, college flirt was gone. I could no longer bury 'the incident.' If he could do this to me, he would do this to others. He had access to girls far less confident—girls without stable homes, girls lacking social success, girls craving his approval. I was not one of these targets, yet he chose me. The guilt of leaving other girls at risk brought me out of the darkness and to the confession table. He had to be stopped—not for me but for them.

During fall break my sophomore year I met with a trusted teacher from high school—the Sheriff's good friend. At least if he knew, he would keep an eye on the Sheriff's behavior.

Bad idea.

He didn't want me to tell anyone for fear of what people would say about ME. The Sheriff was a powerful person.

"Are you sure it wasn't a dream?" he asked. "How will you be able to prove 'the incident' happened?"

He tried to convince me he was on my side.

"I don't want you exploited in the press or the courts over a 'she said, he said situation.' You have your whole life in front of you."

The teacher promised he would keep his eye on the Sheriff—a relief, however temporary, for my guilty conscience.

Six months later my mother and I were on a long, snowy drive to visit my grandmother during Spring break. As usual, she was venting frustrations about my father's behavior on reoccurring offenses—lack of affection, rude comments...etcetera. I had heard it all before. Her words were the white noise of a disconnected television. I tuned her out.

Until...

"Why can't your father treat me lovingly, like the Sheriff treats his new wife?"

My emotional seams burst.

"I hate that man!"

I spit. Two years of anguish boiled through clenched teeth.

Her look from the driver's seat could turn anyone to stone.

She spoke slowly, measuring every word. Her lead foot never wavered.

"Why...would...you...say...that?"

Filtered filth spewed from my no longer reluctant tongue. My mother's hands were glued to ten and two on the wheel as she listened, speechless—a difficult task for a headstrong woman who prided herself on taking charge and solving problems.

When the sting of the "tazers" I fired wore off, she put on her fighting gloves.

"I will kill that son-of-a-bitch! Why didn't you tell me? Why didn't you tell me?" Her despair barely veiled her rage. My two years of silence wounded her.

"I knew you would have gone after him if I told you," I answered calmly.

"You're right. I would have killed the bastard!"

"Which is exactly why I didn't say anything! He would have brought you down. He's the Sheriff!"

"No way! We could have destroyed him if I knew! How could he do this? I had it all wrong, my feelings all wrong. That bastard!"

"This is my fight. You are not responsible. Promise me, you will do nothing. I have to deal with this on my own. Promise you won't tell anybody," I begged.

"Have you told your father?"

My daddy held my hand, while we drove to the police station. Against his better judgment, he stayed in the car at my request.

The Sheriff was expecting me. I walked down the long, cold corridor toward his office. My mind replayed words rehearsed often.

Was I really doing this?

I paused near his office, looking at the floor, wishing for the courage to bolt like a spooked horse.

"Well, if it ain't my favorite college girl."

The hair stood on the back of my neck.

I froze, eyes wide, breath held.

The Under-Sheriff was in front of the Sheriff's desk. He blocked my view of the monster.

"Kristy! What a pleasant surprise."

The Under-Sheriff delivered a big hug, and his warm smile defrosted my rigid body, a little. Although I hadn't expected him there, I was relieved for the momentary buffer. Over his shoulder, my eyes fixed on the Sheriff as he rose from the big black leather chair behind his wooden desk.

"What are you doing home in the middle of the week?" the Under-Sheriff inquired.

"Spring break."

My voice cracked. I needed to harness my nerves and dig deep to unearth my bubbly self. I didn't want to draw undue attention to this visit. We exchanged pleasantries, my mind anxious for my moment alone with the Sheriff.

After what felt like an eternity I interjected.

"I would love to stay and catch up, but I have a private matter to discuss with Mr. Sheriff."

The Sheriff spoke to his subordinate.

"Finish up here. Kristy and I will head to the interrogation room to chat."

I followed him, down a cold hallway to a small room with no windows. He motioned for me to sit in one of the two metal upright chairs. The armrests encased me. He assumed a position of authority in a swivel chair behind the desk.

"So, what do I owe this pleasure?"

The sugar in his voice masked his evil.

"I'm here because of what you did to me."

My tone matter of fact, my pulse racing.

"What do you mean?"

His expression seemed perplexed, but his eyes told another story.

"You know what you did."

I stared into his dark dead eyes, the blue I once admired gone.

"I don't know what you are talking about."

His voice speaking words his body didn't believe.

"Yes. Yes - You - Do!"

My voice was unwavering and direct. His denial did not deter my mission.

"You know what you did."

I continued by spelling out each of his actions, slow and monotone, not losing eye contact. His fingers began to fidget on the desk and his right hand reached to caress his nodding chin. His body squirmed, the power in the room transferring to my side of the desk.

"You did this to me. I trusted you and you did this to me."

I took a breath hoping to reach the finish line.

"I've been a wreck since that day. You've destroyed my relationships at college. I don't trust. I don't sleep. How could you do this to me?"

"I'm sorry. I'm sorry. You're just so beautiful and..."

He lowered his head.

Did my ears hear correct—did he just admit to all of it?

His inaudible excuses floundering, he was drowning—I controlled the life preserver.

Empowered, I cut off his empty words.

"I don't want your excuses. You had no right to touch me."

"But, Kristy..." he pleaded.

"I don't want to hear anything you have to say. What you did was wrong! I told Dr. Kline all about what you did to me. Yes, that's right, your hunting buddy knows EVERYTHING. My parents know. Your best friend knows. They all know what you did."

"Please, please, Kristy, let me explain. You have it all wrong."

The powerful Sheriff looked like a guilty little boy seeking his parents' absolution.

I stood up, throwing up my palm to silence him.

"I didn't come here for you. I came here for me. You are nothing to me now."

As he kept mumbling, I stood and walked out of the room holding my breath. I left the building and walked down the concrete steps smiling at my daddy parked below. His fearful eyes warmed as he connected to my calm baby blues. My daddy was proud. I was finally free.

Emerging from hell, my strong spirit was revived. I had taken on the devil and won.

CHAPTER 35

Kristy, Are You Doing OK?

"You are a remarkable woman," Neil stated with watering eyes.

His compliment was comforting. Neil spoke in a tender voice, "I'm so sorry that happened to you...so sorry."

He looked at me with admiration. My insides squirmed.

"Does Patrick know the details with the Sheriff?"

"Most."

I tried to remember what I told Patrick.

I was calmed by the memory of Patrick grabbing my hand as I told him about confronting the Sheriff. He was proud of my strength, though he didn't say it directly. He loved me, and I longed to escape to that quiet moment with him in my parent's hot tub under the stars. I couldn't return to simpler times.

Neil was getting straight to the point.

"Have you thought of a strong moment in your life after confronting the Sheriff?"

I obliged with another moment stemming from 'the incident.'

I never looked back after the confrontation. I had forgiven the Sheriff and moved on—or so I thought.

Four years later, Patrick and I were returning from our honeymoon, and my parents picked us up at the airport. Once settled in the vehicle she handed the front page of the newspaper back to us. My tanned face turned white.

The Sheriff's photo was on the front page under the headline: Sheriff Faces Charges in Sex Assault Case.

My mother's anger gurgled.

"A lot has happened since you've been off honeymooning. Your dad and I had to listen to our friends defend the Sheriff, while our community smeared a good woman's reputation. I don't know how much more we can take."

My mother pleaded with me to tell her social circle what the Sheriff did to me. My daddy was silent. With the latest allegation, my request for secrecy was destroying them. I was ashamed. Another woman had become a victim, and God only knows how many others were out there. I did what I had to do. I contacted the detectives.

The Sheriff was convicted of assaulting the woman and was sent to prison. My soul was vindicated—strong girl reborn.

Neil's warm eyes spoke to the acceptance for which I longed.

My half-smile accompanied a shoulder shrug and open hands. I was uncomfortable with any praise on the subject.

"I did what I had to do for a woman wrongly persecuted in the court of public opinion."

"Kristy, you didn't have to come forward. You *should* be proud of yourself."

Neil's compliment coddled my fragile state-of-mind.

"I am proud, sort of. I just wished I would have had the strength to stop him earlier."

I thought of my failures in the unmarked car, and my fists tightened along with my chest.

"You were just a girl. You did the best you could."

Neil tried to make eye contact, while my eyes drifted to his worn brown shoes. One of the laces was untied. I couldn't look at him. My face contorted in agony.

"I should have done better. I could have done more."

My volume increased.

"But I pushed ahead through life, trying to *control* my happiness. And I used poor Patrick as my crutch. He doesn't deserve the torture I've put him through."

Neil's face reflected my emotion and he diverted the subject.

"Close your eyes. Picture yourself in your calm, peaceful place. Describe what you see."

Relieved to escape, I visualized the peaceful place Neil had me conjure a few weeks before.

"I'm alone in the hammock at my beach. The calm Caribbean blue water glistens from the sun's rays. There is not a cloud in the sky. A wisp of a breeze cools my skin. The trees rustle gently in harmony with the sweet songs of swallows. Everything is perfect."

"Notice how your body feels now."

I was no longer on the edge of the chair. My core had melted into the cushion. My arms rested at my sides. The clenched fists were relaxed.

"My pulse is slowing. I feel like putty."

"Good. Stay aware of those feelings as you now picture yourself in the interrogation room in front of the Sheriff confronting him."

Neil's directions were leading me to a place I had avoided.

My heartbeat quickened, yet the tension in my body was different. There was a power between my strong mind and the body beneath my armor. I was in control. I was strong. I was no longer afraid to fail like I had that day.

I didn't want to fail Patrick, but could no longer pretend I didn't need passion. I prayed for a changed man, a husband who could open up and share his feelings, not just organize outcomes. Maybe his counseling would also peel back layers of protection. I wished he was seeing his therapist more often.

Over the next few sessions, Neil continued to turn on my verbal onslaught in sessions. Once unleashed, there was no way to stop. When I wasn't with Neil, I was with Sarah. The woman I deemed self-absorbed when we first met became my reliable confidant. She accepted the real me in the mornings with no make-up, hair not done and my *unfiltered* feelings. At the gym, I was my true self,—exposed with no protection from her inquiries. Each day, I revealed a few more horrors of my messed up life. Yet Sarah never wavered despite of her admiration for likeable Patrick. Her friendship was unlike anything I had known or deserved. In my pathetic state, I had nothing to offer in return.

Why would Sarah want a friend like *me?*

When one hour in the gym wasn't enough, we walked outside in the spring air. Sometimes, in order to bridge time until another session with Neil, I'd convince her to hike the trails around the old asylum. We would wander under the canopy of trees and meander up and down the rolling hills. Sarah provided a sponge to my rambling words.

Amongst the brush along the edge of the trail, we would often stumble upon cement structures covered in graffiti. It was rumored to be a popular spot for homeless who roamed the woods looking for their own peace. I was not much different from them, seeking an escape from my unfair world. The smell of smoldering ashes from their recently abandoned campfires triggered my fears...of a burning place where the serenity of this forest didn't exist. Maybe I would be better off busting through the white picket fence to the dark side. I was going through hell. Without Sarah, I may have surrendered to the heat and quit my fake existence. Sarah, the angel, pushed me to walk through the flames. Sounds from the babbling creek encouraged my steps. If the creek couldn't stop the flames, then I prayed Neil had the extinguisher.

The virtuous girl was history. I was a sham of a Catholic and wife.

CHAPTER 36

I Run to You

Had my mistakes become regrets? Had I learned to love abuse?

The weather remained cold. May flowers never came after the April showers. There were no buds on trees or floral scents in the air. The weary weather mirrored my state of mind. The pain piercing my heart distracted me from any discomfort my body was experiencing. My iPod, gutted of snappy pop tunes, blared country lyrics in my ears as I ran. The lyrics rekindled moments lost in time. Tears soaked my face as my strides lengthened.

Happy was gone from my vocabulary. My family deserved better than what I offered. I clung to my marriage by a thread, no matter how hard I tried to forget, Chad had happened to my heart.

I was a failure to God, my family and myself.

I ran faster, words echoing in my head. It did not make sense that one man could change the course of my life in just two days. This was not part of my life plan.

I don't do emotion. I don't do spontaneity. I don't do adultery. What is this thing I have become?

I lost all momentum. The memory of Chad clouded my ability to move forward.

Maybe seeing him would eliminate my convoluted fairytale. My struggling existence yearned for Chad to remember my 5K race on Mother's Day. I needed him.

Patrick didn't put up a fight about me leaving for the weekend with Chloe. I wished he would have. I craved unbridled emotion, and he flunked again, keeping in sync with the nice guy routine.

Fear coursed through me on the drive to Grand Rapids.

Was I scared of running, scared I would not miss home...or afraid Chad would show?

Whichever the source, relief washed over my body once on the hotel room balcony. Here there were no expectations - no struggling to *do* the right thing or *perform* in the marriage. I could breathe. I was able to ignore the mess of my life and relish in the warmth of the spring sun. The balcony door caught a breeze and slammed against my chair. I opened my eyes, and there stood Chloe.

Every muscle suddenly tightened.

"Did you talk to him?"

Guilt swallowed me whole. I did not make the call, yet my heart was sinning. I should not have asked Chloe to contact Chad.

Chloe sat on the other mesh chair, water bottle in hand, and propped her feet on my chair. She slowly laid her phone on the railing.

"Don't make me wait," I spouted.

Perspiration gathered on my neck.

"Yes, we spoke," she answered nonchalantly like we were discussing the weather not my fragile heart. "I could hear his voice quiver when he realized it was me. He thought something was wrong with you. He's worried about how you are holding up."

"What'd you tell him?"

My legs shook. My mouth tasted like sandpaper. I needed a drink.

"I said you were holding up alright, trying to make your marriage work."

"What'd he say? Is he getting the letters?"

The impulsive tone of my loud voice was like a crack addict needing another fix.

"He just kept asking if *'his Baby'* was REALLY OK. He sounded sad. He was distraught at the thought of causing you pain. He doesn't want to be the cause of a wrecked marriage and only wants you to be happy."

Chloe took a breath.

"He's not coming."

My emotional addiction overpowered my moral compass. I grabbed Chloe's phone and dialed. Chloe said nothing. The call went straight to voicemail. I sat in silence.

Why was I so weak when it came to Chad? Maybe I could run from his memory and my guilt. I had to stop the feelings.

A sea of people surrounded me, yet I never felt so alone. Waves of runners propelled my body. My mind was lost. Despite Chad's desires, he refused to be my crutch. I had to figure my marriage out myself with no distractions. Chad couldn't be the reason I quit my marriage, and guilt couldn't be the reason I stayed.

Could I do life alone?

I was alone. I was running!

Pride intertwined with my stride. By myself, for myself, I was running! Three years of fear had dictated my excuses to not run the race.

Why had I given up on my abilities and let fear rule my life?

I turned a corner.

Cheers from the crowd lining the streets energized my steps— the first toward changing my scripted life. I had approached life like something to be accomplished, as if I knew the ending before reading the book. My life of planning hadn't allowed me to live with real emotion. The time had come to throw away the script, set fears aside, and follow my passions.

As my foot passed over the blue pad stopping the race timer, I sensed that a new clock was beginning. It was my time to live, to laugh and to love—not for the approval of others, but for myself. I vowed fear would no longer corral my feelings and paralyze my steps.

But where did that leave my marriage?

For the first time in nearly three months, I was proud of myself and couldn't wait to share my accomplishment with Sarah and Neil. Not including Patrick in my thoughts burdened my heart. As I pulled into the driveway, the suffocating feeling returned. I labored to breath.

How could I disappoint my family?

I walked into the kitchen to find an assortment of flowers on the kitchen island and a big banner hanging with the words—Way to Go, MOM!

Who does these kind acts for a woman as tainted as me?

Patrick. His gestures felt forced—an obligation to do the right thing. He must be an emotionless robot following the role of a good husband in spite of the daggers thrown his way since Texas. I pitied him for loving a woman such as me.

He deserved better.

With the lights off and the children sound asleep, I understood why my *robot* husband was kind on my arrival—he needed someone to oil his parts. Before the past weekend, I would have accommodated him out of fear of failing at my role as a good wife.

Not this time!

Completing the race freed my soul and lifted fear from my spirit. My feelings mattered!

I snapped with a long, loathing sigh.

"Do I have to leave the bed?"

CHAPTER 37

Could It Be

"Why do you do things you hate?"

Neil's question caught me off guard.

"What do you mean?"

I squinted, perplexed.

He leaned forward and looked at me with inquisitive eyes.

"Why do you have to prove people wrong and accept a challenge you don't want to do? You chose an all-girl school to challenge yourself in female friendships. You pursue a degree you don't enjoy because you think it's the right path for security. You say you're not good at being a stay at home mom but do it because you feel it's the right thing. You run a 5K, but you say you hate running. Why?"

I had no answers.

Why do I do things I hate?

I have always followed the plan, accepted the challenge. I was the "good girl" striving to do better, be better. I dug through the cobwebs to reach my memories, realizing that "overachiever" was my reoccurring theme. Happiness or passion had not been my goals. I didn't have to *like* what I was doing. I merely had to learn to do it well to gain approval from someone, anyone—perhaps even just myself. I wanted to be noticed and admired for my out-of-the-box accomplishments. Perhaps then I would be worthy of someone or something great. I kept reaching...

A visual entered my head:

I remembered stomping the snow off my shoes in the foyer of my childhood home as I cradled the envelope I had been anxiously awaiting. I slowly trailed my finger across the return address label from the University of Notre Dame, and then tore open the envelope. As I unfolded the letter my smile faded.

"I'm sorry to inform you, but at this time we cannot accept you for early admission. We will be reviewing your application with the regular admission applicants."

I wasn't fabulous. I was waitlisted!

I immediately dismissed my desire to go there, and brushed off the defeat to make a new plan. I assumed if I wasn't worthy now what would make me worthy in six months. Being a "good girl" hadn't been enough, so I needed to improve myself more. I loved basketball, but knew my limitations as a 5'4" player. Cheers and adulations as a college athlete were not in the cards.

Instead, I settled on an early admission offer to attend St. Mary's College, the all-girls school across from Notre Dame. Maybe an all-girls environment was just the challenge I needed anyway. Through high school and even into college, I never really had a female best friend. I desperately wanted someone to confide in and depend on like a sister. I longed for pure acceptance from another female and never gave up trying to find it. I just started believing that it wasn't in the cards for me, so I stuck with less complex male friendships, until they wanted MORE than friendship. Maybe with only girls on campus, I could focus on my problems of connecting to female friendships and still be involved with Notre Dame's activities—boys—since the two schools commingled social events, including football games.

I figured this was God's way of making me jump through another hoop to better myself. That is until I gave up on being worthy of a "bestie." After a year or so of trying with all girls and after finally confronting the Sheriff, I conjured up enough courage to reapply, be accepted and transfer to the "Dome."

"How's all the achieving and planning working for you?" Neil asked.

"Just fine—until Texas!"

My snarky tone blamed Chad for shaking my picture perfect world.

"What does your chest feel like right now?"

What is he talking about?

Oh, that's strange—I hadn't felt the weight on my chest until he pushed my mind to focus there.

"Heavy, like I can't breathe."

"Do you *really* want to go back to the way things were?"

His question trapped me.

"No...but it was so much easier," I said stubbornly.

I didn't like him having one up on me.

"At least, then, I had security and a trusted man who loved me, and not all these irrational feelings screwing up a good thing with a good man."

Despair reappeared.

"Why aren't you more angry that this 'good girl' who does everything right doesn't feel passion?"

"I don't know...I only feel sadness. I accepted that passion wasn't in the cards and carried on with life—a good life. Chad wasn't supposed to exist!"

Sadness weighted my body like an anchor. Time's up!

I couldn't get back on Neil's schedule soon enough. Twice a week wasn't sufficient. I continued to write every day in my journal, but I was a girl of language. I needed to talk!

Thank God for Sarah.

We took daily walks along the asylum's hilly trails. The once bare hardwoods were covered with greening leaves, and our warm accessories shed in the balmy spring air. The gym lacked the appropriate atmosphere for our ever-increasing in depth talks. Three months of introspective had been exhausting, and left no strength for me to carry protective armor when with Sarah. I was no longer talking at her, but talking with her. Being with Sarah provided much-needed reprieves from the turmoil of my internal war.

Since Chloe was in the rough seas of her own divorce, Sarah was the life preserver keeping me afloat. I needed Sarah. My initial perceptions were all wrong. She would drop her work to walk and talk with me even though I had nothing to offer her in my defeated state. She evolved into my reliable sounding board—my trusted friend.

"Neil asked me if I could think of a time in my adult life when I was strong. I couldn't think of one, Sarah—not one. How pathetic!"

"Kristy, that's asinine!" Sarah insisted. "You're one of the strongest women I know. You're fighting for your marriage. Do you know how many women would have thrown in the towel? Be proud of yourself. In the middle of all this, you even ran that 5K you've avoided for years."

Sarah's cheerleading was a twist to her regular tongue biting during my hours of continuous chatter.

I struggled.

"Thanks, but I don't feel strong. I used to be a girl capable of anything. Fearless in most every pursuit. But 'that girl' is now lost."

She stopped and made eye contact with me.

"I don't think she's lost. I think you know exactly where she is."

Sarah's unexpected feedback rang in my ears. They suffocated unclear thoughts bouncing around in my head. Maybe she was right.

My depressed mind still searched for answers as I waited to see Neil. His waiting room felt more like an old lady's living room than a professional office.

I considered Sarah's observations.

Had fear of failing paralyzed my pursuit of feelings? Had the race liberated my soul?

I recalled the sound of the gun firing that cold morning. My body surged with strength and determination—running! A strong woman full of passion did exist! I didn't have to achieve the best time. I just needed to find satisfaction in the doing.

If only all my running could rid my heart of Chad.

CHAPTER 38

Do I

Nervous energy coursed through me. My fingernails were nubs. It was Memorial Day weekend, and Patrick and I were attending our first social gathering since St. Patrick's Day. That period of social isolation felt like ten years.

Could I survive tonight without exposing my sinning soul?

Outwardly glued at the hips, we walked into the trendy art gallery housed in a converted warehouse that consisted of two areas. One was cozy yet sophisticated with high ceilings, exposed pipes, and various works of art displayed. Bartenders intermingled with the art. The other area was wide open with a band on an elevated stage and random couches scattered about. It reminded me of an underground rave party in a large city, not here.

Everybody who was anybody was there to celebrate my friend's 40th birthday. Being MIA for months, various social circles were gossiping about my absence...everything from Chloe and me leaving our husbands for one another, to me having a terminal illness. I didn't care. I owed it to my friend to be supportive. I had avoided her for fear she would see right through my charade, or I would open my big mouth to her spilling my demise.

"Ooooohh, you're here!"

The tan, blonde birthday girl bounced toward us, drink in hand.

"I'm so glad you made it! I was starting to think you forgot about us. Kristy, look at you. You're fading away! And you, Patrick, where have you been hiding those pipes? What's up...Mid-life crisis?"

She laughed, while never losing her beautiful smile.

If she only knew...

I hadn't put on a face for months and didn't have the strength tonight either. My walls were rubble, and I had no energy to maintain a façade. The pleasing everyone Kristy had vanished in Texas and the new, calmer Kristy was making her debut tonight. For the first time, I wasn't worried about how I looked or what I said—other's opinions were the least of my worries.

Luck was by my side, though. Patrick redirected the conversation to the birthday girl until other guests distracted her.

Over her shoulder, I spotted Sarah, my guardian angel with her husband, Aaron by her side. Her shiny blonde hair framed her fair skin like a porcelain doll. In spite of her window to my soul, her presence comforted me. Patrick however had apprehensions about Sarah and our new-found connection. He wasn't sure how to handle my new confidant. However he *was* relieved that I spent more time with her than Chloe, who was pushing ahead with divorce against her husband's wishes—and mine.

"Hi, friend," I said, smiling.

Sarah's husband responded, "Hello y'all."

Aaron could charm a room with his Tennessee drawl—an anomaly here since most Southerners weren't keen to move to frigid Northern Michigan. His accent resonated as he said hello, and my heart skipped a beat remembering what I was trying to forget.

Aaron grabbed Patrick and escorted him to the bar—a true test as we hadn't touched alcohol since Linda requested we abstain for at least three months during our counseling. We stuck to this pledge despite her suspension of our sessions—anything to try to save us.

Would Patrick break under tonight's pressure?

Sarah hugged me and whispered, "How you holding up?"

"Hangin' in," I replied with a weak smile.

"Pat and you look good. Are you?"

"For now, yes."

I wanted to capture the moment. Tonight, Patrick and I were connected, unconcerned with our surroundings and comfortable in this crowded room.

Then, I shot back.

"Why? What are people saying?"

"Your calmness is raising some eyebrows, but Chloe's issues overshadow everything."

Sarah's voice was comforting, but her words disturbing. Chloe deserved a better friend than me. I was a hypocrite for hiding behind Chloe's pain.

Before I could ask her more, Patrick returned—two glasses of soda in hand.

I clung tighter to Patrick, my security blanket, this evening. Our typical drill at a party would be to work the room separately and compare stories at night's end. But tonight was different. Instead of drifting back to our old ways, we stood together in our tarnished armor. I was proud of the man on my arm, my rock. He loved me even though I hadn't been so lovable.

Was it time to step up and decide the direction of my own life without leaning on Patrick or waiting for him to break?

He didn't deserve the way I chipped away at his kind spirit. I needed a life based on reality AND emotion, and he deserved better than what I gave him. Like a noble captain, Patrick was not abandoning our sinking ship. I had to set him free, just not yet.

Tonight was a night to forget the pain I was causing and honor my husband. He deserved all my attention, and my flirting ways evaporated. Every unsolicited hug and kiss from our male friends made me squirm. Attention that formerly boosted my confidence and stroked my ego now deflated my spirit.

All was changed. I had become someone else. There was no turning back the clock.

Not wanting to acknowledge the looming cliff, I ignored the darkness and danced with my husband.

Every dark night turns into daylight, but I was not ready to give up my crutch in that moment. Patrick continued putting his best foot forward. He planned a romantic date at a new restaurant called *Siren Hall.* That was an appropriate name for what we needed—sirens calling an emergency crew to come save our marriage. After the party last night, I needed to give our marriage one last chance, praying his romantic gesture would spark a fire...maybe a miracle. Patrick deserved that.

After confirming the sitter, I made lunch for the children and a sandwich for Patrick. I found him on the back deck soaking up some spring sun. He had removed his shirt exposing his well-defined chest. I hadn't noticed how toned his physique had become the past few months. His hairless skin glistened in the sun and he appeared much younger than he was. He would have no problem finding my replacement. He sat up at the sounds of my footsteps.

"I made you a sandwich."

"Thanks," he replied half-smiling.

Patrick gestured for me to sit in the lounge chair beside him. As I sat down, he asked, "Did you have fun last night?"

"Yeah, I did. It was nice to get out. But I don't miss the charades."

"That makes two of us."

He paused.

"You know I love you, right?"

His candor caught me off guard.

"Yes...I know."

Darn tears.

He took a deep breath.

"I've been thinking a lot...and we can't move forward until you put Texas behind you. I think you should go to Texas."

What?! Did he say what I think he said?

"What do you mean?"

"I mean you need to figure this out. We can't go on like this. The memory of him is standing in our way."

His words pointed. His expression masked by the glare of the sun.

"Are you sure?"

"Yeah, you can call him Tuesday when I'm out of town to arrange it."

"O-OK, I think."

I had broken him. He was letting me go. But I wasn't sure how to handle this.

"So...now what?" I asked. "Are we still going to dinner?"

"Of course. We still have to eat. I told you, I love you and only want you to be happy."

His words were controlled, unlike the sweat dripping off his face.

We relaxed at dinner. Patrick's courage that afternoon freed me from the pressure to feel something—reminiscent of our summers on Brooks Lake. Patrick expected nothing from me then and nothing from me tonight.

"Let's try and enjoy the rest of this long weekend," Patrick added.

True to our truce, we embraced Memorial Day weekend comfortably, enjoying every moment as an intact family. I loved Patrick and always would. I prayed he could begin to heal, and wished his next week away would be helpful.

My glassy eyes filled with water—I wasn't worthy of him.

CHAPTER 39

I'm In

My hand trembled the Tuesday after the weekend. Maybe Patrick was right. The myth of feelings would be expelled if I saw Chad. The idea made sense to my head, but my heart knew better.

I dialed his number.

"Kristy?"he asked?

His Southern drawl still invigorated me.

"Hi!" I said, hesitating to allow the butterflies to fly from my heart.

"I can't believe it's you. Everything OK?" Chad asked cautiously.

"Fine, I think. What would you say if I came for visit?"

I forced my tone flat to tame my emotions.

"When?" he asked guardedly.

"Whenever you say."

My playfulness peaked through.

"I'm not sure..."

He paused, his voice sounded strangely aloof.

"What about your marriage?"

"It's Patrick's idea. He's beginning to understand our relationship is missing something and is letting me go. I told you we were different. He just wants me to be happy."

A sigh of relief escaped.

"Kristy, I don't know if this is a good idea. You're still married."

His reaction was cold—not what I envisioned. He continued with an apprehensive drawl.

"Don't get me wrong, baby. I want you here. But I can't be the reason you break up your family. I'm not going anywhere. You know how I feel. Find comfort in that. You have to sort through your marriage."

I gasped. Chad refused to be my crutch. At least I had Neil.

My appointment with him wasn't until Friday. It was going to be a long, lonely week in my head. My thoughts were too horrific to even consider sharing with Sarah. I was alone—the place I feared most. I knew Chad would never move to Michigan with his boys' mother in Texas, and Patrick would never move despite us both hating the cold weather of the North. I would have to hope for living next door to Patrick and co-parenting. After all, we were best friends before all else. Divorce was not in my vocabulary, yet here I was contemplating the option despite the repercussions from my church, and the wrath of God.

With Patrick away until Friday, I had no choice but to handle the children's bedtime rituals. I drifted from room to room tucking the children in. A glimpse of how difficult nighttime would be without Patrick's help. Ally, the smallest, clung to me as I sang her an out-of-tune lullaby. Brooke, *Miss Independent*, was asleep when I got to her. After finishing with the girls, I crawled into bed with Seth—usually the chatty night owl. Tonight he said nothing about my awkward gestures and snuggled quietly in my arms. My mind settled just enough to begin feeling his love before creeping out of his room.

His soft voice startled me.

"Mommy, thanks for staying with me. I love you."

"I love you, too," I whispered. "Now, go to sleep."

I retreated to my bathroom to wash my face, and then collapsed in wailing sobs.

Why all this emotion now?

Sleep was not on my agenda this week.

The next morning, after dropping the children at school, I walked alone in the misting rain. Sarah was home with a sick son, which was probably for the best considering my ugly thoughts of divorce. Instead of the wooded trails, I walked the more populated path along the bay of Lake Michigan. The aqua blue bay sparkled as scattered rays of sun peeked through the rain clouds. It was a perfect day for a rainbow.

Despite the discomfort of being alone with no sign of hope, the walk empowered me and I temporarily let go of my mental crutches. I realized my life had been a boring, predictable book evoking little emotion. I was resentful that the life I chose hadn't given me the feelings I wanted and forced me to settle for scraps to fill my heart. My happy moments, however few, occurred outside of the white picket fence, like when the empty flirt got her confidence cup filled by the attention and compliments of others not required to love me.

I sat on a bench to retrieve the number of Chloe's attorney from my contacts list. I asked for the number after the 5K on Mother's Day Weekend, but I had not been ready to call then. I couldn't stop the inevitable and needed to know my options. I made an appointment for Friday, after my morning session with Neil. Two days away.

In the emptiness of Wednesday night, I went to the garage and rifled through my trunk looking for the hidden book. I stoked the fire in the fireplace and checked on the sleeping children for the umpteenth time. Then, I plopped into my favorite chair next to the burning wood and began to read: "How to Handle Divorce."

My gut ached after the first chapter. By the second, I was in the bathroom vomiting.

How could I divorce?

My moral pedestal was crumbling. The over-achiever was becoming the exact type of woman I prided myself in NOT being. How I had been identifying myself was all wrong. I was weak—an imposter. Patrick was the positive in my life and my children needed him. He is a good man.

How could I break them apart, even for one minute?

I curled up on the familiar bathroom floor and cycled in and out of consciousness until sunrise.

Thursday was a new day. I busied myself with planned activities to pass time until my dreaded appointment on Friday —and I wasn't talking about Neil. After neglecting myself for the past few months, I needed a haircut and much needed highlights. Maybe if I looked better, I would feel better able to face my fears and move forward—alone. I knew my appointments with Neil and the attorney would leave my insides rotting, so at the very least my outside should be presentable for the kid's after school talent show Friday.

I left the salon to meet Chloe for soup, about all I could stomach these days. My fingers fumbled for my ringing phone at the bottom of my purse. She was probably running late.

I answered out of breath on the last ring.

"Hello?"

"Hi, baby."

His voice caused an electric current to travel from the phone through my entire body. I froze.

"Is it OK I called this number?"

"Should be," I responded, gaining composure. "I haven't told Patrick yet that I'm not going to Texas. He's been gone all week for work."

My words choked on my heart.

"Well, I've been thinking...maybe we can figure out something. Hearing your voice ripped through me, and I can't get you off my mind. I miss you, baby."

His drawl dripped honey over each word.

"But, I thought you said me coming there wasn't a good idea, unless I was detached."

My head was spinning.

"I know what I said, but I can't deny you, baby. We got whatever 'it' is."

His direct line to my heart was fully engaged.

"I've been thinking too, and it kills me to say this...but maybe your instincts were right. I'm not sure if I should come."

Chad's voice reverberated in my head until it hit the pillow. Unable to sleep, I pulled out my journal hoping to write him out of my mind. The week had been an emotional roller coaster. My vows had kept me strapped into the seat of the coaster preventing my fall from grace. Maybe God would forgive my not-that-bad bag of sins, as long as I didn't travel *south* to Chad. The sixth commandment hadn't been broken yet—*or had it?* Morning couldn't come soon enough.

I needed Neil!

CHAPTER 40

Show Me What I'm Looking For

I gasped.

"What are you doing home?"

Disrupting my thoughts of self-doubt, Patrick stood in the doorway of our bedroom. He wasn't due home until tomorrow night.

I couldn't mask my shock.

He laid his suit coat on the chair next to the bed.

"The meeting ended early, so I decided to drive home. Are the children already asleep?"

"Yeah, for an hour or so," I replied.

I slipped my journal into the nightstand drawer when he went into the bathroom to change.

Instead of retreating to his office, Patrick climbed into bed wearing only his black boxer briefs. His well-defined six-pack abs glowed from the light of his bedside lamp. He must be spending a lot more time in the gym or was benefiting from my lack of cooking these past three months. Either way, he would have no problem attracting the ladies.

His green eyes stared at an uncomfortable me. I wished he would turn his light off.

"Did you talk to him?"

Patrick's blunt question caught me off guard—so much for his salesman-like manner.

"Yes...but I'm not going. Seeing him won't change things between you and me."

I fiddled with a lock of my new blonde hair, twirling it around to distract myself from the pit in my stomach.

"What do you mean?" he asked, before erupting in anger. "He changed everything between us! EVERYTHING! If you think for one minute I want you to go to Texas, you are wrong! I hate him! I hate everything about him and Texas!"

I was confused. Wasn't he the one who told me to go to Texas? Was this the breaking point I feared? Was Patrick finally ready to kick me to the curb where I probably belonged?

Preparing myself for the barrage of insults that would likely come next, I blurted. "Why on earth did you tell me to go then?"

"Because I love you!"

His words drew strength from a well I thought was dry.

Not prepared for his first outburst of real emotion, I froze, locked on his smoldering eyes. His heat made me thirsty. I ignored the need to quench my thirst with his expression of love and listened as he continued pouring out his heart.

"All I ever wanted was for you to be happy. And you're *not*! I don't want a divorce. I never wanted one! A divorce will be your decision, not mine. I will never give up on you until you give up on us. Then, I will move on and you will not be the one I confide in any longer. I can't be just friends with you! I LOVE you! There will be no 'Happily Ever After' divorce."

His words shattered my dreams of harmony and confused my already damaged heart.

This was true emotion from a vulnerable place. I wasn't worthy of his words. I knew it and so did he. Trying to ignore my urges for hydration from his expressions of love, I focused on his failures of verbal expression for the past umpteen years.

Where was all his emotion before tonight?

I pleaded with his rational side, "How can we keep trying to feel something we don't?"

"Kristy, I feel."

His eyes radiated pain I had never seen.

"I buy you flowers. I do housework. I help with the kids, all because I love *you*! Do you remember the surprise vacation last year to the Loews Hotel in South Beach?"

Of course I did.

"It was a five star hotel, and you complained about everything. No matter what I do, you have a different idea in your head and are never happy with my romantic gestures. I can't live up to your fairytale! I don't put myself out there for fear of failing you."

I dropped my head, listening to his long overdue rant. His words continued to sting.

"The irony...I always thought you would wise up and leave me. I knew I was never good enough for you...but then the marriage... the kids. Finally, after Ally, I believed. I let my guard down and WHAM! This happens!"

I wanted to stop his bleeding.

"You're right," I said with a soft, quivered voice. "You do everything right—flowers, surprise vacations, even dancing with me when you hate to dance. I don't know why I critique all your efforts to love me," I said as water pooled in my eyes.

Why can't I feel his gestures of love?

My tongue lashed out in my defense before I could call back the troupes.

"I feel like a misunderstood conquest being pursued for one purpose!"

"That's not fair. You never told me you didn't like my kiss, my touch...until after you came back from Texas. I didn't know what you needed. Now I know."

His volume lowered.

"I am learning to be a better man...for you...or at least for the next one. But I want YOU!"

His eyes had an intense look I had never seen before. This was my first real glimpse behind the wall. Before I had time to process his words, Patrick embraced my cheeks with both hands and pulled me in for a kiss. I lingered in the moment. His eyes remained open, and I fell into the unfamiliar space. My heart felt alive as it explored this new territory. Our eyes bore into one another as he caressed my cheek which sparked an unusual fire in me. I basked in the warmth of my best friend, trying to ignore what was on the horizon.

Passion flowed between us in an unfamiliar way. I felt a difference in his caresses.

Had the true Patrick finally emerged from behind his green barricade or was my fear of the cliff ahead altering my state of mind, leaving me vulnerable to his actions?

As much as I wanted Patrick to save me from myself, he couldn't fix our lack of chemistry.

Or could he?

Tonight was different. He was different.

How can I be ready to move on one minute and be open to Patrick's goodness the next?

I needed strength. He needed a better woman.

CHAPTER 41

Come Back To Me

I couldn't handle all the emotion. I desperately needed strength. I needed answers. I needed help. I needed something.

My drive toward Neil's office went through the dark tunnel of large oak trees lining the entrance to the old asylum. If it was still open, I would have admitted myself—instead Neil would have to do.

Music invaded my thoughts. The magnitude of Patrick's Texas proposal sang through the radio.

"So, I'll let you go, I'll set you free. When you see what you need to see, when you find you, come back to me..."

Waiting for my appointment, I logged in my journal the recent roller coaster of events—from seeing behind Patrick's eyes last night to the song this morning clarifying the feelings Patrick tried to verbalize. If God was sending me a "sign" where Patrick was concerned, I wanted to make sure I didn't miss it.

To Neil, I rambled through the highlights of the past week in classic Kristy fashion—confronting Patrick on my hopelessness of ever feeling passion for him, his proposal of me going to Texas, Chad's selfless love, my appointment with the divorce attorney, and my breakdown after cuddling with Seth. I described Patrick's outburst of emotion that led to our odd intimate encounter in our bedroom, and my fears of being alone without my best friend, Patrick.

As I finally took a breath, I realized Neil was sitting forward on the edge of his seat, not taking his eyes off me. I could feel his compassion. He cared about me, and I him.

Why can't I connect with Patrick like this?

"Neil, why can't I accept Patrick's gestures of love? All I do is critique him? He does the right things, and I can't even be grateful for them...like a 5-star vacation to South Beach awhile back."

Shame clothed me, and I felt myself shrink remembering Patrick's assessment.

"Close your eyes and let's visualize on remembering the hotel."

Neil's voice was calming. His words re-describing my prior description of the South Beach hotel.

"You say the hotel had marble floors, a king bed overlooking the ocean, an elegant pool and a five-star restaurant. Yet, these luxurious items never made you feel what you expected—romance and passion. You weren't mad about the condition of the hotel, you were mad about the condition of your heart."

Neil's words were all too accurate. My heart was void of what I longed for. He changed topics to one of our previous discussions about my peaceful, happy place.

"When you described your peaceful place at your beach, you described it as 'just perfect' and it seems only when you deem things just perfect do you allow yourself to relax enough to feel."

His words ignited my "ah-ha moment."

"I expect perfection or I am never happy. Is that what you are trying to tell me?"

I didn't wait for him to answer. I knew he was right.

"My whole life has been about striving for success—the perfect husband, the perfect house, the perfect friends, the perfect *me*. I can't see Patrick's goodness because I magnify his imperfections, so I don't feel his goodness."

My voice began to quiver from the self-revelation.

"It isn't him. It's ME! I am not angry at Patrick. I'm angry at myself! I wasn't strong with the Sheriff. I didn't get angry or fight back. I did nothing! For a girl who prides herself in achieving and doing the right thing...I did nothing! I DESERVE NOTHING!"

Neil was quiet. His eyes trained on mine. I was shaking.

He allowed me a few moments to process what I had just learned.

"This is good, Kristy. I would like us to continue talking if you are able to stay past our hour."

I nodded yes, still dazed from my outburst.

"Please excuse me for one moment. I need to reschedule my next client. I'll be right back."

Neil's decision comforted my weary soul. He was choosing me. I was worth his time. I'm glad I'm worth somebody's time.

As he reentered the room and closed the door, he said, "I think maybe the events with the Sheriff are clouding your thoughts more than we both realized. Have you ever heard of PTSD?"

"What?"

The acronym was foreign to me.

Neil eased back into his chair.

"PTSD, or Post Traumatic Stress Disorder, is where a traumatic event alters your perception of life. Soldiers can have it, but so can ordinary folks. There is a type of therapy for PTSD, and I would like to try it with you. We revisit the traumatic memories, while you track my movements with your eyes to alleviate any distress your body and mind might be feeling. It might be helpful."

For a girl who only operated in the black and white, I was skeptical of this gray area of therapy. With my old self being beaten down by this emerging new girl, I agreed to try—anything to find my happy.

"Just follow my hand with your eyes, listen to my commands and let your mind take you wherever it goes, even if it doesn't make sense."

Neil made crazy seem safe—anything for clarity.

He asked me again about my kids at bedtime and why I could never open up or *just be* with them and what it felt like when I did. I described how I was relaxed and peaceful when I cuddled Seth in his bedroom two nights ago. I followed Neil's hand movement. My body escaped to the peaceful moment with Seth where nothing else mattered, and I had no need *to do* something.

"What is your body feeling?" Neil asked.

"Calm, relaxed."

"Good," he replied.

Then, with a swift shift in his words he said, "Now picture yourself in the Sheriff's unmarked car laying your head on his lap to fall asleep."

With my body relaxed, I felt safe as if I was with my own daddy. Then, like a bolt of lightning, my body turned stiff like the metamorphism of a rock, and my breathing silenced. My peaceful slumber had been disrupted by the Sheriff's touch.

"Describe what you're feeling," Neil coaxed softly.

"My chest is heavy like a weight is suffocating my existence. I feel trapped, closed, shut down."

"Where are you now?" Neil asked.

"I'm frozen. He's putting his hands on me. I want to get up and run, but my body won't move."

Tears were brimming behind my closed eyes.

"What emotions are you feeling?"

A tidal wave of sadness consumed me, and one word limped from my lips.

"Sorrow."

"Why aren't you angry when you talk about what he did to you? What he did was assault."

Neil's statement caught me off guard.

"I don't know. I'm just not. I'm over it. People have endured a lot worse."

Neil's pity was getting irritating.

"Don't you think you deserve to be angry about what the Sheriff did?"

"What's the point?" I asked, as a sense of hopelessness forced me down into the chair. "It is what it is."

Neil's tone shifted from soft to powerful.

"What he did to you was wrong."

He stood up, grabbed a small pillow and held it in front of me.

"Get mad! Push his hands off you!" he demanded.

I rolled my eyes and gave a wimpy gesture. This was ridiculous. My sense of logic was prevailing.

"Come on, Kristy. Get mad!" Neil urged. "He doesn't get to put his hands on you. Push his hand off and stand up."

Neil was insistent.

His challenge irked me, but provoked a response in hopes he'd move on if I gave in to his request.

I gave a harder shove to the pillow in an effort to stand. Neil's hands held the pillow firm and resisted me, and my body fell back into the chair.

"You can do better than that!" Neil taunted. "Stop him!"

He trapped me in the chair with the pillow.

My hands reacted before my mind could stifle my actions. I pushed myself forward. I hit the pillow with clenched fists in an effort to fight off the Sheriff.

I had to stop him. I had to.

My arms continued flailing, uncontrollably.

Neil's comforting voice broke my frantic movements.

"You were in a car. You couldn't flee. You couldn't fight. All you could do was freeze."

My arms fell. I was out of breath. My spent body dropped backward, but the chair caught me. Shame engulfed me, shrinking my existence.

I didn't do the right thing. I froze!

"Follow my hand with your eyes," Neil instructed.

He moved his hand side to side a few times before speaking in a controlled voice.

"Now close your eyes again. What changes are you feeling?"

My body felt numb. My cotton dry mouth tried to speak.

"I'm numb. I can't move. I want to withdraw, cower in a ball and sob."

Dampness irritated my eyes.

"When it happened, you couldn't withdraw *or* fight. You were trapped in a car. You had to shut down."

Neil took a slow breath.

"Let go, Kristy. Let yourself feel."

His words penetrated to my core.

"Let yourself feel."

My mind caught up with my convulsing body, and an explosion of sobbing dismantled me.

Trying to clear my flooded eyes, a silent Neil leaned in, as though to hug me, but withdrew to resume his professional demeanor.

No one would want to hug me like this.

Instead his side-to-side hand movements continued, and, with leading questions, he tried to bring me back.

"What do you notice?"

My spasms and sobs continued as my eyes remained closed. The fuzzy scene in my head became clearer.

"I'm on the floor...in my bathroom."

I had come full circle to the night of shaking and sobbing after lying peacefully with Seth. My body was remembering...experiencing pain never released.

I had clarity. I finally understood. My mind healed the day I confronted the Sheriff, but my soul never did.

CHAPTER 42

But For The Grace of God

I left Neil's office sobbing with his words ringing in my ears.

"Let yourself feel whatever you feel this weekend."

I drove home with tears still streaming down my face, and dialed my attorney with shaking hands.

"I thought I was ready, but I'm not."

My car passed beneath a canopy of trees that defined the street like soldiers at attention with swords arched overhead. I was being set free. My self-inflicted prison of perfectionism had confined my senses and protected me from being vulnerable to pain—or feeling worthy of joy. Pardoned from perfection, I emerged from the darkness of the trees and was transformed by the light at the end of the tunnel.

By the grace of God, a rainbow danced across the bay. Its hues were vibrant through my cleansed eyes—the colors more beautiful than I had ever seen before. My physical sight had been altered with God's mercy to a "seeing" from my soul. My new vision made everything feel more intense, more alive. I now understood the excitement felt when people spot a rainbow. Not only could I see the glorious celebration of color, but I could feel the joy of the miracle.

For the first time in a very long time, I felt hope.

I pulled into my driveway. Though the rain from my eyes continued to fall, a speck of sunshine slipped through the dark clouds to illuminate my dream house on the hill. I fumbled for the garage door opener. The white panels, disappearing one row at a time, exposed Patrick's car.

I took my first breath—the weight of my icky off my chest.

Through a blur of tears, I staggered into the house and looked for Patrick. He was still in bed, under the covers—a scene I wasn't prepared to see at 10:30 on a Friday morning. He had obviously been far more impacted by my withdrawal than I had been aware. Still sobbing, I crawled on top of the bed and buried my face in his warm chest. The blankets separated us. Neither of us said a word. He wrapped his strong arms around me as I wept.

He must be thinking the worst. I don't cry.

For more than twenty minutes, I struggled to compose myself. When my wails finally subsided, I gathered enough strength to lift my head off his chest, and, for the first time in twelve years, I saw *my husband.*

Before today, my damaged eyes only caught glimpses of him, but now my vision was unobstructed. I could finally see all of him. I could see down into his soul. Patrick's selfless, unconditional love had triumphantly breached the dam that had been restraining my ability to return love for so long. I was flooded with feelings. His goodness overwhelmed me.

A switch had been flipped.

I explained my morning journey to my husband, a man who loved me selflessly despite my brokenness—a brokenness that I now understood couldn't be healed simply by constructing a perfect life or a finding the perfect man.

Patrick had been brave enough to let me go and, in that process, I found myself.

Patrick's eyes spoke right to my heart—a heart now open and filled with intensity. His expression looked skeptical, but the spirit behind his eyes wanted to believe. He crawled out from beneath the sheets, removed all obstacles between us, and embraced me—his soul fully enveloping mine.

"But how?" he asked.

Patrick had questions. Of course he had questions. I still had questions about my crazy journey in Neil's office. I knew my questions could wait. His couldn't.

"You, that's how."

I smiled, noticing my black mascara was smeared across on his white t-shirt—a happy occasion just like the day he proposed. My mind flashed to our wedding day and the births of our three children. I wanted a do-over on all special occasions, yearning for every feeling I'd been cheated out of over the past umpteen years.

Patrick's twisted expression pulled me back to the moment. I needed to explain more.

"You set me free. By telling me to go to Texas, you released me of my obligations without me having to fail. There were no expectations for me to perform and achieve 'good girl status' in order to be worthy of my life. But then I had to ask myself what life did I really want? I didn't know who I would be without you. My head wanted you, but my heart resisted."

I took a breath and placed my hand on his chest.

"I didn't know walls were barricading my heart from you—walls I built to protect myself from being hurt the way the Sheriff hurt me. My heart didn't know how to let people in after 'the incident'—not you, not even the children. My life was built around control and predictability. If I was in control, then I felt safe to feel something. When I felt overwhelmed, I'd clam up and run."

Patrick seemed baffled.

"Why the kids?" he asked.

"I know it's a hard concept to understand, but my body prevented itself from being open—to anyone or anything. The other night when I cuddled with Seth longer than normal at bedtime, I relaxed enough for my heart to open. For a brief moment, I felt peace. But, before long, my body couldn't handle the level of vulnerability. In the deepest parts of my brain, my subconscious was replaying the horror that came from leaving myself vulnerable with the Sheriff. I broke, not realizing why at the time. After talking to Neil, I was able to come full circle to connect my mind with my feelings. I was living life numb, Patrick. My heart cut off from the world, protected and preserved, in order to avoid more damage and pain. You gave me the best of yourself, but it wasn't enough to break down my walls because I didn't know I had walls. I didn't know my heart was protecting itself."

Patrick sat there listening, anxiously rubbing the seam of his t-shirt between his index finger and thumb, trying to make sense of what probably sounded to him like cryptic messages.

"So, now your heart isn't protecting itself anymore?"

"That's what I've been trying to tell you. I can feel! It's like I was living life void of raw emotion."

My excitement took over as a reinvigorated Kristy bloomed.

"I can only explain it like this. On the way home, I saw a rainbow with colors more amazing than I have ever experienced. It was as if I had been color blind and God gave me the glasses to see. Before, I couldn't see true colors or feel love fully...like everything had been muted. I had no idea I was living like this...numb to my real feelings."

I stayed in his eyes, smiling, even though I was experiencing every pain I had inflicted on his soul. Thankfulness washed over me for feeling emotions with this new intensity—even if it hurt.

With cautious lips, Patrick asked, "What about Chad?"

His question was well warranted and explained the distress on his forehead.

"The only reason I could let Chad in was because logic couldn't keep him barricaded the way I barricaded you. Only God knew the inner secrets of my heart and could shatter my false sense of control by bringing my impossible Prince Charming list to life. Perceived perfection broke through and made me believe there was more to life than black and white living. Resentment of my 'good girl' way of life had settled on my heart, making me question my life choices. I couldn't ignore my heart any longer. Chad was simply a catalyst to awaken my dead soul. God was saving me from myself."

"Yourself?" he questioned.

"My self-loathing over failing to stop the Sheriff left me incapable of loving or being loved. God knew I was missing the best part of living—feeling *you!* I may have gone my whole life without realizing I was not whole. My fear of being hurt again stood in my way of an open heart. I focused on your faults so I didn't have to let you in. Now, I feel safe to feel—the icky is gone! God's grace showed me forgiveness for not being perfect, and I hope you will too."

Tears welled in Patrick's eyes.

He quietly pulled my body to his chest. His eyes said more than enough. He still loved me.

"I love you!" I blurted. "You loved me through the icky and now I feel. I feel you!"

The moment of epiphany ignited a fire between our imperfect souls. His body intertwined with mine and captivated my soul unlike any other embrace. Tears of joy flowed. I was alive. Our love consumed the room. Patrick's apprehensions were crowded out, for now.

So this is what love feels like.

My emotional barricades were gone. I was finally *one* with my husband.

With the afterglow of newlyweds, we rushed to the children's end of the year school talent show hand in hand—LATE. The word late hadn't been in my vocabulary until today, and despite failing my responsibility to show up on time, I was on cloud nine and couldn't wait to tell Chloe what happened. I knew she would be there to watch her children perform, and maybe, just maybe, this would give her hope.

After getting Patrick seated, I floated my way behind the stage to help with whatever I was supposed to be doing.

There was my angel to greet me.

Accosting Sarah with open arms and watery eyes, I whispered in her ear, "I had a breakthrough with Neil this morning...I saw Patrick as my husband for the first time. I can feel him!"

One happy tear escaped in my rambling.

"I cancelled my appointment with the divorce attorney."

Sarah looked at me like a deer in headlights.

"Divorce?" she asked.

Had she not known my real thoughts? Maybe I hadn't been as transparent as I believed.

I brushed over her bewilderment.

"I had been punishing myself for not being perfect the day of 'the incident' with the Sheriff and closed off my heart without even knowing."

Sarah's smile spoke volumes. A peaceful relief washed over my exhausted body as if I had completed the dreaded 5K run again—this time with my full heart intact.

"I had forgiven the Sheriff, but I had never forgiven myself."

I prayed Patrick would forgive me too.

CHAPTER 43

Just Got Started Loving You

Patrick rolled over to face me.

"Good morning, beautiful. How was your night?"

I gazed through his sparkling emerald lenses to a soul shining with a love more deep than I could fully understand. A whole new world had been opened through an unexpected door, and I wasn't dreaming. This was my life. This was *my husband*.

Gratitude for Patrick's courage to love me consumed my soul like a tidal wave. Patrick did not understand, he trusted. I thought I was so smart and was humbled. I did not know, but was shown the way via a patient and selfless husband, talented psychologist and perfect resumé—all united at the hands of something bigger than any of us, something bigger than I deserved.

I ran my fingers through my tangled hair before pouncing on top of his chest like a pro wrestler.

Grinning ear to ear, I suggested, "We have lots to make up for..."

Laughing, Patrick jumped in with a quick rebuttal.

"Yeah—a whole honeymoon and then some."

I appreciated his humor, especially after months of my brutal words.

"You up for the challenge?" I taunted, while batting my bare eyelashes. "Watch out! This is the new, Kristy. You might have your hands full!"

"That's the hope," he teased with a mischievous smile.

My playful swat landed on his harder than normal bicep. His buff body was the bonus to getting a do-over honeymoon phase of the relationship. Raw emotion was a much better high than perfectionism, alcohol or any other substance I could envision. I was looking forward to staying drunk on Patrick.

Ally snuck into the bedroom and jumped up on the bed yelling, "I want in...Family hug time!"

I missed those words...*family hug*. Another new high entered my being. She buried her face in my back and wrapped her tiny arms around my sides. I caught Patrick's sparkle and smiled until I lost my breath. Seth had jumped on top of the pile, laughing.

Patrick yelled, "Come on, Brooke! Where are you?"

I noticed Brooke standing next to the bed shaking her head at us. Patrick reached out with one hand and flung her onto the bed. Her coy smile said it all. She worshipped her daddy, and, now, I knew I did too. He was the pillar holding us all up. I owed him a rest for carrying the weight these past months.

Laughter was back in the house because of the infectious love of my husband. I felt pure joy, and it was contagious to our children. I hadn't realized how contained their behavior had been the past few months. They must have felt the tension in the house and were trying not to rock the boat. My mind had been absent from them since my failure in Texas—my soul for a lifetime.

I missed so much.

After a quick breakfast of cookies and ice cream—my rules were thrown out the window with the rest of my internal baggage—we ventured outside. The sky was clear blue, making it hard to tell where the water ended and the sky began. I spotted a lone cloud, yet the sky was still beautiful. It didn't have to be perfectly clear—one blemish wouldn't diminish its beauty. If anything, the single cloud made the sky more unique, more amazing.

Hand in hand, Patrick and I followed our children's footsteps through a sea of white Trillium in the woods adjacent to our property. Trillium was a beautiful white flower, rare and endangered, just like our intact family. Yet, both were in full bloom outside our home.

I could see these miracles now with my new soul vision.

Patrick suggested a family hike to start the morning. I was the one who liked to walk, not him. I buzzed with electricity at the thought of him being adventurous. This was the family I longed for. Despite Seth and Brooke squabbling as to which direction we should explore, I was relieved to see they were back to their old selves and not the reserved children of the past few months. Their mother had been lost, and I realized they had felt my angst even when I couldn't. I thanked God the children were too young to fully understand their mother's withdrawal and for the time we'll have together in the future to connect without the shadow of the Sheriff haunting my heart.

Even though we were scaling logs and moving branches, I didn't want to let go of Patrick's hand. I didn't want to lose the connection I finally experienced with him. Each breath I took felt like a gift from above. The air cleansed my lungs, boosted my spirit and brought hope to my heart. Life was different, and I had no intensions of ever going back to needing things and achievements to feel whole. My heart didn't need that kind of boost—a honeymoon, maybe, but not things to fill it. My emotions were boiling over with an amazing elixir, and I didn't know how to turn off the burner—not that I wanted to anyway.

With the children each having play dates for the day, Patrick and I were left alone to explore foreign territory—our hearts.

Despite months of my evil tongue lashings, Patrick had deciphered my heart's desire for spontaneity—a risk I had never been willing to take. He decided we would take a drive, just the two of us. With the sunroof open to the sweet fragrance of spring air, Patrick meandered along the winding shoreline of Lake Michigan to an undisclosed destination. Resisting the urge to control the day's activities, I didn't ask what he had planned. I honored my husband.

We stopped at random turnoffs to stretch our legs and explore each other. The tranquil sound of the waves rolling ashore freed my soul from past rough waters. My heart was now able to feel a life I had only experienced through my physical eyes. I was a kid in a candy store wanting to experience everything in sight, even at the risk of an overload.

We ended the day at the Sleeping Bear Sand Dunes, normally only 35 minutes from our doorstep, but, today, it took a six-hour drive. We laid out a blanket on a 450 foot bluff above Lake Michigan. There were breathtaking views in all directions—endless blue water to the West, lush green forests north and south, and a crystal clear inland lake to the East. I felt happy. I was no longer overshadowed by a closed heart.

Our unspoken words sang in harmony like the blending colors of the sunset laid out in front of us.

As Patrick uncorked a bottle of wine, he exposed his thoughts hesitantly.

"I dreamed about this moment, but thought it would never come."

His lack of eye contact reflected his wounds from my betrayal.

A tear dripped down my cheek.

"I'm so sorry I put you through this."

I struggled for the right words to explain my miracle.

Despite the rigidness of his body, Patrick's sly smile betrayed his sarcastic wit.

"You think?"

JUST GOT STARTED LOVING YOU

Thank God, I hadn't killed his spirit.

My hands rose in playful defense.

"I know...I know. I'm crazy! But at least now I feel."

I leaned over to kiss him with passion pulsing from inside out. I was a gooey mess like the scenes in the movies I once disregarded. My impulsive move spilled the glass of wine he was pouring. He didn't flinch until I sensed the wetness and giggled through our embrace. Laughter was a welcome improvement to our past twelve years of uptight behavior. I prayed my emotional change would last and my raw heart would remain open to feel.

"Thank you for the great day," I said.

My smile glowed from a light shining within.

He touched my wedding ring, slid it back and forth, and squeezed my hand.

Patrick's eyes locked with mine, giving me the courage to speak from my heart.

"I thought I had our marriage all figured out—that is until *Mr. Perfect Resumé* came crashing into my life. He could have taken advantage of my vulnerability and pursued me for his own, but he didn't. It's a miracle you both had the courage to let me find the true me on my own."

My new essence overwhelmed me. I needed to be pinched.

Patrick's words were uninhibited.

"As they say...If you love someone, set them free. If they come back, they're yours. If they don't, they never were yours to begin with."

"I'm glad you're back," he smiled.

"Me too."

I pressed my palms against his, fingertips to fingertips.

"Our love was stuck," I said, while interlocking our fingers. "But now it's intertwined the way God intended. We had been missing the best parts of each other, and we would have spent a whole lifetime not knowing the truth if I hadn't been shaken off my protective pedestal."

Patrick touched my cheek. My core quivered from the intensity, as I melted into his soft kiss.

CHAPTER 44

Goodbye Girl

The text read: "Hi baby can you come next week? I miss u!"

My heart stopped.

Five days had passed since I communicated with Chad and a lifetime of events had occurred. With my heart opened to the infinite possibilities of Patrick, I now had to address my feelings for Chad.

Patrick was lounging in my favorite chair next to the cozy fireplace. Disrupting his calm after our three month rainstorm was nowhere on my priority list. I preferred to jump into his lap and smother him with the love I hadn't felt since before the Sheriff stole my soul. But I had to clear the air first.

"Hey, Sweetheart!" he said as I plopped down.

The voltage of his voice charged my heart like I never dreamed possible—my icky gone.

"I got a text today," I said.

"Oh," he replied as his eyes sank to the floor.

This *feeling* thing was not all it's cracked up to be. I didn't know if I would ever get used to living without a protective barrier.

I took a deep breath and shared the rest of the message.

"He wanted to know if I was coming to visit."

Patrick crossed one arm across his chest and his thumb and index finger began rubbing the seam of his t-shirt sleeve.

He asked, quietly, "Are you?"

"Of course not," I declared, while kneeling at the bottom of the chair. I placed my hands on his lap. "I'm forever yours, remember?"

I tried to smile away his fears.

He touched his ring—a signal he remembered the inscription on the inside band of his wedding ring, which read: "Forever Yours 4-19-97."

My eyes glued on his, my voice raspy.

I said, "It took a perfect stranger to set me on this path of healing...and I didn't even know I was sick. I will forever be grateful to him, but I belong with you."

Tears welled in our eyes. His face was rightfully skeptical, but he leaned down and placed his arms around me anyway, saying nothing.

I had destroyed his trust and would have to reassure him of my love, no matter how long the road.

I tried explaining.

"Before, I didn't believe I was worthy of love, especially from someone as kind and honest as you. I tore you down to protect my heart from being vulnerable. Chad was the dynamite needed to blow-up the walls of my self-inflicted prison of self-doubt. He could have tried to lead me down another path—but he didn't."

Patrick placed his hands on mine.

Realizing the time was now or never, I took a big breath without exhaling and spoke.

"I know it's a lot to ask, and I'll understand if you say no...but I would like to call him and explain my miracle."

"You do what you have to do."

Patrick's words were void of detectable emotion.

"Are you sure?" I asked, questioning his sincerity.

Patrick shook his head side to side with a slight smile.

"No...but I'm telling you yes anyway," he joked.

"Seriously, I won't call if you don't want me to. You're my priority...forever and always."

I wanted reassurance that I wasn't being greedy with his compassion.

"It's fine," he urged.

His answer was more convincing this time.

"Promise me you're OK with this," I requested.

"Now you're sounding like the kids. If you keep asking, I'm going to change my mind."

"OK."

I put my hands up before wrapping my arms around him.

"I don't deserve you!"

He smiled broadly and said, "I know."

The kids piled out of the SUV eager for their Tae Kwon Do class. I, on the other hand, was shaking. Tonight was the night. I drove to a nearby parking lot with an open view of the green, rolling hills that lead to the blue water in the distance, turned off the car and dialed up Chad.

"Hi, baby. I thought you would never respond."

His drawl released my butterflies again. This was going to be more difficult than I imagined.

"I'm sorry," I said, my voice cracking a bit.

"Are you alright?" he asked.

His change in breath reflected his connection to my fluttering chest.

No, I wasn't.

His exhale inflated my depressed lungs.

"Yeah—It's good to hear your voice."

"I'm the one happy to hear you, baby. You spoiled me last week with your call. I'm trying to be strong, but I just want you with me, and I know I shouldn't."

He was throwing off my equilibrium. My mind drifted to being in his arms. I tried to regain my balance.

"You're not failing. Your strength saved me," I said.

"Saved you?"

His voice changed. I sensed confusion by his tone. My statement had perplexed him.

"Chad, you were my miracle—a fantasy I deemed could never happen."

I struggled with more words, not wanting our connection to end.

"Our stars align, Kristy. It is what it is."

My cheeks flushed. His voice filled with the reassuring calm I loved which helped ease the burden on my heart.

"I believe that too."

A smile began to form on my face.

"Without you, I would have never understood the void in my heart and would have gone my whole life missing the best part of living," I explained. "Your existence challenged me to question myself and my choices."

I paused knowing what I was about to say would come as a shock after our last conversation.

"I had a breakthrough with my therapist on Friday."

The can of worms was opened. I squirmed my way through the uncomfortable details of the Sheriff and my journey of PTSD therapy with Neil. Chad had questions, which I expected.

He asked, "If the trauma with the Sheriff left your heart numb, then how could you feel for me?"

"You were a living, breathing Prince Charming right from the pages of my dreams—the man with the perfect resumé. You shook my whole world to its core leaving me vulnerable. Logic couldn't defy your existence, and my mind felt safe to open my heart."

Silence—I didn't like silence.

"I'm so sorry you had to go through this alone," he said, the inflection in his voice connecting with my struggle.

"Don't be sorry. You were my dream come true, a gift only God could have used to save me from the hatred of myself. If you would have pursued me, I would have never discovered the assault that was plaguing my heart."

"I never thought a woman like you could connect with a man like me," he added, falling more quiet.

He was desperate to get back on solid ground.

"Are you still coming to Texas?" he asked.

After a deep breath, I said, "No."

The word felt like a nail scraping across my tongue, and the long pause spoke volumes. I tried to resuscitate his heart.

"I know what we have is real. The timing is just wrong," I suggested to ease the blow. "I couldn't feel or receive love until you came along. You helped save me. You are my miracle."

I could hear his deepening pain with each breath he took. It was as if I could feel the beat of his damaged heart through the phone.

"No...You are mine. I found myself in you, Kristy. I want you in Texas with me forever," he pleaded. "We're connected. You're my heart."

I had no more words to console him. My heart was also in pieces, jumbled with his.

"I love you." he said, his voice shaky.

CHAPTER 45

Crazy Girl

The conversation with Chad was replaying in my mind.

His "I love you" hit my heart hard.

It was one thing to feel a connection, but quite another to hear the words. My heart ached knowing that I had rejected his outpouring of raw emotion in a manner that caused him such heartbreak. Despite the pain he displayed on the phone, I prayed his heart would trust him to love again the same way he had helped my heart open up to Patrick in a way I never dreamed possible. I will forever be grateful for his selflessness, but it was finally time to focus on my family.

I walked into the restaurant with walls covered in a red, white and blue nautical theme. Ironic because I was living the "American Dream" or so I thought. My pursuit of happiness compass was no longer focused on the external and was pointing inward. It was time to share my newfound journey to my concerned parents. I prayed there would be no familiar faces other than those of Patrick and theirs this far off our typical beaten path. Patrick had driven twenty minutes north to this small fishing village. My personality had made a 180 from the boisterous woman my parents knew, now dressed in a calm spirit and conservative clothing. We sat around a circular table, all eyes on mine. The hair stood on my arms as I felt their eyes pierce my vulnerable soul.

My parents seemed as if they were sitting on pins and needles asking themselves, "Why would they have asked us to dinner without the kids?"

We knew they were worried about our marriage even though they hadn't come out and asked since our spring break trip.

Patrick distracted the tension with a bold statement.

"I think you both need to order a drink first."

He always knew how to silence my parents—a task not easily accomplished.

Drinks firmly in hand, I proceeded to tell them of Patrick's and my journeys since returning from Florida—the marriage counselor, the individual counselors, the divorce thoughts and the PTSD therapy. I explained how I couldn't be open with Patrick, my kids, or anyone until I had things perfect and in complete control with no surprises—an impossible task until Chad defied my logic by showing up with his *perfect resumé.*

My dad didn't look at me. The details were far too intimate to penetrate his walls. He kept eyeing Patrick for levity regarding the uncomfortable situation. I could sense my parents were worried about his state of mind in light of my revelations. Their mouths hung open, yet nothing came out—a rare occurrence for such opinionated people. The gray of my story and Patrick's ability to listen to my candid words were difficult to absorb.

Raw details rolled off my tongue without a filter to hide my icky. My broken walls left no protection for my emotional heart, and my crying was foreign to my parents. They remained speechless as if they had been zapped with a stun gun.

As the sting wore off, my daddy looked at Patrick and asked, "So...this is all a good thing?"

Patrick grabbed my hand and with a smile answered, "Yes. No worries, Gary. We aren't getting divorced."

My daddy turned to me.

"So, you're OK now?"he asked.

"Yeah," I replied with a peaceful smile. "Crazy, but OK."

The sting from my candid story would take awhile to wear off. I prayed my parents wouldn't feel more pain or guilt over 'the incident' with the Sheriff. It wasn't their fault.

Despite not being able to control my parent's reaction to the strange shift in my life, verbalizing my truths helped set me free. Control had been my tool for shielding my true emotions, and now my true feelings were exposed to the open air and vulnerable to rejection.

I was learning to accept the real me—icky and all. Telling them had been another step forward.

A few days later, my daddy called. I wasn't prepared for his inquiries after his uncomfortable demeanor the other night. Maybe he had been listening more than I realized. I prayed this was true for his benefit as well as my mother's.

"Kristy, I don't understand how this has anything to do with the kids."

This comment caught me off balance.

"Well, I know it seems strange to link them with the Sheriff. But let me try to explain. At bedtime, when the house is peaceful, I try to lay down with each of them. As I start to relax, just as I had in the Sheriff's car, my body stops my heart from opening up for fear of reliving the same pain."

"Like a child who touches a stove and instincts kick in?"

"Sort of like that," I replied.

"I'm sorry. I didn't realize you were still hurting. I thought you were OK when you emerged from the Sheriff's office with your blue eyes all sparkly again."

His voice trailed off.

"I didn't know," he said.

"You couldn't have known," I assured him. "I didn't even know."

"You'll be OK now, right?"

"Yeah, dad, I'm alright now. I'm alright."

Many times we say what people need to hear, but I meant what I said. I really was beginning to be "alright" with the real me, icky and all, and I was getting closer to being the authentic self I was created to be. Each session, each day brought me to a place I never knew I needed. Through emotional ups and downs I became acquainted with the "new Kristy."

I remembered a turning point in one of my sessions...

"Close your eyes. Now, what are you feeling?"

Neil's words moved me to the police station during the confrontation. I sat taller in the chair.

"I'm strong, invincible...as if I could conquer the world."

"Do you remember crying when you were speaking to the Sheriff?" he asked.

"No!" I responded forcefully.

I opened my eyes and stared, trying to understand this silly question.

"Why not?"

"I don't know. I told you I didn't cry before Texas."

Annoyance crept into my tone.

"Kristy...when you were confronting him, you were strong, but you didn't release your feelings. Tell the Sheriff how you feel about what he did to you."

"Huh?" I groaned.

It was one thing to follow the pencil and have my body do strange things, but now I had to act out my proud moment of confronting the Sheriff?

"Neil, I didn't go there for his pity," I said, somewhat annoyed. "I went to take back my life. I was no longer the weak girl he controlled. He couldn't hurt me anymore."

"I understand you took control and forgave him. But, you have never stopped blaming yourself for what the Sheriff did to you."

Neil's voice escalating with each word.

"You admired him. You trusted him. And he betrayed that trust. He assaulted you!"

Trying to absorb Neil's boldness, my eyes again followed his moving pencil until he told me to close them. His voice returned to normal.

"You are in the chair, sitting across the desk from the Sheriff in the interrogation room. Tell him how you FEEL, not just what he did."

My body tightened. The Sheriff's steel blue eyes were staring at me. My fragile words slipped out.

"How could you do this to me?" I asked.

He didn't respond.

Clinging to my soul for stability, my heart tumbled out through my words.

"I loved you like a father and you did this to me!" I yelled.

My cascading tears exposed my heart and his betrayal. Feelings from the past bombarded me, including the love for a man sworn to protect and serve, and the pain and guilt having trusted the wrong person.

I sobbed uncontrollably for what seemed forever. Slowly the waterfall subsided. I mumbled through my sobs, defeated and vulnerable...

"Can I have a hug?" I asked.

I collapsed back into my chair and let Neil console me for the first time.

CHAPTER 46

My Heart is Open

I relished how open Patrick had become to my feelings. Only two weeks had passed since my breakthrough, but I felt like a lifetime of emotions inflated me.

So much time squandered.

It was if I had supersonic powers to absorb any and all emotion to the Nth degree, and I didn't want to miss a one—not with Patrick or our children. I was making up for lost time, relishing in the simplicity of each new moment experienced. I danced on the furniture in the living room with our children, ignored bedtime rules and hugged them every chance I could—each moment more special than the last.

I knew what a radical change my behavior was for Patrick. However, he embraced my raw heart despite the apprehension I could sense in his movements. He was trying to be more verbal with his feelings, and I was learning to explore the unknown without past demons interfering with my openness. I felt no pressure from him to move beyond my comfort levels. He remained cautious in pursuing me, letting me take the wheel and determine the speed with which we reconnected. My heart had been cracked wide open, but I was hopeful of Patrick being everything I ever wanted in a husband.

I found myself pursuing him.

Is this what bliss is?

I held Patrick's hand everywhere we went, sat on his lap at little league games and kissed him anytime I felt the need—which was every other moment. I couldn't get close enough to him, smothering him like a blanket. I didn't care if we were drawing attention to ourselves with our public displays of affection. We just laughed at the bemused smiles on curious bystanders' faces when they saw us—a middle-age married couple—acting like teenagers. I was radiating happiness. This indescribable feeling had entered my heart, saving me from the numbness of my prior existence. I was alive. An internal joy awakened my soul at a level deeper than even Chad could generate. I was finally alive and free to feel—even sadness.

Why couldn't I have known this sensation earlier?

Each happy moment followed with the opposite—a moment of sadness. Valuable time with my loved ones had been wasted in my numb state. Mourning the missed moments of true emotion, I wished for a do-over.

Patrick granted my wish by arranging an impromptu second honeymoon. He convinced my parents to watch the kids, while we ventured away for a long weekend. I told him I didn't care where we traveled to just as long as we could be together. My days of complaining about locations were hopefully over. I discovered I didn't need the perfect environment to unlock the vault around my heart. It had been cracked open thanks to Neil's help. I was available to feel each and every moment—good and bad. My emotions were as volatile as a toddler, one minute laughing and the next sobbing. I had no sense of control, a far cry from how I had lived in the past, and my anxiety was skyrocketing to new heights worrying if the pressure from a romantic hotel room would cause an explosion.

What if I was moving too fast and this tsunami of emotions would crash on me?

A weight returned to my chest.

Panicking, I halted Patrick from pulling the trigger on the reservation. I didn't want to throw a wrench of negative emotions into the progress of our relationship by adding extra pressure to feel more than I was ready to feel.

I needed a therapy session—fast.

"Neil, do you think it's a good idea Patrick and I go on a second honeymoon so soon? I thought it was what I wanted, and now I'm second-guessing myself."

Neil slid his chair away from his desk and turned to face me. My worries were transparent.

"Kristy, Patrick is not the Sheriff."

"I know that," I said with a look of disgust.

"Do you? Because based on your words from the last few sessions, you keep focusing on negative emotions about sex instead of your anger at the Sheriff's behavior. His actions were *assault*— NOT sex. Stop commingling the two!"

I sat motionless and wide-eyed. Neil's forceful convictions caught me off guard.

Was he right? Had I blurred the lines between sex and assault?

I flashed to an earlier encounter with my husband in the bedroom. As our kissing progressed towards more intimate expectations, I left myself. My open heart closed with his pursuit for more. My passion went cold, yet I didn't stop him or verbalize my feelings.

265

I had checked out of the moment. After all was done, a burning anger consumed my core. I kept quiet once again.

The sound of Neil's notepad hitting the floor brought me back to the present.

As Neil leaned down from his chair to pick up the notepad that had *slipped* from his lap his words echoed in my head.

"His actions were assault—NOT sex."

"You're right."

I snapped, dropping my head—just another area where I had punished Patrick for *my* failure to connect.

"Emotions don't make you weak, Kristy. They make you human. Do you believe Patrick has your best interests at heart?"

The mention of Patrick's name brought life to my ashamed soul.

"Of course I do. He's been incredible through all this."

"Then it shouldn't matter how the vacation goes. You don't know what life has in store and no matter how hard you plan and how much you think you're in control, you're not. Good things happen and bad things happen, but Patrick's intentions are good."

"But I'm afraid I'll shut down if it gets too physical, and I'll disappoint him further."

"Be honest with Patrick about your emotions in those intimate situations. You have to have faith in him...and yourself."

Neil paused, set his pencil and notepad on the desk and turned square to me. His warm eyes connected to mine.

"You trust Patrick, right?" he asked with great seriousness.

"...with my life!" I told him confidently.

"Then believe you will make good decisions based on what you know. You can't keep punishing yourself if someone chooses to mislead you. That's their fault, not yours. It's the Sheriff who assaulted you, and you could not have predicted his evil actions. Don't focus your anger on your husband's loving acts...or on your own."

"The Sheriff is to blame. Be angry at him."

CHAPTER 47

Come A Little Closer

My conversation with Neil continued to repeat in my head like a nagging mom.

"The Sheriff is to blame. Be angry at him."

"The Sheriff is to blame. Be angry at him."

"The Sheriff is to blame. Be angry at him."

I had freed my heart from its protective force field. However, my body was still trying to decode my exposed feelings commingling sex with assault. The lines between the two had been blurred by the Sheriff, and I was eager to sort through them. Even though I didn't want to accept his assessment, Neil was right.

Maybe a second honeymoon would help me do just that. I didn't want fear to hinder my ability to function in the unknown, so I took a leap of faith and gave Patrick the green light to schedule the trip. Feeling empowered, I rummaged through my closet looking for the rest of my secrets.

Patrick was nestled on our bed roaming around on his laptop, narrowing his choice for the location.

"You sure you want me to pull the trigger?"

Patrick's expression was like a neon billboard of apprehension. He didn't want to be vulnerable to complaints that might arise if he picked the wrong resort, or if I changed my mind about choosing him.

I took a deep breath, sat down next to him and placed my secret, prepaid cell phone on top of the bed, hoping this isn't the straw that breaks the camel's back.

With conviction I said, "I choose you. No matter where we go, or what happens, I choose you...forever and always."

Patrick's eyes shifted from his screen to the phone, then back up to my eyes. I didn't wait for his reaction. My voice filled the empty space trying to abolish my fear of his rejection.

"I'm so sorry I didn't give it to you sooner."

"Thank you for giving it to me, but I've known all along you've had it," Patrick confessed.

"What?"

"After my night with Ralph, I started snooping for anything that would explain your withdrawal, and I found the purchase on the credit card statement that confirmed Ralph's suspicions."

"Oh," I said ashamed and deflated. "Why didn't you tell me?"

"I wanted YOU to tell ME."

His eyes softened, now believing that relinquishing the secret phone confirmed my explanation about my transformed heart.

"Fair enough," I said, knowing the next blow might not be cushioned by his prior knowledge. "No doubts anymore that I'm all in... here's the last of my secrets."

I threw a wad of money on the bed.

"You can pick any resort you want. This is the cash I secretly stashed from grocery store purchases in case you kicked me to the curb where I felt I belonged."

I pulled back a little just in case he exploded.

Patrick laughed.

"Great minds think alike. I opened a bank account in my name just in case you were the one doing the kicking," he confessed. "I guess we won't have to worry about paying for the vacation."

Tossing the phone and money aside, he pulled me into his chest for a tight embrace. We giggled in our intimate moment of honesty. Then we moved forward with our 2nd Honeymoon plans.

Patrick chose a beachfront hotel and spa in a quaint coastal community of Florida. The boutique hotel was recently renovated into a masterpiece. The lobby was tone on tone whites with shades of turquoise splashed throughout. The glowing blue water of a center fountain was a focal point of bold color. The environment evoked tranquility with a modern edge and soothed the waves of my feelings, for the time being.

The trip was a well-deserved break from the marathon of emotions we had been running blindfolded. Thank goodness we had the perseverance, and he had the patience, to push forward during those dark days.

Each new sunrise presented a new reservoir of emotion. I was no longer walking through life as if mindlessly playing a video game. I was simply enjoying each moment, taking good with the bad, learning perfect doesn't really exist. And that was OK. I kept reminding myself that the uniqueness of each moment is what makes life special, not trying to reach the impossibility of perfection in order to feel safe to remain open-hearted.

We walked the beach hand in hand, wandering without purpose along the shell strewn sand. Patrick passed by the solid white and solid black shells that were catching my attention, and stopped only to grab a few odd-looking ones. Their unique blemishes made the collection more interesting to him. I hoped he would view my flaws in the same light after all his relief of winning me back wore off.

As we splashed our feet in the shallow pools lapping on the shoreline, I paused and said, "Thank you for taking me here."

I twirled a tangled lock of hair.

"A vacation without the kids was long overdue," Patrick answered stoically.

He was trying to deflect the openness of my gratitude from knocking on the door of his heart.

"No, I mean it. After all that I put you through."

I was redirecting the conversation without making eye contact.

"I really appreciate your willingness to be here with me."

"You're my wife. Of course I want to be here," Patrick stated.

He wasn't ready to go deeper.

Absorbing the beauty surrounding us and smelling the salty air were bonuses to my senses. The day was full of magnificent moments, including my bond with Patrick. I was open to the simplicity of Patrick's love. He wasn't one for grand gestures or heartfelt speeches, but his attention never wavered. His unique essence seeped deep within my core in a way I never anticipated. He wasn't Chad. However, Patrick made me feel special in a different way. I wondered if he had always been this attentive and I hadn't felt it before, or if he was still in crisis mode trying to survive. Either way, I was relieved to be feeling Patrick's presence, even if he felt a little guarded. At this point everything felt new and exciting, and I was grateful for the second chance.

Following our day of relaxing along the beach, we retreated to the comfort of our oceanside room. We washed off the grit, and then snuggled in the plush complimentary robes on our private veranda. His warmth stirred feelings. I was breathing in a language foreign to me. This man loved me in his own way, and I didn't deserve him. We were in unchartered waters, our connection different. The light of day blinded my fears and I tried to experience my husband in this new light.

With our bodies rejuvenated, that evening we strolled hand in hand to the tiny beachside town. The open air restaurant was filled with bold primary colors splashed about. Hopeful birds perched on the open beams of the roof and on the rails along the edge of the restaurant and sidewalk. The casual atmosphere helped bridge my nerves as darkness fell. I didn't want to slip back to my old way of relating—expecting to be disappointed so my heart had to accept mere scraps, just like the birds. Before Neil entered my life I had walls to protect my heart so I wouldn't get hurt, now the walls were knocked down, and my freed heart beat rapidly with the anticipation of what may come next.

After dinner, Patrick wanted to stop at a beach bar for another drink. I thought I would be relieved to escape the pressure of a dark bedroom a little longer, but I wasn't. My thoughts couldn't be kept quiet if I wanted to stay open-hearted to the moment.

How could I expect Patrick to "get me" if I didn't voice my feelings?

"I know the three months of abstaining are over, but I don't want to go back to the way things were—alcohol as an escape from feeling reality," I said as subtly as I could.

Patrick grew irritated.

"I'm fine. I can have a few drinks."

I gently grabbed his arm.

"I didn't say you couldn't....I just want us to be fully present with each other tonight."

"I'm here, aren't I?"

His sarcasm made me cringe. I hadn't accused him of anything, yet he took my words as a critique, not a request for connectivity. This feeling thing was tougher than I realized, and I didn't like feeling vulnerable. Trying not to retreat to my own self-pity, I reached for his hand despite a flood of negative emotions.

He ignored the gesture. I wasn't going to regain our connection from dinner.

"It would have been nice if you told me you didn't want me to have a drink! You have all these expectations I can never fulfill!"

His irritation intensified.

Against my better judgment, I defended my point.

"I didn't have any expectations. You were fine to have a drink. I just didn't want that to be our whole night. I want us to just be."

Uh-oh...Wrong words.

"Just BE?!" he barked. "Just be like...Chad?! I don't know what you want from me, Kristy! The way I see it, this is just another one of your excuses to pick a fight before bed!"

Maybe he was right.

CHAPTER 48

Heads Carolina, Tails California

With the second honeymoon behind us and the chill in the air gone, my thawed heart continued to warm in the summer heat.

Life felt different.

My body expressed the natural ebb and flow of feelings. I felt like a disoriented toddler learning to walk. I relished in each passing day. My day planner was empty except for numerous appointments with Neil—each session an unmapped journey. Neil held my hand as I sorted through the baggage my body had been carrying. I became a believer in the gray, trusting my emotions to lead me, not the detailed road map I had once followed in hopes of avoiding pain and finding joy.

Could I let myself be vulnerable to the unpredictability of life—starting with my husband and children?

Following the disappointment of the getaway, Patrick and I spent the rest of the summer enjoying life's simpler things. The fresh air, blue sky and warm waters of the lake were balms for our healing spirits. I tried to push my disappointment for missing so much of life to the back burner, the same burner on which I kept Chad.

Neil's words would echo in my head.

"You can't control your feelings. You have to let emotions flow. Trust yourself to make the right decisions for your life."

Could I trust myself to make decisions without society's "Happily Ever After" manual dictating my worth? I must try.

As the hammock blew in the light breeze, Patrick squeezed my hand. I was nestled beside him, my head propped on his bare chest. We watched in awe at our children taking turns jumping off the dock into the turquoise waves stirred up from speeding boats. Their smiles were brighter than the sun, melting my heart. I no longer needed to be alone in my perfect place to feel peace.

"What do you think about jumping in the Suburban next week and going on a Southern tour before the kids go back to school?"

My eyes caught his.

"What...do you want to do?"

He smiled.

"Let's load up the Suburban and go south...our very own *Chevy Chase* vacation."

I couldn't believe my ears—us diving into a vacation without set plans?

In seemingly slow motion, I asked again, "Ser-i-ous-ly?"

"Yeah, we can kill two birds with one stone...get a much needed vacation and explore places to move."

My ears were captivated by his intensity.

Was I hearing correctly—move?

My expression must have been dazed and confused because Patrick continued to sell the idea.

"I am serious, Kristy. I have been listening, and you're right. We have done everything with a plan. So let's screw the plan and start living! I want to list the house for sale and see if I can land a transfer somewhere greener, somewhere warmer."

His green eyes sparkled with adventure. I was mesmerized.

I rolled on top of his bare chest wrapping both of my arms around his neck almost flipping us both out of the hammock.

Through my crocodile tears, I mumbled, "Let's do it!"

He froze.

"Why are you crying?"

With tears streaming down my face, I smiled and blubbered, "I don't know...I feel everything now...sometimes too much!"

He wrapped his arms around me caressing the small of my back until my tears subsided.

Locked in his eyes, I tried to explain my crazy.

"The only way I can describe my roller coaster of emotions is to compare the change inside me to someone who can't hear and is given the gift of sound. You remember the news show where the deaf girl was given cochlear implants and the doctor turned on the volume for the first time? She covered her ears—the sound was overwhelming. My feelings are as intense as her first sounds, except I can't control the volume."

His full lips curled upward.

"I'm gonna have to get used to this new you—but the palm trees should help."

My elbow found its way into his ribs and we both started laughing.

I didn't deserve such an amazing man.

He was willing to change directions for me. He must have been listening to my years of ramblings about muggy heat and live oak trees lining the streets like in the movies we loved—*The Notebook*, *Doc Hollywood*, and *Gone with the Wind* to name a few. I even remember telling him how watching *Shirley Temple* as a child had left an everlasting imprint on my heart. Maybe he had been listening more than I realized and connected with my soul deeper than I ever knew.

Doubt again shadowed my excitement for a moment.

Is living in the south his dream too, or is he still trying to be the perfect man for me? Either way, I embraced his offer hoping I had found my *Noah* and *Lon* wrapped into one man.

He didn't waste time pursuing the Southern tour. His Type A personality in full gear, Patrick contacted realtors to list the house and started looking for open Southern sales territories within his current company. He mapped out a few potential cities to visit based on accessibility to water and available transfer locations. Spontaneity was not lost in his planning. We discussed flipping a coin to see if we would explore the Southwestern States or the Southeastern ones.

Heads won.

We left Northern Michigan headed to the gulf coast with a goal of traveling across the state of Florida to Jacksonville and scooping up the Southeast coast through the Carolinas. We had no hotel reservations or set schedule. We were free to explore.

The kids did better than expected traveling by car instead of plane, our usual transportation choice for long hauls. Throwing our usual structure and rules out the window, we stopped at a park to devour a box of popsicles for lunch, ran into the ocean with our clothes on, and pulled over once to dance in a field of flowers. We were learning to laugh and live without inhibitions.

In each city we liked, Patrick would contact a realtor to schedule a peek at a few houses to see if we could envision living there. On the fifth day, we climbed out of the jammed SUV to view a house in a small town along the gulf coast. Once inside with the realtor, I remembered how the August heat melted my lipstick in a matter of minutes. I excused myself to grab my purse from the vehicle before anything else melted.

As I opened the door my phone was ringing—the screen read Houston, Texas.

The ringing of Chad's call was like a tea kettle's whistle reminding me of the passion simmering in my heart for him. No matter how hard I tried I was unable to keep him on the back burner. His outpouring of emotion on my voicemail overwhelmed me. Chad had broken—his love withstanding, his strength shot.

It was undeniable. Chad had hijacked a piece of my heart.

Since the visit to the Gulf was tainted by Chad's call, I was happy to be traveling toward the Atlantic. I believed the farther we traveled from Texas the better off I would be. I didn't want to ruin Patrick's first taste of free spirited living, so I decided to wait to tell him about the call until after our trip. My husband deserved all of me, and I prayed Chad would vacate my heart during the journey.

We buzzed across Florida determining its coastlines were too busy to raise our family. Savannah, Georgia was a strong contender with its live oaks and palm trees—until we landed in Charleston, South Carolina. Charleston lured us in with its low country landscape and Southern hospitality. We knew with our goal of spending less and living more we would have to give up life on the water. However with Charleston's vast waterways and bridges, we could live here and still be able to drive past blue ripples every day. We stayed in Charleston longer than anticipated exploring neighborhoods, schools, and beaches, and skipped the rest of the Carolina coastline.

Charleston captured our hearts with its charm and small town feel, not to mention the bonus of Patrick's college roommate, Jon, living here. Over the years Jon and I became trusted friends — he was even a groomsman in our wedding —despite our flirty encounter at Patrick's college bar excursion fifteen years earlier. After I graduated from Notre Dame, I helped Jon land a job at the bank where I worked. Jon changed the course of his life midstream by giving up his banking career to go to nursing school in South Carolina. He even bought a Harley and grew a long goatee-beard that he braided. At the time we thought he was crazy—now I understood his change of heart!

I wanted the same thing as Jon—to let go of the logical plan I had always pursued and follow the uncharted waters of my open heart pulling me to South Carolina.

CHAPTER 49

She Never Cried

Back home and hoping the other shoe wouldn't drop, I settled into the routine of fall and focused on becoming more acquainted with my new self.

Ally was starting her first day at all-day kindergarten. I struggled to let her go. Tears streamed down my face as I stood with all the other parents and Patrick on the playground watching the children march into school. When our first two had gone off to kindergarten, I didn't understand parents' distressed reactions over a few hours away from their children. I watched them smugly and thought, "Get a grip!"

Now I understood!

Sadness engulfed me realizing I had missed so much emotion with our other two. My life had only been black and white and now EVERYTHING was in vibrant color. I was grateful for my tears.

Not being used to my public display of emotion, I turned away from the crowd to wipe my wet cheeks on my sleeve and compose myself. Out of the corner of my eye I saw a man I didn't recognize pull Patrick aside with a distressed look. As I approached them, the stranger rushed away avoiding an introduction. However I over-heard him insist that Patrick call him. When I questioned Patrick, he blew off the encounter saying he was a doctor from the hospital who wanted to discuss a case.

Well that was peculiar.

In spite of being late for work, Patrick grabbed my hand with-out saying a word and walked me to my vehicle. His face remained void of emotion as he pecked me on the cheek and hurried off to his car. I wasn't sure if my emotional state scared him away or if his mind was preoccupied with his to-do-list. Either way I was left alone in my sorrow as Patrick set out on a mission. He had be-gun a full court press —the only kind he knew —on his company for a transfer south. I prayed he wasn't pursuing the transfer just to please a changed me. With the numerous stones I had cast in his direction before my breakthrough with Neil, I wondered if his good guy routine would tire. I was afraid the hurt from my betray-al would cause an explosion to his spirit like a shaken can of soda being opened for the first time.

Please God be with Patrick.

I missed the depth of emotion I experienced from him the first few weeks of my breakthrough. If only Patrick could express his feelings the way Chad could, then maybe I could rid myself of Chad's hold on a part of my heart.

I continued to pray...and walk with Sarah.

Following our morning stroll, Sarah and I tracked the aroma to the coffee shop where we continued our discussion about the new *emotional me* and my worries about my surgery in two days. I had a complicated hysterectomy a few years prior, and an area causing pain again needed to be repaired. The original hysterectomy nev-er scared me, but now with my heart exposed I was freaking out.

For a supposedly healthy woman in her thirties I had far too many ailments, inheriting the nickname "chronic" from our good friends, Mandy and Ralph, who listened to my full confession soon after we told my parents. I was fortunate they had forgiven me and were still able to crack jokes even after knowing all my icky and the pain I put Patrick through. I was discovering the meaning of true friends, and that included Sarah.

As she and I stood in line, man hands grabbed my waist from behind, throwing me off balance. I spun around to one of Patrick's friends wrapping his arms around my shoulders and greeting me with a quick peck on my lips.

"Hey! Good to see you, Kristy," he said with a smile.

The hair on the back of my neck was standing at attention. I muttered a subdued, "Hello."

"Gotta run. Late for an appointment," he said as he grabbed two coffees from the counter and headed for the door.

He turned back around.

"Tell Patrick I said, Hi," he shouted, and disappeared onto the sidewalk.

The coffee line had moved forward, but I was still in the same spot—frozen.

The self-admitted touchy-feely flirt had been replaced by an ice queen.

Why was I so uncomfortable with his greeting?

My mind drifted to an intense session with Neil.

My eyes were shut, my body shaking. Methodical words left my lips, "He's putting his hand over mine and placing it on the stiff of his jeans."

"What happened next?" Neil's calm voice encouraged more visual detail.

My voice unsteady, not wanting to go there.

"He's moving my hand back and forth on himself."

"Open your eyes and follow the object in my hand."

Holding a pencil, Neil waved his hand back and forth in front of my eyes for a few seconds, then asked, "Close your eyes again. Which hand is touching his private parts?"

Hesitating, I tried to envision the position of my hands, while following Neil's fingers. I couldn't. My pulsed picked up pace.

"It's OK. Keep your eyes closed. Focus on what your body is feeling."

A pit returned to my stomach. My knees weaken. I wanted to collapse, to hide. My right hand began to shake uncontrollably.

Fighting tears, I mumbled, "I can't control my right hand."

"That's good, Kristy. Let your body remember."

The involuntary trembling of my right hand consumed my whole body. I opened my eyes to impede my movement, but the shaking continued. I couldn't stop.

Neil's hand holding the pencil continued to move. I tracked the movements, his verbal commands guiding my mind to my peaceful place at the beach in the hammock. The convulsing slowed. My apprehension subsided.

"Relax...Allow your mind to take you wherever it needs," Neil calmly added.

I saw myself lying in bed on my side, my back to Patrick. What did he have to do with this? Guilt swarmed like a disrupted bee hive. My insides quivered.

"What images do you see?"

Shame blanketed my words.

"Patrick is spooning me, trying to wake me."

A knot tightened in my gut almost buckling me over. I could feel my skin charring from his heat. I wanted to curl up and die. Disgust boiled in my veins. I did nothing to stop his pursuit. I went numb.

"Don't resist the shaking, Kristy. Let go."

Neil's tranquility blanketed my anxiety. I surrendered to the unraveling of my emotions through the convulsions of my body. Neil guided me back to my peaceful place. My foggy state lifted. The intersection of paths I traveled was still hazy.

"Why is the touch of Patrick igniting painful feelings and causing my body to go haywire?" I asked.

"Your body is remembering feelings your mind blocked out—a body flashback."

My face scrunched.

"I don't understand. What does that have to do with my husband?"

He leaned forward with hands open to explain.

"When you wake to Patrick's touch, your body remembers the fear and the helplessness of the Sheriff interrupting your peaceful sleep for his own pleasure. You shut down all emotion."

My struggle to connect the dots must have been apparent since Neil continued.

"Let's look at it a different way," Neil said, sitting back. "When a young gazelle is attacked by a lion in the wild, it plays dead—freezing until the lion gets bored and leaves...since it only chases prey that runs away. When the gazelle deems the situation safe, it gets up, shakes profusely for a period and then prances away. The gazelle is able to recover because of its ability to discharge residual energy. You, on the other hand, were unable to release your nervous energy when you froze during the assault. Humans in survival mode can't always give their bodies time to process the feelings associated with a traumatic experience. These feelings can haunt their body sometimes oblivious to the mind."

The dots began to form a clearer picture in my mind.

"So, whenever I feel relaxed and am disrupted by something unexpected, like Patrick's touch or someone else's, my body gets anxious and numbs down in anticipation of the assault?"

"Exactly."

"You OK?" Sarah's voice pulled me back.

"I think so."

Hesitating to elaborate, I moved forward catching up with the coffee line. Patrick's friend's behavior was not out of the norm for our interactions in the past. However mine was. Living without walls for protection from feelings was changing me.

"That felt weird!" I blurted, as I tried to shake off the uncomfortable moment with a huff of disgust.

"It's about time," Sarah said, chuckling. "I always wondered how you could be such a 'hands on girl' with everyone and feel nothing. The wives of the husbands certainly felt something. And from the look on your face, you're not numb anymore!"

We laughed in unison.

Sarah had been on one heck of a journey with me. Our relationship was like driving in the dark without headlights. Sarah never knew where my ride was taking her or if I was going crash and burn.

"Yeah...It's no wonder people don't believe I never sleep around."

CHAPTER 50

Hard To Love

"Why aren't you wearing your wedding ring around school?" Patrick asked, agitated.

"Huh?"

That question caught me off guard. I shrugged.

"I always wear my ring," I said.

"Well, I had a strange conversation today with one of the doctors at the hospital. He called me all concerned about you not wearing your ring around the school."

Patrick's face grew redder with each word.

"He told me his wife quit wearing her wedding ring then—BOOM—she leaves him for their builder. He believes you're having an affair!"

I giggled—which was an odd response for someone who took serious pride in her righteous reputation. I would have been infuriated in my old skin at the mere hint of this type of accusation. I had tried to control rumors in the spring by disappearing from the social scene and allowing Chloe's pending divorce to be my scapegoat. Now, when I wasn't worried about my reputation the simplest thing is misunderstood. The irony shocked me. I could not control people's perceptions of me and had wasted a lifetime trying.

"Well? Is that what's going on here?"

His green eyes were like a painful laser from a sci-fi movie.

I found myself on the defensive.

"No! Of course not!"

Then, like a light bulb flash from a paparazzi ambush, I remembered.

"Oh...Ally's first day of school! The doctor you're referring to must be the man who insisted that you call him. Now, I understand. I wasn't wearing my ring because I was meeting Sarah to work out."

My tone softened as I tried to regain my composure.

"You know I never wear my ring when I exercise."

Going against my long pattern, I reached out for an embrace. Instead, I received a cursory peck on the cheek as Patrick bolted for his office.

"Can't you just sit with me for a minute?" I asked with a slight tone of frustration.

He responded in kind, "I've got stuff to take care of."

"Can't it wait?"

"Kristy!"

His irritation signaled a line in the sand I knew not to cross, but I usually crossed it anyway in the past. Either he didn't want to deal with the rumors, or me, but whichever—I was being punished and left alone to digest the rest.

Despite the spark, Patrick's fuse never lit. Part of me wished it had. At least then I would see the passion he had in our bedroom the night before my breakthrough at the end of May. With his defenses surrendered, he expressed his vulnerability and connected with my heart. Since then, however, Patrick's heart was back under lock and key. I couldn't blame him, I suppose. I had pulled the rug out from under him just as his father had with his abrupt disappearance. Patrick deserved stability and didn't need the rumors, my erratic heart, or my upcoming surgery rocking his boat. He calmed my rough waters with his patience and unconditional love. I owed him the same.

The next day in my session I tried to describe my moments with Patrick, the talk around town, and my upcoming surgery.

"Neil, the more I voice my true feelings and wants, the more Patrick pushes back. He assumes I'm criticizing him personally."

"Are you?"

Neil's voice felt like my conscience.

"No. I'm just trying to tell him what I want instead of being disappointed when he doesn't get my hints for affection."

"Well, that is a step in the right direction—letting your heart *be* vulnerable."

Neil's smile radiated approval.

"I don't like vulnerable," I said with a pouty lip.

Neil chuckled responding, "I know, but without it you can't have real intimacy."

Neil was right. My heart hurt. Patrick's to-do-list always seemed to get in the way of our connection, and he still viewed my verbalization of feelings as complaints.

What if Patrick was only performing as the dutiful husband and his emotions were not there?

Feeling the weight of frustration my chest tightened and my voice strained, "I need him to understand that I'm not trying to change him! I'm trying to find the 'real' him beneath the layers of perfection."

"Kristy."

Neil's voice stopped me.

"You can't control how Patrick reacts to your wants nor can you force him to open up. Remember, his emotional walls were the reason he could endure your pointed words about your feelings for Chad."

Neil slid his chair closer.

"Maybe a better way to explain things to Patrick is that you aren't trying to change who he is but are asking him to join you in trying new things. For example, when you try a new food, that doesn't mean you have to give up your old favorites, it just means you get to experience new tastes."

Neil's examples had a way of smoothing my rough edges, but my disappointment lingered.

"I know, Neil, I understand. I just want his heart to be freed from external restraints the way mine was, but the more I express my desires, the more he accuses me of trying to change him into Chad."

Unlike most visits, I left Neil's office with my insides still in knots. My unaddressed emotions overwhelmed me, like a small town girl lost in a big city.

Trying to sort through Neil's advice, Chloe's pending divorce, and the rumors, the last thing I needed was dealing with the emotions about my upcoming surgery. Without my usual protective field, I felt alone and petrified of what may come next. Not because of the rumors swirling outside like a tornado, but because my heart was exposed. I didn't want to feel alone in a house left standing if the winds never died. My life was now being shaped from the inside out, and I became more terrified about my vulnerable physical and emotional state.

Meanwhile, Patrick continued his superhero routine, but never exposed his inner spirit the way Clark Kent exposed his true identity to Lois Lane. On the other hand, I had become a blubbering idiot, mushy with emotion. He did not understand my needs for

affection or reassurances about my upcoming surgery. I was starting to experience unbridled living and feared I may never get the
chance to enjoy it to its fullest.

I had wasted a lifetime trying to avoid destructions. Where had that
gotten me?

My life had been miserable trying to please everyone, an impossible task. Now freed of the chains holding my heart hostage,
the challenge now was fighting the urge to find a substitute to
soothe my heart when it was at risk of pain and disappointment
from Patrick's inability to connect. I couldn't force his heart to
spill out, but that didn't mean I didn't yearn for a human connection to support my struggles, as Chad did. I longed to hear a voice
like his, reassuring me that I was going to be OK, even when I
didn't feel at all OK.

What if something terrible happened in surgery?

I picked up the phone.

His Southern drawl answered with a skeptical edge, "Hello?"

My heart skipped a beat.

"I'm sorry. I shouldn't be calling."

"You OK, baby?"

The concern in his voice busted through to me. I burst into tears
as I explained my fears over tomorrow's surgery and the thought
of never seeing him again if something happened. He assured me
that everything would be fine, but avoided the warm fuzzies. Chad
felt restrained, his feelings guarded. My call hurt him. My need for
comfort was selfish. I had crossed the line. I wasn't being fair to
either of them.

CHAPTER 51

If Tomorrow Never Comes

Tears formed as I waited to be wheeled down for surgery. Patrick stood next to the bed scrolling around on his phone. I wished he was here in mind and not just in body. Maybe then he could sense my fear about the surgery.

Where was the old me when I needed her?

I was probably being irrational, but that didn't matter since dread had already penetrated my senses. The call to Chad had made things worse.

What if I don't wake up? What if? What if...

The worst possible outcomes kept running through my mind, each scene scarier than the last. Maybe my character was being killed off—*I had my miracle of a healing heart that was enough for one lifetime.* My fears skyrocketed at the thought of never having the chance to truly live life. I wanted Patrick to help lift my burden, not because he was obligated to, but because he wanted to. Wishing Patrick hungered to connect with my inner feelings, my mind drifted to Chad.

Why am I thinking of Chad again? Stop it, Kristy! I said my goodbyes. In that moment, I realized just how alone and vulnerable I really was. My prior-self felt strong behind the armor, protected from being disappointed by people's actions *or inactions.* Any attention thrown my way was a bonus. But now, with my armor removed, I was no longer in denial about needing someone in my life for love and support. I wanted that person to be Patrick, but he didn't know how to fully give what I needed—at least not yet.

He was making every effort to change his actions. However, I couldn't force his heart to be able to empathize with me. I understood what it was like to live behind walls, numb, oblivious to what was missing, so I kept giving Patrick a pass. His devotion was far more than I deserved, yet I couldn't control the palpitations of my heart yearning for more. I desired to be taken care of and protected from the unknown—even if just for a moment.

I wondered if Patrick would ever be able to break out to give me his heart and soul. Tears continued as I drifted off, wondering if this was my new reality.

"How's she doing?"

My eyes tried to focus on the face standing over me in front of the light. I wondered if my groggy state was playing tricks...*were there two faces, or one?* I closed my eyes and focused on listening. The voices were talking about *me.* I wondered if I was crazy *or dead.* Both options were not very appealing. The longer I listened the more I understood.

"Better now. She was freaking out with tears before the surgery."

"Kristy? Tears?" the voice said bewildered.

"Hard to believe, I know—Miss Independent."

"You know what they are saying around the hospital about the two of them?"

"Yeah, I heard."

"Sorry she's getting dragged into our mess."

"Don't be. She's capable of taking care of herself."

"No—I'm not!" I blurted into the light realizing I wasn't dead.

"Looks like she's back—but definitely *not* her old self," Robert chuckled.

"Chloe isn't capable either. She needs you," I whimpered.

"Not anymore—That train's left the station. Leave it alone, Kristy, or I'll put you back under."

Robert's joke hid his real feelings. Chloe had moved out of the dream house they built. The divorce would be finalized in a month or so.

Patrick placed his warm hand on mine and squeezed.

"That sounds like a good idea, Robert. She can't give me back talk then," he teased.

He wanted to avoid the subject of Chloe as much as Robert did.

I didn't have the energy or guts to push back, knowing I was already walking a thin line with Robert. His presence was a miracle in itself, realizing he probably wasn't my biggest fan after being Chloe's partner in crime, and was most likely there to relieve Patrick's anxiety, not mine. I couldn't fault him if he held me responsible for her departure. I blamed myself. There was so much to say, but now was not the time to bombard him with my guilt. Instead choosing to tell him how much his visit meant to me, before the weight of my eyelids closed everything down.

I wasn't sure if it was the pain of the surgery or the ache in my heart that prompted my withdrawal of consciousness.

Surgery hadn't cured my sadness. Knowing Patrick should have left my station a long time ago, I still felt guilty for wanting more from him. He was already doing so much to keep the house afloat, while I recovered. I didn't like missing so much time with my children. I didn't like being afraid or feeling alone.

However, alone was where I found myself. Despite Patrick being *with* me, he was too consumed with his work, the kids' schedules and the state of the house. My sensitive state wasn't helping, and seemed to push Patrick away further, as if I were an "emotional time bomb" primed to explode at any moment. Even I was afraid of what feeling would unleash during this quiet, recovery time.

"Please just stay here with me," I whined, still recovering a week after surgery.

"You'll be fine. I don't know why you're so emotional. The surgery was a piece of cake compared to your hysterectomy."

"I want you here," I said, choking back tears. "You've been gone two days for work and now you're leaving again?"

"Stop guilting me! I have done everything around here, while you've been laid up."

"Except be with me!" I barked.

Not the right thing to say.

"I have been taking care of things around here! If I don't do it, who will? You don't appreciate a thing I do for you! I've agreed to change jobs and move south. I've done everything you want! But you're never happy! I deserve to go out!"

When I unexpectedly refused to enter the argument, Patrick stormed out. He wasn't grasping the fact I needed HIM, *not* the things he was doing.

Why couldn't he choose me over his to-do-list or friends?

The quiet bedroom felt like a prison, but I refused to retreat to my protective shell like a turtle.

I texted: "Sorry for making you feel guilty. Have fun with your friends! I'll be fine."

Despair crept back in worrying that Patrick may never be able to share his heart. However, I could no longer use the white picket fence to guilt him into staying with a changed woman.

My entire life I had tried to *perform* the right way so people would perceive me as a good person. I controlled my environment to maintain this image, but now my defenses were down. There were chinks in my armor...first Chad, then my failure as a Catholic and now the physical weakness of surgery.

Rumors were swirling around town. I was stuck in my bedroom recovering, thinking, and writing in my journal.

I never felt so lonely.

CHAPTER 52

Days Gone By

Patrick remained buttoned up, his soul protected. Mine yearned for more. I still hoped.

Our dream house of the North remained on the market as Patrick moved through interviews for his transfer. With our hearts yearning for Charleston, he was making a concerted effort to change our structured way of living, yet expressing his feelings remained difficult. I struggled to relax in his tense arms. We hadn't regained the passion from early summer, and resentment was settling into my heart—and probably his.

One evening, with the local news on mute, we sat at the dinner table with our children discussing Halloween costumes.

Patrick interrupted, "Hey, the ticker on the TV says school will be closed at least two days due to a swine flu outbreak."

"What? There's already no school Friday. How am I going to get everything done for Halloween if the kids are around the next few days?"

My mind began to sort through my to-do-list. I must rearrange it to deal with this change.

Patrick continued, "Seeing as how the kids are off most of the week, why don't we jump in the car and go south?"

I was half listening, until I heard *south.*

My eyes squinted trying to catch up with his statement.

"What do you want to do?" I asked, to make sure I heard him correctly.

"Let's head toward Florida...tonight. We could go to your parents, recheck Charleston again, or wing an oceanside resort. It doesn't matter. I have vacation days left, and the kids wouldn't miss much with this swine flu thing and Halloween on Friday. What do you say?"

Our kids, bubbling with anticipation, sat nervously watching us go back and forth, as if we were in a playful tennis match.

"Tonight?" I processed his odd proposal—or maybe it wasn't so odd. He did initiate the two-week trip in August.

"Well, I'd like to get on the road in the next two hours. Think you could have everyone packed then?"

His voice had no hint of humor. He was serious.

"I guess," I responded.

My head was still spinning.

"Let's get moving then. We'll drive through the night. The kids will sleep."

I stood. Shaking my head and smiling, I wrapped my arms around his neck.

"Who is this guy and what have you done with my husband?"

The kids started chanting, "Florida! Florida!"

His boyish grin was back.

I kissed him and said, "You clean the kitchen. I'll pack."

Maybe there was hope after all. I kept my fingers crossed. I hoped Patrick's walls would disappear and his heart would escape. He had already made a huge step by initiating the spontaneous vacation. Instead of revisiting Charleston, we kept driving to Florida's east coast. In our quest for a quick get-away, we forgot Ally's shoes and didn't realize it until our first bathroom break in West Virginia! Luckily we were able to laugh it off with our new-found impulsiveness.

With the whimsical side of Patrick unleashed, I had hopes of our intimate connection rekindling as it did the few weeks after my June breakthrough. Yet, though he was no longer functioning me-chanically like a wind-up toy, his playfulness was directed toward the children, not me. I settled for baby steps—hand holding and a few small public displays of affection were better than nothing. The alternative would have been dire, and I was thankful for his mercy.

After a few refreshing days at the beach, we made our way inland to my parents' quaint home in orange grove country. Returning there stirred up uncomfortable feelings from the spring visit, and squashed my hope of passionate openness. We were learning to live without a plan, yet distance remained between us in the bedroom.

Patrick's heart barricaded itself further, and I couldn't find the door.

He felt I needed time alone to sort through my feelings. But separation was not what I needed, I needed intimacy. Instead he booked Ally and me on a flight home for later in the week, and he drove back to Michigan with Seth and Brooke. He was doing everything to accommodate me except express his deep feelings.

My parents focused on Ally, and I spent the remainder of the time lying by the pool...thinking.

My feelings for Patrick were tainted with the cloudy memory of Chad's openness—his perfect resumé without perfect timing. I was longing for a relaxed soul to embrace and comfort my new existence. Maybe if Patrick unleashed his spirit, the clouds would cease to block the aura of a soulful connection. However, I think Patrick felt pressure to perform perfectly, while remaining restless within his fallible skin. I feared he was still comparing himself to Chad by trying to be the better man for me. The problem was, I didn't need him to be the *better* man. I wanted him to be *my* man. I jumped into the pool hoping to cool off the destructive fire burning within me.

The nagging questions remained. Would Patrick be able to let his guard down to connect our souls and quench my desire for Happily Ever After? Could he learn to just be without the need to achieve perfection?

My hope was fading and discouragement was taking root. Patrick did not want to be vulnerable to heartache and eliminating his walls remained a complex task. Despite my efforts to tell him that I wanted *him* and not the things he was doing for me, he only saw himself as failing to connect with me, "Ms. Ungrateful," and therefore erected even more barriers. Patrick was a doer, not a feeler. Maybe I needed to accept him as is.

But where did that leave the new feeling me?

I wanted a life prioritized by love not accomplishments or wealth. My appearance, achievements and adherence to religious rules no longer defined my sense of self. I was peaceful in my own flawed skin. Patrick wasn't. He was still comparing himself to Chad and trying to win my love by being the perfect mate. I just wanted him—imperfections and all.

I flew home more confused.

Could I wait for Patrick to connect to my emotional needs?

We would have less than twelve hours together before leaving for the Chicago film festival. More time away from each other was not what either of us needed. We were trying to bridge our intimacy gap, but skipping the festival was not an option. David, my pseudo-sibling, was coming all the way from Sweden to debut his short film in the United States. David was the exchange student who lived with my parents and me my junior year of high school.

He moved in the same year Patrick left for college and as I said earlier, probably not a coincidence.

David and I had a rocky relationship. I was a conservative rule follower into athletics and academics. David was and is a free spirit into the arts—a world I did not understand. Too much gray. As young adults, however, we found common ground through multiple transcontinental visits and developed a true bond. I treasured our relationship and wouldn't dream of missing his film debut in the states.

Knowing how much David meant to me, Patrick offered to be with the kids so I could go. I worried about his real feelings about me traveling with Chloe, but also knew he thought highly of David and trusted him to keep an eye on me. With Chloe's divorce finalized a few weeks earlier, I thought an escape would do her some good too.

Our bedroom looked like a tornado hit. I was unpacking from sunny Florida, while packing for chilly Chicago. Patrick sat on the bed watching.

"I'm not thrilled about Chloe going with you."

Patrick's comment made my blood curdle.

"Don't you think it's a little late to be telling me this five minutes before I'm picking her up?"

"Kristy, at this point we are just roommates staying together for the kids."

I thought this discussion was about Chloe.

I didn't know how to respond. His sarcastic tone wasn't altering his voice, so I resorted to my own mockery.

"*Now*, you decide you want to have a *feeling* discussion?"

Sadness smothered the room.

"I'm just stating the obvious," he said, still calm. "I know Chad is still a part of your thoughts, and I can't compete with that forever."

CHAPTER 53

Love Like Crazy

Patrick's harsh words this morning had pierced my heart like a knife.

A parade of emotions consumed me on the five-hour drive to Chicago and I had the next four days to assess the damage. Patrick was right. We didn't connect the way we should with Chad's memory still crowding my heart. There wasn't room for both in my life and my prayers for Chad to vacate weren't being answered, despite my heart being opened to Patrick. I could feel Patrick's love and every other feeling to the Nth degree since my breakthrough, but didn't know if that would be enough after feeling Chad's passionate words for *me*.

I wish Patrick could express his heart instead of me trying to pry him open like an oyster.

Maybe looking into Chad's eyes would explain why his spirit haunted my dreams. I turned to Chloe who sat next to me in the car with a blank stare.

I recalled a similar look on her face a few weeks prior, while sitting in the back of a courtroom watching Chloe on the stand as her divorce was being finalized. Throughout her testimony, the judge pressed her decision about divorcing a man she seemed to speak so highly about. Having no concrete answers, Chloe's broken eyes kept scanning the room for her lifeline. Robert wasn't in court and was no longer protesting her decision. He had given up the fight. Their divorce was final. I knew that look all too well, most of my life I too had felt disappointed, alone...disconnected.

"Chloe, I'm lost."

"Haven't you driven to Chicago a hundred times?" she asked with her eyebrows raised.

"That's not what I mean."

"Oh, back on the men topic," she said, as she turned to look out the passenger window. "I should've known."

"I'm lost for what to do. Patrick is a good man and doesn't deserve only half of me. I need Chad to vacate my heart, so I can move forward with Patrick."

I took a deep breath.

"It's been nine months, and I can't shake the two days I spent with him. Maybe once we get to Chicago, I should jump on a flight to Texas and see for myself why this fantasy has a hold on my heart like a boa constrictor?"

Chloe didn't flinch. Instead she began making calls to the airlines as I drove.

"Found one—Leaves tonight, back Sunday in time to see David's film," she said. "I think you should check with Chad first."

Where was Chloe's usual indifference to my actions?

"I guess you're right, but..." my voice quivered. "...you call him."

"I'll do whatever you want me to do, but if my husband would have been half the man Patrick is to you, we wouldn't be divorced now."

Chloe's candor was like a bolt of electricity.

I turned to look into her eyes.

"What? You never said anything like that to me before!"

"Well, I'm saying it now," she said nonchalantly. "You have a good husband who loves you, and I don't want you go through the hell I'm going through."

Chloe's words reverberated. Patrick is a good husband, and he loves me. But why?

The answer smacked me like a sucker punch.

The love I had been pursuing was not *real* love at all. I had been so consumed with *my* wants and *my* fairytale dreams...*my, my, my*... that I missed the example of real love right in front of me—Patrick! The more the dots connected the more my head throbbed. Real love isn't earned, but given freely—no strings attached. My authentic faith came to life. I had been a zombie, following the dictates of the church without a connection to God's love or any love. The thought was too much and suddenly too obvious to bear. The rush of emotion flooded my eyes and blurred my vision making it difficult to keep on the freeway. My heart and mind united in powerful revelation, bursting the dam holding the water back. "Happily Ever After" is not a fairytale where the perfect prince saves you from yourself. A true prince loves you for yourself—faults and all.

Tears streamed down my face. I was free from the self-centered fairytale love I had felt for Chad. I had forgiven myself for not stopping the Sheriff and now felt an overpowering love radiating from within. Stammering, broken, humbled—my prayers had been answered.

God had drawn a perfectly straight line with a crooked stick.

CHAPTER 54

The Book You Never Read

I wanted to turn the car around, rush home to Patrick's arms, and tell him how much I loved *him*. But how could I leave David unsupported? He had flown halfway around the world to debut his first movie. As I drove the Skyway into the city, I decided to text Patrick why I loved him every waking hour...reminiscent of my lost pre-wedding journal. I wasn't sure my texts would be enough, but I had to try something.

Thank goodness I was sharing the weekend and my epiphany with David. He was the anchor I needed, grounding my present state of mind to my past existence. He had in-depth knowledge of Patrick's and my relationship and knew how I ticked. I thought I knew David too, until I realized I was attending the Chicago *Gay and Lesbian* Film Festival—a shock to my conservative system.

Being immersed in gay culture was a first for me. I'm not sure I would have been comfortable before my breakthroughs, but was grateful my heart could enjoy the moment now. Although Chloe and I were probably the only straight people in the crowded block of restaurants and bars, I didn't see any difference in the eyes of the patrons than I did at the straight bars I frequented. Some eyes were peaceful, others were vying for attention to prove their worth, and others were empty and wounded—my eyes were opened to many levels I hadn't seen before.

I realized David for years had battled his own internal fight masking the fact he was gay. We were one and the same—living life empty of purpose, looking for validation and struggling to accept our real selves. David and I were discovering how to *just be* ourselves without requiring outside validation. I was grateful for my time with him and my new understanding of love.

"I must say I was worried about what you would think and how you would handle the weekend," David said as he hugged me in the middle of the Chicago sidewalk.

I missed his Swedish accent.

"I know what a rule follower you are and I'm definitely out of 'that' box."

He smiled.

"You are what you are, and I love you," I said. "I may not understand your choices or feelings, but I sense your peace."

David pushed back from our embrace and stared, his brow wrinkled.

"What's up with you? You're way too calm to be my sis, Kris."

"Well, let's just say we have a lot to catch up on."

I hugged him again, smiling.

Chloe stayed at the hotel to rest and skipped the movie to give David and me time alone. We walked arm and arm to a nearby coffee shop to talk before the debut of his movie, titled *My Name is Love.* As I realized how appropriate the title was to my second epiphany, a chuckle escaped. I didn't waste another second as my mouth became a runaway train. David listened as I exposed the gory details of the past nine months. I could call my relationship with Chad what it was now...an affair. The words felt odd rolling off my once virtuous tongue. To my surprise my shame had vanished, my soul cleansed, I felt the love of my Creator.

I had peace.

The self-righteous woman I once was would have judged things I didn't understand to validate my own worth and choices—I would have judged David. Now, with my heart opened to real, *unconditional love,* I could give of myself without having to understand the heart of another. My view of love was no longer tainted by selfish wants, desires, or need for validation. I finally understood that true love is not about what you receive, but what you give of your authentic self. David was giving of his true self. Now it was my turn.

I was ready to give my whole self to Patrick without condition. I was accepting of myself, feeling the love of my Creator, and ready to love with an unconditional heart.

I prayed my hourly texts throughout the weekend would penetrate Patrick's heart.

Friday's texts read:

I love that you talk on the phone with me and share your day.
I love that you buy me flowers for no reason at all.
I love that you put up with this spoiled girl even when she doesn't deserve it.
I love that you take time to truly hold me tight.
I love that you vacuum something almost every day.
I love that you are so polite and loving when I kick you awake because you are snoring.
I love that you do projects with the kids to lessen my load.
I love that I'm missing you. Sweet dreams.

Saturday's texts read:

I love that you haven't given up on me and us.
I love that you are not self-centered even when I am.
I love that you always like my cooking.
I love your willingness to improve our intimacy (which we need to start practicing immediately).
I love that you give everything your all.
DON'T GIVE UP ON ME.
I love that you rub my neck (next we will have a whole session on kissing it—up for the challenge?).
I love that you told me I'm Yours is a song that makes you think of me.
I love that you are trying to understand me.
I love that you are my husband.
I love that you help pick up the house.
I love that you clean the kitchen after I cook.
I love that we both are going to learn the new meaning of fore-play (R U game?), no need to reply, just think on it. Be creative! Slow, seductive, teasing, messy, tantalizing, invigorating, soft, breathy, loving, exploratory, imaginative, just to name a few of my thoughts.
I love that you love me, 'Cuz I love YOU—I do!
Sweet dreams!

Sunday's texts read:

I love how you blow your nose in the shower like a goose—LOL.
I love that you lay with Seth at night and chat.
I love that you are our daughters' knight in shining armor.
I love that you never leave laundry on the floor and put up with me when I do.
I love that you can handle the kids without me.

I love that you can get the girls ready and out the door without me, just don't get used to it—LOL.
I love that you are interviewing for Southern jobs—good luck tomorrow.
I love that you want to throw out the plan and take a risk with me.
I love that I want to be with you right now.
I love that we are open and honest with each other.
I love that you are my heart.

And Monday's texts read:

I love that I love YOU more than I could ever have imagined I could love someone.
I love that I am coming home to you.
I love that no one can love me like you do! (I finally get it!).

Patrick's lack of response was abnormal. Maybe I had chipped away one too many times at his spirit and killed his love. I couldn't turn back the clock or worry about the consequences, however. I could only move forward and hope our love prevailed.

I prayed I wasn't too late.

CHAPTER 55

God Gave Me You

Fear shackled my footsteps. For the first time in my life since "the incident," my heart was truly vulnerable.

Had I lost Patrick forever?

I was ready to accept the consequences of my misguided ways. I held my breath, and opened the back door. On the center of the kitchen island was a huge bouquet of vibrant yellow roses—my favorite.

I dropped my bag and ran to Patrick who had paper towels in his hand from cleaning the granite on the island. I wrapped my arms around his waist as my knees gave out. Catching me, he gathered me into a tight squeeze.

We didn't let go.

Tears overpowered me, and I whispered breathlessly, "I'm so sorry...soooo sorry."

Our embrace was so long the children began hugging around our legs wanting in on the love. Over Patrick's shoulder I saw Chloe smile. She set down my other bag and quietly slipped out.

Patrick leaned his head back to connect with my weepy eyes.

"I'm glad you're home."

"Me, too," I whispered, smiling through the tears.

We shooed the children away, then retreated to the quiet of the bedroom. As I locked the door behind me, the clicking caused Patrick to halt and swing his head over his shoulder catching my baby blue sparkle. My impulses exploded. I pounced onto his back and smothered his exposed neck with my kisses. I pursued my husband without expectations of how he should love me. My existence was a whole new adventure. It was my turn to exhibit boundless, grace-filled love to the one man who loved me with all his being— imperfections and all.

"That was different," Patrick said with a mystified grin creeping up his cheek bones. "Who was 'that woman' and what have you done with my wife?"

I wondered the same thing.

Where had this woman come from?

I giggled.

Relaxed, we propped ourselves on the throw pillows of the bed. I began a candid reflection about my weekend in Chicago. Patrick fidgeted with the seam of the sheet. He didn't want to relive the past. I scooted closer to his chest and rested my hand on his. I realized my nine month journey with Patrick in the passenger seat had been a long, bumpy ride for both of us—yet Patrick stood steadfast, while I discovered the real me, his love barely wavered. I wanted him to understand my love for him would never again be conditional.

"If you don't you like this wife I can send her back," I said seductively.

"No, No," he responded putting his hands up in defense.

The sunlight filtering through the blinds glared off his wedding ring and into my eyes—a small price for the relief of knowing he hadn't given up on our vows.

Mocking a reprimanding schoolteacher, I waved my finger at him before switching to a more playful voice.

"Good! This new woman is your fault, anyway. But that's why I love you! You helped me find my true self beneath the walls. You loved me even though I was a runaway train of emotions the past five months, and I'm sure that wasn't easy."

"To say the least..." Patrick interjected sharply.

His body language betrayed his apprehension toward this second change of heart. I couldn't blame him—my actions needed to speak louder and longer than one escapade in the bedroom that could be dismissed as a guilty conscience.

"I know," my voice danced on hot coals. "I deserve everything you throw my way. But, how 'bout a little life line here...my soul was in a protected world like the character in *The Truman Show*. You liked that movie."

Patrick nodded reluctantly.

"And?"

"And, well...*Mr. Truman* wasn't aware his life was controlled by producers and actors, and I wasn't aware of the restraints and limitations imposed on my heart by the Sheriff. Like *Truman*, I was living in a world of fake emotions manipulated by others. Then an unbelievable storm shook our worlds forcing us to bust through the walls imprisoning our spirits. Once free, I yearned to feel the genuine feelings I missed. I thought I wanted YOU to make *me* feel special like my Prince Charming fantasy. But that was the lie! I had *love* backwards—focusing on *my* wants. There is no perfect person that can make me feel special 100% of the time. We are human, after all."

"I'm human—you're still up for debate," he said.

His familiar teasing tone eased my tension, a bit.

"Hey."

I nudged him. Patrick has a way of getting me back on track during my ramblings. Before I could get to my point, worry hijacked my inner peace. Maybe the mere mention of a Prince Charming slammed the door on his open heart.

What if he wasn't teasing?

I recanted my playful objection.

"Uh, I guess you're probably right considering the next crazy stop I'm going to reveal."

His smile lessened my fears. We were still on the same page of the love story...

I took a breath.

"On the ride to Chicago, I considered going to Texas to rid myself of Chad's grip on half my heart...until something deeper, something stronger united my spirit. Chloe's words sparked this second moment of clarity. 'If Robert was half the man Patrick is to you,' she said, 'we wouldn't be divorced.' In that instant I realized you love me the only way you know—unconditionally. I felt love from a whole new dimension, because of your example. I know I'm hard to understand..."

I fidgeted with a strand of hair.

"You, think?"

He couldn't always say what I wanted him to say, but I finally understood the language of his heart.

My voice grew more confident.

"As we drove on the Skyway, the spirit of unconditional love hit like a lightning bolt. My selfish idea of love was not real love at all, and I have you to thank for my epiphanies—the first in June where I felt God's grace cleanse my soul and free my heart from my own prison, and now an unconditional love merging heaven and YOU. I love you, Patrick...only you. I just didn't understand how to love before, but I'll never make that mistake again."

His grassy eyes radiated tranquility. He gently embraced my face, pulling me into a soothing kiss.

CHAPTER 56

Loves Gonna Live Here

I was home.

Yellow petals blanketed the kitchen island. While gathering the fallen petals, I noticed two of the most beautiful roses remained alive. I placed them in a small bud vase and moved them to Patrick's bedside nightstand. I was mesmerized by their beauty. The yellow no longer symbolized a thorn of disappointment. It was now a "sign" of connected hearts. The vibrant hue was like that of a rising sun on a day full of new possibilities.

I sat on the bed. Clutching his pillow, I breathed in the clean, fresh scent left from his smooth skin and sighed. My heart was intertwined with his and I knew being without him tonight would be painful. He was in South Carolina for his final meeting before the transfer and wouldn't be returning until late the next day. The reality of Charleston was so close I could almost taste the salty air. I had faith in what was meant to be.

The last six months of living with authentic emotions had been like hiking along unmarked trails through the mountains trying to reach the ocean. I never knew what I was going to experience next. The expedition was frightening and exhilarating at the same time.

Reflecting on all the stops, each memory reminded me of Patrick, I realized he had withstood pain for my benefit—his sacrifices, my salvation.

I didn't deserve a second chance, yet I was getting one.

Our love has endless possibilities. Longing for his presence, I fell asleep with the two roses comforting me to an unknown journey ahead.

A vivid dream jolted me awake.

In the dark of night, I rummaged through the drawer of his nightstand for a pen and a pad of sticky notes. When my eyes adjusted to the moonlit room, I scribbled the words from my dream...

The Majestic Roses

After all the rain had stopped,
And the storm had passed,
I took a breath,
And two of the most amazing
Flowers remained.

The two of them weathered the storm
And awoke to an entirely new and beautiful world

After that, they knew together
Their love could withstand
All obstacles on this earth,
Because their love was God's love.

Placing the note next to the two roses, I drifted back to sleep. Wondering...

Who was this new spirit in my imperfect body?

The smell of crisp air and damp leaves reflected the change of seasons, and like the naked hardwood trees surrounding our home I had been transformed. Thanksgiving was upon us, the season more meaningful than ever before. My self-centered self had fallen with the leaves, and a blissful, contented soul remained. I had more than my share to be thankful for, especially Patrick.

Only by the grace of God could I have found such a profound love on earth, and a man open to a change in life's plans mid-stream.

Patrick's tenacity landed him a devoted wife and a transfer to a new division in Charleston. Together, we awaited the paperwork from corporate, delayed by the Thanksgiving holiday that would outline his new territory, and the timing of the move.

However, before the paperwork could be approved, his company imposed a hiring freeze due to the sluggish economy. The newly created position vanished overnight, along with our hopes of transferring to South Carolina. Fortunately he hadn't given his notice for the Traverse City position. Despite our disappointment, we couldn't control the economy and figured perhaps our mission in Northern Michigan wasn't complete. Even if moving south wasn't written in the stars, material things and achievements no longer controlled our identity. We agreed to leave ourselves open to whatever came first, a new job South or a new way of living North. Either way, the dream house we built had to go. We were starting from scratch.

"Come here, I have something for you."

The glow of the Christmas tree illuminated the room. Patrick was in his favorite leather chair next to the stone fireplace. His emerald eyes sparkled.

"You do?" I asked, giggling.

Reaching under the chair, Patrick slid out a large box wrapped with a big red ribbon and handed it to me.

The weight surprised me, almost pulling me into his lap.

"Careful."

I giggled again.

"Sorry."

His nervous energy increased my anticipation as I ripped open the gift.

"A computer?"

Patrick took it out of my hands and said, "Not just any computer..."

Patrick opened the lid, unveiling two tickets to a country music concert on New Year's Eve.

"You're getting me," I squealed.

Patrick shook his head and said, "You I'll never get. But the country thing I understand."

I dove in for a kiss, almost knocking the new laptop off his lap.

He pulled back.

"But wait. There's more."

As he hit the power button, he said, "Remember when you woke me in the middle of the night to tell me you had a dream where a mysterious figure told you to write a story—our story?"

I reluctantly muttered, "Yeah...?"

Where was this going?

"I want you to tell it..."

What? Air my dirty laundry?

My knees shook.

I'm not a writer.

Patrick gently laid his hand on my knee. With a matter-of-fact smile he said, "Your password is...snowglobe."

Goosebumps covered my skin.

Patrick remembered my entire dream. The figure had also said, "Title your story 'The Shaken Snow Globe.'"

Breathless by his gesture, his touch, his kiss—I experienced true love yet again. His open love transcended my fairytale expectations.

CHAPTER 57

Only Want to Be with You

In Patrick's arms was the only place I wanted to be.

His arms wrapped around my waist like a seatbelt as we swayed to the music. We were ringing in the New Year with Dierks Bentley.

On stage in front of us, he was singing, "Come a little closer baby, I feel like letting go...of everything that stands between us."

Patrick's embrace warmed with each lyric. His chest melted into my back as we swayed. A sweet ballad captured my wish to cleanse all of Patrick's hurt. Maybe the lyrics would seep into Patrick's protected heart the same way country music first shined a light on my lost soul. Maybe he would begin to feel the depth of my love without fear of an outsider swooping in on a white horse to rescue me.

Like an old slide show my mind replayed Patrick's past jabs about us and marriage:

"You can't marry a guy from a State school!"

"What would your daddy say about you not getting the Notre Dame MRS degree?"

"Kristy and I are like *Lady and the Tramp*."

For the first time, my heart registered the pain behind his sarcasm and the depth of his nightmares about my "perfect partner" surfacing.

I put my hand to my chest to settle its pounding. No longer hearing the lyrics, my past words about Chad replayed in my head like a broken record. Hearing about Chad's perfect resumé must have been like kryptonite to Superman, hitting one of Patrick's vulnerable spots. I made his fear of not being good enough become reality, and he may never let his heart fully bask in my love. Tears couldn't wash my guilt. I prayed my actions would.

I vowed to shine love his way without condition, the same way he never wavered in loving me. Patrick deserved a blissful heart disconnected from selfish actions from me or his fleeing father. If *sinning* me was worthy of peace, then so was noble Patrick. I was done looking over my shoulder. Maybe Patrick was as well. He was, after all, at a country music concert in cowboy boots...smiling.

We couldn't go back to the start. But we could start over and create a brand new ending. Together, we were moving forward to uncharted territory, or, as Neil would say, "learning to experience new tastes without declaring the old favorites bad."

It was to be a new year, and a new way of living.

With the map to the "Happily Ever After" thrown out, I enrolled in a writing class at the local community college, and Patrick continued to pursue jobs south. We were just enjoying the journey, one day at a time.

"I know I said I would be open to staying in Traverse City as long as we lived simpler, but after tonight on the slopes there is no question I belong somewhere warm," I said as I snuggled under the covers in my flannels and wool socks still shivering.

"Don't you mean we, Ms. Only Child?" he questioned with *that* look.

"Yes, WE!" I recanted, still getting used to being this vulnerable.

"Better, much better," he responded as he thawed my numb toes with his warm hands. "I think you spent more time in the lodge than skiing."

Our evening of braving February snowfall on a Northern Michigan ski slope reinforced the family's desire to go South. Simply put—snow is *cold* and far too much work. The only benefit was cuddling in a warm bed with Patrick.

Patrick flicked on the television. On screen was the face of South Carolina's governor. We listened as he attempted to justify an affair with a woman he claimed as his soul mate. My heart sank.

"I know the guy feels this woman is his 'soul mate', but giving up his marriage and career to chase a 'feeling?' Sounds too familiar."

A tear escaped.

"That could've been me."

"But it isn't," he said, releasing my toes to hold my hand.

"He chose to go to New York to meet his mistress when his wife gave him the option," he said. "You didn't go to Texas."

My lip quivered thinking about how close I had come to losing my way.

Fearing the governor's plight was mine reincarnated, I wished someone would save his heart the way Patrick, Neil, and Sarah rescued mine. Their unconditional love showed me the answers had been within me the whole time. I had to find peace within, before I could feel this true love.

Patrick coaxed me out of thought with his playful tone, saying, "Hey. Maybe the show is a "sign" we're headed to South Carolina, so you can save the guy from the biggest mistake of his life."

I poked his thigh.

"Who knows. Maybe I will."

The ringing snapped us like a rubber band.

Fearing the worst, I handed the phone to Patrick.

CHAPTER 58

Cowboy Cassanova

Patrick answered, "Hello?"

10:30 at night? Never a good time to get a call.

With my ear towards Patrick's, I faintly heard someone say my name. He handed me the phone. I spoke with apprehension, "Hell-o?"

A woman with a sweet Southern drawl said, "Stay calm. I didn't say anything to your husband. My name is Jolene. I'm Chad's wife."

I must have misheard her. Did she say *ex-wife?*

"Can you talk?" she asked.

I looked wide-eyed at Patrick and mouthed, "It's Chad's wife!"

Patrick's green eyes were the size of palm leaves.

Before I could respond, she continued, "Just pretend you know me from high school or wherever. I really need to talk with you."

My body under the spell of her request proceeded to leave the bedroom and stumble downstairs to a quiet corner. I found myself in Patrick's over-stuffed chair that cradled my body like a mother cradling an infant as I continued to listen.

Jolene was telling a tale of a man who was foreign to me—portraying Chad as a still married, philandering con-artist from the wrong side of the tracks.

What?!

My ear remained glued to the receiver for two and a half hours, while my body remained in shock.

Chad wasn't divorced and had been married longer than us. In addition to me, Chad was allegedly having an affair with an oil tycoon's wife—a woman he met the weekend before me at the same honky-tonk bar.

According to Jolene, Chad never went to college, never played basketball and never owned his own business, unless you count his involvement in the drug and prostitution ring his "business partner" was just arrested for allegedly orchestrating. This was the *Prince Charming* who had walked off the pages of my fairytale with his perfect resumé.

He wasn't real! Not even close! I had almost lost everything based not on a fantasy but a fraud!

I kept the phone pressed against my ear, while Jolene rambled from one unbelievable story to the next. Her voice seemingly never stopped to breathe.

"In August, I filed for divorce, while he was in jail," she said.

"Jail?!" I blurted.

I had entered The Twilight Zone.

"Yes, ma'am," she answered. "He spent the first week of August in the slammer after pushin' me around the night I confronted him about the affair with the oil tycoon's wife."

Reflecting on the timing of Chad's last call, it made sense. Chad's release from jail lined up with his call in August, while we were on the Southern States tour.

Chad was simply looking for an ego boost after failing his wife miserably!

"I'm so sorry," I stuttered.

"Nothin' to be sorry 'bout. Chad was the one ragin' and pinnin' me against his car, threatenin' to kill me if I left—until the cops showed up."

"The cops?" I questioned, trying to absorb what Jolene was saying.

"Can you believe Chad's own boy called the cops? His boy protected me, and I'm not even his real mamma. Chad snatched him 'way from his ex when the boy was just in diapers. I've raised him like my own ever since. I was afraid Chad would take my two boys like he stole hers so I put up with his drinkin' and insults. But now that his best friend ends up on the front page of the paper arrested for a drug and prostitution ring," she said, finally taking a breath. "I'm afraid Chad's next."

As I tried to wrap my head around her mind-boggling tale, I said nothing and Jolene continued to vent.

"I've got me a court appointed lawyer. She's filed a restrainin' order and divorce papers. But Chad's been tryin' to sweet talk me back using *that* smile of his...says he's a changed man. Sending me roses and lett'rs—somethin' he's never done in all the years we've been married. I don't know how to walk away from our marriage. But my lawyer's afraid I'll end up missin' or dead if I drop the case...that's why I'm calling you."

Her voice lowered.

"The night the cops took Chad away I broke into his car and found a letter from you tucked in between the seats. I didn't want to believe there was more than one woman, so I hide it away until now. But next week I have to be in court to face Chad, and I'm scared I won't be able to go through with it."

Jolene took a deep breath.

"Did you have an affair with Chad?"

Her question stung. My protective bark gone. The once virtuous, over-achieving perfectionist exposed for what I was...human.

The real Kristy emerged from behind the white picket fence. I no longer needed to be perfect, just perfectly humble.

I searched for, but could not find, the right words.

"We had an affair—but mainly of the heart. I'm so sorry. He told me he was divorced, and his wife had cheated."

"I never cheated on that S.O.B. He's the one's been cheatin'. Who knows how many more women there are. For God sakes, you aren't even in the state." Jolene sniffled, and then continued, "How could he do this to me? I'm a good person. I take care of myself. I'm 100 pounds of nothin'. I raise his kids, make my own money, and give him what he wants when he wants it. Why am I not enough?"

Her question provoked my tears, realizing Patrick had probably asked himself similar questions.

"This isn't your fault. It's Chad's," I said. "He's living in a world full of lies trying to be someone he's not, in order to fill his emptiness."

"How am I going to get through this?" she asked.

"You will," I assured, trying to boost her confidence. "But if your lawyer thinks he's dangerous, then you need to listen to her."

"He will never let me go with the kids."

"I think he will. Even though Chad told me you cheated on him, he never said an ill word about you. And when I asked him why he gave up on his marriage and three kids he said, 'I didn't give up, I woke up.' In court, all you need to say to him is 'I didn't give up, I woke up,' and he will know you talked to me. I believe Chad wants to be the good and noble man I thought he was, and by letting you go he can be."

My dropped jaw reverted to a smile as the reality of the conversation sank in.

This call was Patrick's miracle.

I regurgitated Jolene's words, true or not true, to an anxious husband lying in our bed. The moonlight illuminated the relief in his expression. His eyes softened. His mind was at ease and I prayed his heart was as well. The call confirmed what I had been telling Patrick since Chicago, no one could love me like he does—not even Chad.

CHAPTER 59

Loves Me Like Jesus Does

Jail, wife, con artist, affairs...WHAT?

The conversation with Chad's wife reverberated. I needed to take the craziness of the news off my mind and conscience. Failing to reach Chloe, I turned to my angel in disguise who responded, as all true friends would.

"That's insane! I can't believe you find this out after you've gone through all this crap," Sarah said as she shook her head in disbelief trying to sort through the unbelievable tale.

At my request Sarah had dropped everything on a Saturday to walk and listen to a recap of the surreal conversation with Jolene. Her beautiful round eyes displayed warmth greater than the sun shining on our path. She connected with me in a way I always hoped a friend would.

"Ironic isn't it?"

I smiled.

"Thank God you didn't leave Pat for that. You see this stuff in a movie, not real life!"

"Isn't that the truth," I said with a reluctant chuckle, knowing how close I had come to self-destruction after a lifetime trying to be virtuous.

"Wow!" Sarah's astonishment was palpable. "I'm so glad you figured yourself out before this news came crashing down."

"Me too," I agreed with a huge sigh of relief. "I would have never forgiven myself for being naïve and destroying my family over my need to be validated."

My voice trailed off thinking of the fate I could have met. Relief washed over me like a refreshing rain.

"I don't need Chad or anyone else to determine my worth—I know who I am now."

Sarah asked cautiously, "So...you're not going to contact him?"

"I should confront him about her allegations, but I've closed that book. Nothing he could say would change anything anyway. I'm a new person. For that I'll always be grateful to him for helping crack my hardened heart, even inadvertently."

Hearing those words was surreal. I couldn't believe I was so peaceful, but I was. There was no need to look back. I had been transformed.

Sarah smiled.

"It's official then. You really have changed. I felt you were over Chad when you came back from Chicago...now I know. I feel your peace."

Her words provoked another light bulb moment. Sarah felt peace within herself when I never did.

A casual friendship of convenience had transformed into a friendship of a lifetime. My tears flowed like a raging river. Walking beside me was the friend I had prayed my entire life to find. I wasn't alone. I never was. Sarah didn't *need* me as her friend. She *wanted* me as her friend—my icky and all.

I had one more person to tell about Jolene—Neil.

I missed my confidant. I was thankful for an excuse to reconnect. Neil's quick response to my voicemail confirmed how much he cared.

"Everything OK?"

Neil's voice always made me feel important and loved in a way I never deemed possible from a shrink. I understood how a patient could fall in love with her therapist in those vulnerable, intimate conversations. I realized how much I missed his authenticity.

"No worries. Everything's fine," I answered.

"Oh."

"That is why I was hoping to see you."

"If there isn't a problem, then maybe we should discuss it on the phone," Neil suggested.

I was not expecting hesitation. I was the one to graduate myself from his services, but I still believed our connection was stronger than a call. My mind flashed back to the frank exchange of emotions during our final session in November. With tears in his eyes, Neil wrapped his arms around me, while saying a heartfelt goodbye. My heart loved Neil, and he voiced those same feelings—not in a romantic sense, but in the spiritual sense of "Love thy Neighbor as thy Self."

In Neil's eyes I saw Jesus—his love unconditional despite my flaws. Neither of us wanted to let go of the connection, but the time had come for me to discard my last crutch and trust in my changed spirit. I realized I couldn't go backwards despite wanting to reconnect with him. Maybe he just didn't want another painful goodbye, so I didn't argue. A phone conversation was probably for the best.

"You won't believe what I'm about to tell you."

"OK...I'm ready."

"You know...we talked about how my fantasy of the perfect resumé gave me the excuse to sit on the sidelines and not open my heart up to anyone who wasn't perfect. Then, when the perfect resumé became reality, my whole rational world gave way."

"Yessss...?"

"Well, Chad wasn't real—Not even close!"

I recounted the unbelievable story in Jolene's call. Neil didn't say much, but I could see him tilted back in his chair, relaxed, one leg crossed over the other. As the details of Chad's alleged deceit poured out, he probably uncrossed his legs and sat upright, pressing his worn brown shoes into the carpet for stability with his jaw hung open. When I finished all the crazy details of how close I came to throwing away my life for a myth, I heard him swallow, take a breath.

"How are you doing with all this?"

The uncertainty in his voice made me think he was questioning his decision to push for a phone conversation instead of a face to face.

"Neil, I have no emotional unfinished business, so Chad's supposed lies don't hurt me. If anything, his words, true or not, woke me from my numb state by playing into my fantasy. The concept of Chad saved me, and for that I am truly grateful. I'm just saddened his own self-loathing required him to concoct an elaborate act to feel loved. I saw the amazing man he could be if he could only believe in the good person he had been created to be...his icky and all."

"Wow! You really have grown," Neil said, sounding like a proud father.

"Crazy, huh?"

I laughed.

"I'm having a hard time believing it myself. But this is my life and I'm grateful."

"How is Patrick in all this?" Neil's question diverted topics.

"Still amazing. I think Jolene's story was Patrick's miracle. He's off the hook for comparing himself to 'Mr. Perfect Resumé' and more receptive to my transformed heart. The peace I now feel comes from knowing real happiness can't be found in people, places or things, but within yourself. And, when you find it, you want to share it with the world."

How lucky I was to be connected to Neil—even if only for a short while, Neil hadn't known the exact direction to take me, and, yet, he never gave up. His guidance freed me from the demons haunting me. Neil was a good man, another of my angels.

Without Patrick, Neil, Sarah, Chloe, and, yes, *even Chad* as the spokes in my emotional wheel, I would have never moved forward on this incredible journey. My heart would still be stuck in cement—hardened and alone.

CHAPTER 60

Say A Prayer

Patrick and I continued to restructure our life. The barricade of the white picket fence was torn down. The existence of a perfect resumé was debunked. We were finally moving forward.

Our house remained for sale and so did Chloe and Robert's— the last item tying them together other than their children. Chloe was trying to move on with her new life. I was lucky to get one-word texts from her. Not that Chloe was readily available before her divorce, but I was hoping the latest chapter of my saga would entice her.

When I finally got a few minutes with her, my news was anticlimactic to Chloe. She appeared distracted by her own thoughts. Getting her to open up had always been difficult. Chloe had bigger concerns than the myth of Chad. She had divorce.

The dissolution of her marriage haunted me. I had been a lousy friend to Chloe hiding my dirty laundry behind her suffering. I should have been brave enough to speak the way she had spoken to me in the car ride to Chicago. My fears of living life without her stood in my way of being vulnerable.

I felt Chloe blamed me for not doing enough or meddling too much. Either way I wanted her forgiveness and friendship. I would have to live with the pain of loving someone who won't love you back—a consequence of living with my new unbridled heart. I was learning to love unconditionally, even if it hurt.

I was taking flight like a butterfly leaving its cocoon. I transformed from an over-achieving socialite who craved attention, to a calm thinker who professed my faith. Thank goodness Sarah recognized and accepted the changed me. She even supported my desire to move to a warmer climate.

With our hearts still pulling us south, Patrick broadened his job search to include other companies and careers. During spring break, we all made a return visit to South Carolina so the children could visit a potential Catholic school. My feelings for Charleston warmed when my family entered the school's front office and were greeted by a large collection of snow globes—a "sign" (or so I thought at the time) we were on the right track.

However, just before Memorial Day weekend, Patrick was offered a transfer to Wrightsville Beach, *North* Carolina, not *South* Carolina, which I felt was our destiny. The offer was a new test of faith. Don't control the journey, but be open to life's detours. Patrick already turned down one offer from his company to move to an inland Southern city because of its lack of waterways. Maybe Wrightsville Beach was the Southern place to which God was calling us. After all, the city had been a planned destination on our summer tour until we fell in love with Charleston.

Wrightsville Beach *did* fit our hearts' criteria of beautiful beaches, live oak trees and Southern hospitality. Charleston would be only a three hour drive south along the coast. Turning our words into actions, we accepted the transfer and jumped into the unknown of Wrightsville Beach. Having that confidence our house would sell after a year on the market was another story. The economy continued its downward spiral since a year ago when that couple knocked on our door asking us to sell. Doubt deflated our spirits.

What if the house didn't sell?

Patrick, worried about the financial strain, questioned the decision to accept the transfer. I told him not to worry if the house didn't sell. We would embrace moving to a small rental apartment in Wrightsville Beach as long as necessary. I suggested we leave all our things behind and act like we were going on vacation with just our clothes, computer and photo albums. I knew this was all I needed to truly be happy, but Patrick was still in "white picket fence mode." For the first time ever, I prayed out loud under the protection of our dark bedroom with Patrick listening and holding my hands. I asked God to take away our fears about the house not selling and give us peace to trust Him.

"I can't just sit around all weekend and wait. I have to do," Patrick said, as he walked out the door in his ripped jeans and old t-shirt.

The yard was Patrick's escape. He needed to control something and making the landscape perfect could help bait a buyer. Asking him to rely solely on faith was too much at this point—even for me. It was going to take a miracle to sell in this economy, and giving up his amazing job yesterday for the unknown was a big leap for him. Guilt corroded my excitement since I was the catalyst for these changes. It was going to be a long Memorial Day weekend.

"Where is Da-Da going?" Ally asked as she yawned at the breakfast table.

Brooke yelled, "Daddy, wait!"

She pushed herself away from untouched pancakes and ran out the back door in her polka-dot pajamas before I could stop her. She was probably the hardest worker in the family despite her size, and her presence might give Patrick's mind a distraction from the stresses ahead.

Still casually chewing his pancakes, Seth said, "Wouldn't it be easier to pray around the for sale sign?"

"Maybe," I replied.

He might be right. Praying would be easier than spreading mulch in landscape beds, but we chose yard work.

The simple things I once dreaded as I had too much on the to-do-list now touched my soul in a way I could explain only in tears. Exhausted from our long day of family yard work, we all snuggled under a blanket in front of the fireplace to watch a movie. Peace penetrated my soul, knowing no matter what the journey ahead I had found home—not in this physical structure, but a place of contentment within my own flawed skin and less-than perfect family.

Ally began to drift off to sleep so Patrick scooped her up from the couch and climbed the stairs toward her room.

Brooke and I were following when Seth blurted, "Wait!"

We froze in mid-step.

"We NEED to go outside and pray again! Someone's heart wasn't into it last year when we 'planted' St. Joseph under the for sale sign for good luck."

Ally perked up.

"Yeah, Da-Da. Let's go!" she squealed as she squirmed out of his hold.

Humoring Seth, we marched outside in our pajamas. The sun hadn't set thanks to the longer days of summer's approach. Holding hands around the for sale sign, I chuckled to myself.

What must the neighbors be thinking?

Standing in a circle, Seth read the prayer card from on our bulletin board, tacked up there when we first "planted" St. Joseph late last summer after our Southern tour. Brooke, not wanting to be outshined by her older brother, interjected with her own intentions.

"God, please take us to a place where we can better serve you... or give us the peace to stay here..AMEN."

Patrick and I peeked up from our prayerful pose and smiled at each other.

Who are these children?

Perhaps Catholic school was paying off.

The setting sun cast an orange glow on our day's hard work. We all stood quietly looking at the house, an unusual disposition for our chatty bunch. The calm of the moment penetrated my senses like a dose of anesthesia. Brooke was the first to break the spell, grabbing Patrick's hand and heading down the blacktop toward the house. I reached for Ally's and Seth's hands and proceeded with them down the driveway. My mind, reflecting on the accomplishments as a united family, was interrupted by the tender voice of Ally.

Her bright blue eyes gazed up through strawberry blonde locks, as she said, "Isn't this the steps where you first brought me into this house—my first and only home?"

I took a deep breath. Patrick glanced over his shoulder with glassy eyes and smiled a smile unlike any I had seen before.

Peace settled on my heart. It was almost as if Ally was saying goodbye for all of us. The moment was as pure as a first snowfall covering the ground. Change was inevitable, yet I felt no fear. Wherever we were going or whatever we were doing, our family would prevail amongst the chaos thanks to faithful hearts full of love.

"Mommy, Mommy!" Seth hollered from the backseat on our way to school.

I was lost in thought—consumed with yesterday's excitement at the house. I hadn't had much sleep. It had only been two days since spreading mulch and so much had happened.

"Mommy, don't forget your phone on your walk with Sarah. You need to take it today. When they call you to tell you you've won, promise you'll come to school and tell me."

I was distracted by my excitement to tell Sarah the good news.

"Mommy!"

I reached for the volume button to turn down the country music.

"I'm sorry, Seth. What are you saying?"

"They're calling the winner this morning at 8:20. You need to have your phone!"

He was relentless.

"I'm sorry, honey. What are you talking about?"

I stopped at the curb of the school and looked over my shoulder to refocus full attention on him.

"Today the radio station is calling the winner for the trip to the country music awards, and you need to take your phone on your walk with Sarah!"

"OK, OK, Seth," I said, raising both my palms toward him trying to appease him. "I will."

He flung his backpack over his shoulder and paused before shutting the door.

"Promise, you'll come to my class when you win?"

"I'll definitely come if I win. Now, go!"

I dismissed Brooke and him with a wave, anxious to drop off Ally at kindergarten and catch up with Sarah to share my unbelievable news.

I was beaming brighter than the sun reflecting off the glassy waters of Lake Michigan—a fabulous day for walking the path there. The birds threw in a good morning hymn and the temperature cooperated at a comfortable 72 degrees. There was only a week before summer vacation, and we were making the most of our time. Sarah was tying her shoe on her back bumper as I walked up.

"Sarah!" I yelled like a giddy school girl.

My enthusiasm tumbled out, "You won't believe what happened last night!"

Before she could answer, I blurted, "We sold the house!"

"What?"

Sarah stood and looked at me with dazed eyes. My monologue began as we started our walk along the shoreline.

"After we talked Friday about Patrick accepting the job, we freaked out about whether the house would sell—almost gave us cold feet about the move. I told him it didn't matter to me when it sold—all we needed to be happy was our clothes, computer, photo albums, and each other."

"Of course," she said.

"Seth said, 'someone's heart wasn't into our prayer last fall when we planted the St. Joseph statue in the yard for good luck, and we need to pray again about the house selling.' We felt silly."

"Of course," she said.

"But we all marched out in our pajamas and held hands around the 'for sale' sign, while Seth and Brooke said a prayer. Crazy thing—the realtor called the next morning to set up an afternoon showing. I drove around with the kids after school waiting for the realtor to call and say the coast was clear to go home. Then BAM! The phone rings, and the realtor says..."

I took my first breath and changed my voice to imitate the realtor.

"I've never had this happen in all my years of real estate—I was waiting outside for the couple and their realtor to finish looking around your house and after about 15 minutes the husband walks out the front door and tells me: 'I will give them 97% of what they are asking. Will they sell me all the furniture? Can they be out in two weeks? And I'm a cash buyer.' And I wept!"

Sarah stopped and looked at me like a deer in the headlights, when my phone rang.

Caller ID did not recognize the number, but I did.

I screamed, "NO WAY!"

CHAPTER 61

God Must Really Love Me

"ME? No way! Nooo way! NO WAY!"

My continual screams of disbelief echoed on the radio as I jumped up and down on the sidewalk. Cars zoomed past. My appearance was of no concern to me. Time was moving in slow motion, while my brain tried to catch up with my body's celebration.

"Yes, Kristy—YOU! You are going to the Country Music Television Awards! We will be flying you and a guest to Nashville to see the show—LIVE! That's right, Kristy—rubbing elbows with country music's biggest stars. And if that's not enough, we're giving you two tickets to the Country Music Hall of Fame. But wait, there's more...."

In his sultriest radio voice, the deejay described details of the all-expense paid package. I had no idea what he was saying, yet words of excitement kept flowing out of my mouth. The amazing chain of events ran through my mind in a loop—all out of my control.

How could I be worthy of all this good fortune?

I must be dreaming—the amazing job offer South, the house and contents sell as we prayed, and now a trip! And not just any trip, a trip to the home of country music, the same music that opened my heart to feeling the life I was meant to lead. It was too much to handle. Tears poured down my cheeks as I gasped for air.

Being saved from my numb existence and Patrick choosing imperfect *me* to love was already more than I deserved. I was NOT worthy of all this!

Overwhelmed, I dropped to the sidewalk.

Thoughts of me as a little girl yearning to be chosen first by someone or something flooded my mind. I always wished to be the one picked from the audience to help on stage, or the one whose name was called after a big drum roll, or the one important enough to be chosen as a best friend or maid of honor. I would think maybe if I tried a little harder, did a little better, then I would earn the right to be chosen by someone or something—but that didn't happen. Instead I spent years feeling less than as second best: being salutatorian—not valedictorian, being waitlisted at Notre Dame—not first choice, and being a consolation prize for Patrick—not pursued with all his heart and soul. I never won my heart's desires until I no longer needed to validate my soul!

I chuckled. Now that my heart didn't need confirmation, external, crazy things were happening—unbelievable things! My biggest dreams were becoming reality, one after the other in ways I could have *never* imagined possible.

"Kristy, Kristy. You still there?"

The voice of the deejay brought me back. I gazed upward from the cement and connected with Sarah's concerned eyes. She had removed her sunglasses and was leaning over me to assess the situation.

I exclaimed into the phone again, "I can't believe this. NO WAY!"

"Believe it! You're our winner Kristy! Where are you calling from?"

"Crazy enough, I'm outside your studio walking along the lakeshore."

"Well, give us a big wave and tell us who has made you a winner?"

"Sunny Country!"

"Kristy, stay on the line and my assistant will get your info."

I couldn't talk. Realizing I needed time to compose myself, I decided to end the call and walk to the station to discuss the details in person. Plus, I would have Sarah to remember specifics that I would miss. We reversed direction, and headed toward the huge sun mural on the side of the building. I filled Sarah in on the unbelievable nature of what just happened. The turn of events from one year ago was hard to comprehend. Thank God Sarah had been my witness to all of it or I might have walked myself over to the old asylum and committed myself as delusional. Today the sun shone brighter than we both could have ever imagined.

After getting things sorted out at the station, we resumed our walk but with another detour—the children's school. A promise is a promise, and I owed Seth big time for forcing me to take the phone. As we rounded the final corner, children were playing in the courtyard. A group came running toward us like a stampede. Seth's big blue eyes were sparkling.

"You won didn't you!" he yelled as he and his friends approached.

I couldn't contain my smile, or my composure. Sarah stood speechless watching her friend's miraculous transformation continue.

Seth hugged me and said, "I told you, you were gonna win! You did, right?"

He backed off slightly from our embrace and gazed up for confirmation. My stream of happy tears said all I couldn't. I was thankful I had paused my own overwhelming thoughts long enough to hear my son's advice on the way to school, making the win that much more miraculous for all of us.

"Yes," I finally muttered.

My uncontrollable excitement made for a good radio promo for weeks, and a reminder of just how far I had come. Resentment of the unrewarded "good girl" no longer festered like a disease in my heart. Instead 'that girl' had been replaced by a humbled woman, worthy of nothing, yet receiving all the whispers of her heart—including unconditional love from a husband and a best friend.

A new roller coaster ride had begun, with our arms extending upward to reach for life's new chapter.

With the Nashville CMT Country Music awards behind us, my head was a spinning like a tilt-a-whirl at the fair—enjoying the ride that made me dizzy, but concerned too much of a good thing might take a turn for the worst.

"You sure you can handle all my changes?" I asked, while gripping Patrick's arm like a vice as the floor vibrated with the landing gear hitting the pavement in Traverse City.

"Handle all your changes?" Patrick repeated playfully. "Besides you making us late to the show with the twenty minute cab ride back to the hotel to change into the second perfect outfit?" He raised his eyebrows with a look of mischief knowing full well that wasn't the change I was referring and continued, "But you did alright relaxing once the twang started."

I nudged him with a spunky sparkle in my eye.

"Are you mocking me and my music?"

"Never the music." he said, smiling.

His boyish grin packed a punch with my thawed heart. Every day with him was like opening another present, not knowing what exciting surprise I would find next. What a better place to start than Nashville. Country music tied our hearts in ways our words couldn't and allowed me to shed my shell of the past that had moved to a mainstream beat. I didn't want anything to do with 'that girl' and was relieved Patrick didn't miss her either.

We were writing our own love song. Even when the sun refused to shine light on my emotional roller coaster, Patrick *and Sarah* had shadowed my unbelievable journey.

CHAPTER 62

Leavin' On My Mind

Before leaving the dream home we built in Traverse City, Patrick and I decided to throw a goodbye party, inviting families who had touched our lives the past seven years. Sadness tinted the occasion when friends with whom I invested years of my life never bothered to show, not even Chloe or the blonde birthday girl I ventured out of my hiding last spring to support during her milestone. But by acknowledging my pain and disappointment, without bitterness, I was taking a big step forward from my prior existence.

I treasured those friendships and the memories we created together, but understood my transformation had been hard to swallow, especially after I pushed people away during my dark days of shame. I was blessed that Sarah was still standing by my side, supporting my every effort to move forward, even if that meant she was losing her workout partner and friend in the process.

In the middle of the kitchen, Sarah stopped prepping the food and hugged me. She felt my pain.

I was learning to connect with people on a whole new level—a level I didn't even realize existed until the walls supporting my façade were dismantled. Emotions on this day were difficult—both extreme highs and lows. I struggled with the disappointment of realizing friends I believed were friends were not friends at all, which also meant the flip side was true about *me*. I had disappointed people who thought I was their friend but had failed to connect with their needs the way a real friend should. I thanked God for cracking my heart. The authentic me was finally exposed, and all I could think was "better late than never!"

The pain hurt, but the newfound joy was unimaginable. I discovered deep friendships I never knew I had because they didn't *need* me, and instead had been walking strong beside me the whole time. Thankful not to miss another moment with people who treasured me for me, I relished their presence.

Hand in hand, Patrick and I wandered about, absorbing the amazing friends assembled in our home. The scene felt different than past parties, maybe because we were different. The empty conversations, surface pleasantries, and our need to please didn't exist. There was a calming energy to both our spirits, despite kids running through the house with open juice boxes and grassy shoes. The hodgepodge of food and drinks randomly assembled on the downstairs patio overlooking the water was of no concern. The party had no fancy theme or organized menu, no agenda, and no advance planning, yet still people wanted to be with us.

I reflected on a past charity event we hosted at our home. Patrick's friend Ralph, the same guy he drowned his sorrows with the night he suspected the worst of me, had snuck into our bedroom to use the bathroom. He saw a group of women he didn't know, but knew of, huddled in my closet rummaging through the labels on my clothes and gossiping. When he was done using the facility, the ladies returned to the closet without concern for the *off-the-radar* guest. Ralph didn't tell us the story for years. Instead, he avoided subsequent functions with our new found "friends." My appearance and ability to throw a good party had probably been more important to this new, high-profile group of "friends" than my frozen heart could feel at the time. I didn't blame them for their priorities. I knew I had been just as blind to the worth of others. I couldn't see my own worth through society's unattainable label of "perfect success."

Pulling me from my thoughts, real images of success were walking across the expansive decking toward me with big round eyes focused on a target. Sarah and an army of woman were on a mission—I was the bullseye. The old me would have paid top dollar to be the focus of attention in hopes of filling my void and confirming my worth, but all I could think now was, *uh-oh, what did I do?*

Sarah's expression said nothing. I still couldn't read her despite the time we spent together the past year. She really should use that poker face in Vegas where it would take her far.

"We wanted you to have something," she said, while handing me a beautifully wrapped object with curly ribbon sprawled over the polka-dot paper.

I rambled who knows what, while trying to deflect the undeserved positive attention. My face turned multiple colors of red, as if I had tried all the colors of blush at Macy's makeup counter. Today was supposed to be about me giving my true self to them, not the other way around.

I didn't deserve this, *or them.* With reluctant fingers, I pulled off the wrapping paper. Unveiled was a photo album crafted by Sarah, the most amazing gift I had ever received. The cover was a beautiful image of the blue waters of Traverse City—the beginning of a tribute to our life here. With the turn of each page, the tears in my eyes grew. I discovered a family photo of each of our friends. Contact information was neatly aligned beneath each family, so we wouldn't forget to stay in touch. There was even a photograph of my parents with the affectionate label *Papa & Mammie*, the names our children called them. Knowing Sarah's affection for simplicity, this gift was truly a labor of her time and love.

I turned to the last page and read, "From your friends of Traverse City. You have touched each and every one of us!"

Glancing up from the page, my soul connected with numerous sets of eyes and my dam burst. I buried my face in Patrick's shoulder.

Unsuccessful in my restraint, I whimpered in Patrick's ear, "How could I have missed all of this—all of them?"

"At least you see it now, and that's more than most."

He squeezed his arm around me.

Before my outburst of emotion could suck Sarah into tears, she tried to lighten the moment.

"I know there's a few blank pages, but I'm gonna fill it with pictures from today. This is just a sneak peak, so don't think you're keeping it just yet."

Trying to distract myself from my sniffles, I started talking with my hands waving around.

"I'm not crying over the empty pages. I'm crying 'cause you guys are crazy for putting up with me and now you'll never get rid of me since I have all your contact info at my fingertips."

"Yeah, they're crazy. But so am I!" Patrick interjected, as a grin crept up his flushed cheeks. "Looks like we're all stuck with you, Kristy."

"Hey!" I shouted, jabbing my forearm against his ribs. "It may be true, but you're not supposed to agree with me!" A snort snuck out between my sniffles and giggles. Their laughter at it was terrific.

"Maybe you're right about the book," Sarah smiled. "I better take it back before we get besieged by Kristy correspondence."

She reached for the album, but I wrapped my arms around her and squeezed. Over her shoulder, I saw Robert walking up the deck stairs. The faucet behind my eyes turned on again.

How could I be worthy of all these amazing friends?

My past needs to impress guests in order to fill my void and confirm my worth had been replaced by a love greater than I ever believed could exist. The quality of friends willing to love a flawed me was overwhelming. These were real friends, our children's real friends, and we were leaving them behind. Disappointment knocked on my heart from the regret of missing so many good souls over the years as I hid from my own. If only I had more time to enjoy the openness I could now feel. But, I couldn't look back. I had to move forward.

My new beginning was being celebrated by letting go of the *old me* and my old things at this party. Our intentions were to lighten the load of the move by giving away all the wine in the wine cellar and emptying the cupboards of all the food. However, something else happened at the party in addition to my epiphany of friendships.

Parents came up to me confused, saying things like "You have to come see this!" and "Your kids are giving away all of their stuff." and "We can't take their toys!"

Before I could process what our friends were saying, I walked around the corner of the house to a parade of children coming out the front door arms loaded with things—robots, snowboards, balls, fish, dolls, you name it. The tiny guests were carrying it away as they said their goodbyes to our children, who were grinning ear to ear.

My mouth dropped open—speechless.

An airless gasp escaped as I watched an electric scooter being wheeled down the driveway.

Should I stop the hemorrhage of things?

My eyes connected with Patrick across the driveway. His sparkling eyes said it all. I held my tongue, blessed to have a man AND children willing to embrace my change. Even though my logical side was still under reconstruction, I was happy to know my family was listening to the words of my heart.

Watching our children give away their prized possessions, without prompting, reaffirmed to me that all of us were changing for the better. Our family would not be defined by material things. We had each other and trusted that God would provide for our future.

We were ALL letting go of the past and moving forward with hearts filled with faith.

CHAPTER 63

The House That Built Me

I never imagined this moment, saying goodbye to the existence we had built here. My life had been an All-American girl's dream—marrying my best friend from high school, building our dream home, having three healthy children and reaching the social "A list."

What more could a girl want?

The chilling white blanket covering the ground for months had disappeared. There was a warm breeze blowing, leaves unfolding, birds conversing, and tears trickling down my cheeks as I looked back at my marvelous, forever house. Its cream-painted wood and fieldstone skirt sat atop a hill framed by towering hardwoods. The backdrop was the magnificent view of God's freshwater rippling with shades of blue, and a single white triangle dancing from the mast of a large sailboat. It was breathtaking—picture perfect!

I had convinced myself that true happiness could be found within a picket fence. I was so wrong!

Sure, on the outside, my life looked like one portrayed in movies and seen in magazines, but not *my* "Happily Ever After." The path I had created was ending. As I wiped the tears and took in the fresh air, my spirit was rejuvenated. I was ready. It was time to pursue the life that had been raging deep within my soul. A passionate life I had given up on, and now felt destined to follow with my one true love—PATRICK.

Thanks to Patrick's display of unconditional love over the past year and the Catholic rules binding me to some moral standards, I hadn't given up. Instead, I woke up and discovered that what I'd been looking for had been there the whole time.

Patrick was my true soul mate, loving me even when I wasn't loveable.

Our perseverance through hopeless times freed us from our frozen marriage and was changing the course of our lives forever. The impossible whispers of my heart were coming true—just not via the route I planned. I was moving to the unknown of the North Carolina coast and releasing the identity I worked so hard to define in Michigan. No longer needing achievements or accolades to mask the icky I felt about myself, I now knew and *felt* who I was—a child of God.

Imperfect on earth, yet perfect to Him.

With my hands off the wheel, I opened my heart to a new journey—lucky to have Patrick by my side on this unpredictable ride. Despite circumstantial evidence giving a false read on what God was planning, the cascade of miracles continued beyond my wildest dreams—dreams I deemed impossible were coming true in the most unlikely ways. Despite all this good fortune, we were scrambling to find somewhere to live for the next month so Patrick could finish his work in Traverse City.

I questioned if I made a mistake trusting in the unknown.

I had stepped out of my comfort zone and used the dirty four-letter word to a Type A, over-achiever—*HELP!* I was learning to embrace this vulnerability and reached out to an acquaintance in our neighborhood. Their house had been on the market for nearly two years, and they had moved into a newly built home on the other end of the lake. I knew it was a long shot, but hoped maybe they would rent us the shell so we could enjoy a last taste of the Michigan summer before digging up our well-established roots.

"You did what?"

Patrick's expression was more distressed than I would have hoped.

"We need to go somewhere, and I thought it might help them out too."

"That is a lot to ask someone, Kristy."

His eyebrows were furrowed.

My apprehension grew into a high-pitched crescendo, "I know, but they said...YES!"

I took a deep breath before my sheepish smile appeared.

"Isn't that a good thing?"

He wrapped his muscles like a straight jacket around my shoulders, pressing my cheek into his tie.

My baby blues looked up at him with eyelashes fluttering.

I mustered out breathlessly, "Aren't you proud?"

He shook his head and smirked.

"You don't even like to order a pizza."

Our neighbors allowed us to stay in their vacant house for the next month, until Patrick's transfer to North Carolina would kick in. They even let us store our remaining belongings in their garage until the company move—a huge relief to us and our pocketbook.

When the owner stopped by with the key, she joked about Seth praying for them to sell as well. Owning two homes was a heavy burden.

"I'll see what he can do," I said with a laugh. "But no worries... for you to let this crazy family of five move into your clean house, I'm sure God will reward you generously."

She smiled.

"That's not my area of expertise, but I hope you're right."

Crazy enough, that's exactly what happened!

The day before we left for North Carolina, they received a mind-blowing offer. Our neighbor's good deed has been rewarded—their burden lifted. Some will call it a coincidence, but I know it was God's intervention. I was learning that the more you pray with specific detail, the more it feels like a miracle when your prayer is answered.

Leaving our home without most of our material possessions to move to a temporary house just down the street was only the first step in letting go. It was eerie leaving behind all that we built together—the furniture, the framed artwork on the walls, the decorations—everything from candlesticks to the hose reels. All that was missing from our dream house were personal photographs and *us*.

We had erased ourselves.

The chains defining our lives were being cut. We were free from the weight of trying to maintain a perfect façade and ready to write a new definition for our family—imperfections and all.

The true test was coming next, moving from the comfort of Traverse City to the unknown of the South. We had no home, no furniture (except for our formal dining room set which I kept in a moment of panic during the final negotiations), no friends, and no expectations, only each other and a small storage unit. I was taking the biggest leap of faith in my life, and Patrick was jumping with me, making me the luckiest woman on earth!

When the last box was on the truck, we watched the movers drive away. They were headed for a storage facility in North Carolina, courtesy of Patrick's company. The moving package was a bonus we never anticipated since Patrick was requesting the transfer.

Our suburban was loaded down with the remainder of our personal belongings, minus the kids. My parents offered to keep them for a couple of weeks to give us time to search for a house and get settled into our temporary housing at a Residence Inn in Wrightsville Beach with one month paid, courtesy of Patrick's company. Seth and my daddy were heading west for a camping adventure in the mountains of Wyoming for three weeks before coming to North Carolina, and the girls would be arriving after only two. Patrick and I had never been away from the kids for this long before. However, we didn't mind since we were rewriting the honeymoon phase of our marriage—first with a trip to Nashville and now a detour to Canada for a Keith Urban country music concert before heading south.

Patrick and I were floating together into the unknown. Despite not being in control, I couldn't be happier. We were *Defying Gravity* just like the title of Keith Urban's album.

I had a feeling our new adventure would be out of this world.

CHAPTER 64

Temporary Home

Laughter was our new toy, and we were enjoying it. Highway exits missed became opportunities of exploration rather than excuses for yelling matches of anxiety. We were savoring our new journey, and Patrick was embracing his *new wife* every chance he could. His fondness for affection was more than I could have hoped from a man I deemed too controlled for passion. He was proving me wrong, daily.

"What are you doing?"

I screeched as my seatbelt locked up. Patrick had whipped the packed suburban off the highway onto the grass along the side of the road, and come to a screeching halt.

"Don't you see it?" he asked wildly.

There it was, in big bold letters —Welcome to North Carolina.

I turned to smile at him, but instead of his emerald glow, all I got was a great look of his tight tush exiting, while cars zoomed by.

Patrick opened my door.

"You gonna get out?" he asked, while extending his hand.

"Here?"

"Yes here, unless you're gonna take my picture sitting down."

I grabbed his hand and shot out like a cannon, knocking him down onto the grass.

"I love you, Patrick Dominiak. I'm so sorry I underestimated you for so many years," I said, while smothering his lips with mine.

"Easy girl," he said as he put his hands up. "Remember, we're on the side of the road."

Our laughter was drowned by a truck whizzing by. For a girl known to have a big mouth, I sure missed years of opportunities to open up about my wants for fear of being disappointed. I could've been being spoiled sooner by Patrick's affection, and avoided my resentments. Patrick "got me" more than I ever realized. He had just been too reserved to act on his impulses—until I opened the door.

I snapped the photo. In all the excitement, I hadn't noticed the brilliant sea of yellow flowers lighting up the landscape around us. Yellow flowers signified friendship, but to us...so much more.

Patrick and I walked hand in hand on the gritty sand as the children kicked off their sandals and splashed in the water slapping the shore. The smell of salty air combined with the serenity of live oak trees soothed my soul. My dream of moving south was a reality.

Our children's free spirits were opening Patrick's and my eyes to all we had wasted in our structured life. They celebrated our change like the comfort of an old familiar melody. They embraced this new location with eager eyes and open arms. Patrick and I were floating in their current, trying to resist the urge to swim to solid ground and find a permanent place to land—Patrick a little more than me.

I couldn't blame his wanting a home to call his own. After all, I had shaken his world. A permanent location might stabilize his fears of me pulling the rug out from under him again.

The pursuit of a place to settle moved at a snail's pace. One would think finding a home in the slow economy would be easy, especially for a husband who lived and breathed real estate—but not so much. Wrightsville Beach presented its share of roadblocks. Despite having more money in our bank account than ever before, we made a pact to spend less than our Traverse City home—a decision we were beginning to regret. We made two strong offers on houses—neither stuck. By our fourth month with two offers rejected, our pact was being tested. Then a new listing came on the market. Our third find seemed like the charm.

On one of my daily phone walks with Sarah (not quite the same as in person, but the beach scenery made up for her lack of physical presence, sort of), I was describing random life at the beach and the recent listing. I described the home as *like heaven.*

I said, "I can only imagine how great heaven will be, but I know once I get there it will be better than I could have ever imagined, and *that* is this *house!*"

This third home felt perfect, right down to the smallest detail. The price was higher than our pact, but still within our means. This house must have taken years to assemble. Each architectural detail, chosen from various historical venues in the south, was intricately placed as if one master puzzle had been created from select pieces of many others. Its uniqueness spoke to our individual personalities—from lizard embossed tiles around the pool, to unique antique finishes that included rustic barn doors used throughout, reclaimed wood beams, and pillars positioned as one of a kind trim pieces. There was even a fireplace mantel from the 1700s—a complete opposite of our Michigan home of clean lines and new materials. The place felt like the perfect security blanket to warm Patrick's fears—and maybe mine.

The aroma of salty, plough mud permeated the interior. It stirred strangely familiar feelings, like those I get when smelling Grandma's cookies baking at Christmas. The labor of love house grabbed our hearts like a one-of-a-kind masterpiece. It was priceless in our eyes. We didn't hesitate to make an offer, even though we couldn't make it our home for another eight months. The house hadn't officially hit the market yet because there were renters contracted until May. This stipulation was of no concern because we could live at the beach rental until spring. Our situations fit like a pair of gloves, perfect for each other.

"What?"

I couldn't believe what was coming from the realtor's lips, but I continued questioning.

"In this economy with those move in parameters? Really? Another offer?"

I hung up and paced on the covered porch. Patrick was inside washing the dinner dishes and watching with anticipation out of the corner of his eyes. When he came outside we rocked on the porch for hours, bantering back and forth about whether to throw money into the bidding war in which we found ourselves.

"We can afford it," I said. "If you want it, go for it."

I didn't want to be the one holding him back from feeling somewhat stable in our new way of life.

"Just because we can doesn't mean we should," he argued.

"I know, but I love it too. We've always been house people and the place is beyond amazing."

It was true. Houses had always been our weak spot—not toys, electronics, vacations or other vices, but real estate. Since we were first married, we loved looking at houses and agreed our home was the one investment that was worth the sacrifice. This location AND this house were beyond fabulous.

"I know but you said you wanted to live lighter," said Patrick, parroting my earlier words.

"Now you're sounding like me. Make up your mind," I whined.

"You make up yours," he poked back.

"We could be happy in that house. We don't have to live in a box just because you want to erase the old you. You're worthy of nice things."

"I know, but I don't *need* nice things. I've got you and that's enough!" I leaned into him for a kiss.

"Oh, so now you talk sexy so I can't think straight and you can blame me if I screw this decision up," he smirked.

"Yep, I've screwed up enough for one lifetime."

I walked my fingers up his exposed leg.

He grabbed my wrist.

"You're not getting off that easy."

"Fine," I huffed. "The place is amazing, and much smaller than our last house."

"The girls would have to share a room...not ideal for them and their sleeping habits," Patrick said, contradicting me.

There were a lot of "signs" for the house, but not the right ones.

We concluded we weren't going to buy our way out of the discomfort of not being settled. We would not have thought twice in the past about pushing forward to win at all costs. Instead, we stuck to our pact and had faith that if the house was meant to be for us, it would happen.

We lost.

CHAPTER 65

God Is There

We were heartbroken. The direction of our lives was still uncertain.

Though disappointment and uncertainty reached for my un-protected heart, I remained peaceful. I had Patrick by my side, which was enough of a prize. Yet I still wasn't sure if I was enough for Patrick. He had given up familiarity, which wasn't easy for someone who liked things neat and orderly. Maybe I was asking too much.

I had second thoughts about stripping him of everything that gave him comfort and an identity in Michigan—his job, his home, and his friends. Here there were no familiar faces to ease anxiet-ies, no comfortable belongings, and still no home to call our own. We were adrift in unchartered waters, and I was asking him not to row.

Was our faith being tested?

Patrick continued combing through real estate magazines, while I groomed my new-found soul. The beautiful beach rental, about a quarter of the size of our house in Michigan, was the safe haven I needed to continue my journey of living light. Here there was no temptation of the self-inflicted busy to fill any voids, or should I say fears, that may have surfaced from the old me. With the kids settling into their new school and Patrick exploring his new sales territory, I found time to relax without guilt and get to know my *new* without all the distractions from being "seen." This social butterfly learned she didn't need to fly, even though she had new wings, and was content absorbing the simplicity of each moment on the ground.

Who is this "new Kristy?"

After dropping the children at school and cleaning the tiny rental, I walked to the beach and plopped my chair a comfortable distance from the water. The thickness of the air discouraged unnecessary steps on the hot sand. Since school was in session and beach season was technically over, it didn't matter where I lounged. There was no one between the blue horizon and me, except for an occasional walker or jogger. With my outer voice silenced, I could turn inward to mediate with the "new Kristy." My guilt was gone. I stretched my legs and dug my toes in the sand. As the waves reached my buried feet, I wondered where the time had gone. Even as an only child, I don't think I spent this much time alone enjoying the moment.

I flashed back to my childhood, before my adolescent move to the rural lake community where I met Patrick.

I remembered wandering through our suburban subdivision hoping to be noticed. Most days, I was out of luck and would end up at the end of our street sitting beneath a stop sign watching the cars zoom by on the adjacent busy street. I was alone. I wanted to be missed by someone, seen by someone, found by someone. I wanted to feel special.

A single tear dripped from my eye. I felt its slow movement as it ran down my cheek and hit my lip with its salty flavor.

I paused, as relief washed over my skin like a cool breeze, knowing I would never be alone again. A spirit I wasn't worthy of had entered my soul, comforting my struggle to believe in a changed me. I found my worth in the most humbling of ways, and was learning to wear my faults with dignity and openness. My worth wasn't measured by people who wanted a piece of me, but by living as the authentic me despite what people gave me in return. This extrovert was feeling more balanced.

So this is what peace feels like.

I was aware I had a story to share—a story of hope, of love...but this was not my time to write. Besides I had no idea how to begin.

The words of the professor in my writing class replayed in my head.

"Who would want to read about *half* of an affair or *half* of an assault."

Since I *half* agreed with his logic, I decided to read books to see if there was even an audience for my kind of raw thoughts— women in the middle living unfilled lives and feeling guilty in the process of wanting more.

So, reading at the beach became my new past time, and I hated to read. I was a s-l-o-w reader, which was probably one of the reasons I was waitlisted at Notre Dame (reading SAT score—yikes!). Luckily, now I had plenty of time since I wasn't looking to conquer the world to be happy. I was fulfilled just being me—faults and all, knowing God would in due time open a passageway to somewhere amazing, even if I couldn't see the door.

This new alone was much different than my withdrawn days of shame. I sat in the park alone. I drank my coffee at the coffee shop alone. I worked out at the gym alone. I walked the loop at Wrightsville Beach alone. I ate lunch alone. Surprisingly, my anonymity in this new place made me feel alive, not alone. I was fully free from past failures and the shackles of my achievements and status that had defined me. For the first time in my life, I did not need approval from others to fill my soul. I felt comfortable with myself, and the smile on my face reflected my true joy.

With my bold blonde exterior intact, I walked the hallway of the children's new school feeling different. My strong girl armor had been dismantled and was replaced by vulnerable openness. Strangely enough, I didn't feel weak amongst the sea of new faces, but more peaceful than ever. To my surprise, people pursued my friendship without me reaching out to be noticed. I was invited to lunches, coffees, and dinners. It didn't matter where I came from, where I had been, or what I did, the women seemed to appreciate me for me...the new girl with a smile living lightly at the beach.

I was being seen, but in a whole new light.

"Me?" I asked questioning Brooke's teacher who sat across the desk.

I was in school for a private meeting at her request. I assumed it was to discuss Brooke's ADHD needs, which Patrick and I had openly discussed prior to the start of the year. But I was totally off the mark.

"Yes, you," she repeated, her smile infectious. "I think you would be just what my class needs."

I wasn't prepared for this.

"Uh...room mom isn't...uh...really my thing," I stuttered. "Plus, being new to the school and all...I don't really...know the ropes."

I searched my mental Rolodex for more plausible excuses in hopes of staying under the social radar.

"Don't worry about that. I have you as co-room mom. I shouldn't say this, but this is a tough-girl class, and...well...Brooke has been my angel. The girls love her and vie for her attention, but she doesn't play the catty games for which this class is known," she said, lowering her voice. "And even some of the mothers."

I chewed on my lip. Oh no, the exact reason I didn't want to volunteer was fear of the *one-up-me* game, or worse yet, risk slipping back into old patterns. Alone was much more predictable—and peaceful.

She continued, embarrassed her feelings about some of the mothers had slipped out.

"I know I should be relieved I have so many mothers wanting to help, but some can be a bit overbearing, and well, this class can be tough enough to navigate. Your daughter has been a much needed calm in the storm."

Her brown eyes sparkled with hope and voice lightened.

"Brooke is my star student—not just academically but socially. She isn't afraid to raise her hand and ask for help. The other girls look to her for answers, and approval. She beats to her own drum, is unphased by the games, and includes girls being left out, even at the expense of being cut out herself. She has shaken things up here—for the better."

"Wow! Really?" I asked.

I had underestimated my daughter.

"She's a godsend, and I think you are too! So, I won't take no for an answer."

I was so wrapped up in my transformation that I hadn't realized Brooke was getting a new start too. She was no longer the shy girl with ADHD who wouldn't connect with peers —or adults for that matter —for fear of being less than perfect. At the new school she reinvented herself with no prior labels defining her, and was becoming everything God intended her to be. She was proud to be who she was—ADHD and all. It was time I took a lesson from her lead.

I could do this.

Building friendships without a need for a protective shield was new, but I drew strength from Brooke's example, and Sarah's words. She kept up our daily talks, even though I was miles away, and she continued to rewrite my idea of a true friend. At first, I resisted invitations from women at the gym and the "it" group of blonde bombshells from the school for fear of being sucked back into my old ways. Sarah convinced me to stay open to whatever came my way. Luckily, I did.

I was no longer defined by my exterior image and material things.

CHAPTER 66

Alright

"So you just gave it all up?" Meg asked, as her big blue eyes doubled in diameter.

I had met Megan, who preferred to be called Meg, at the gym earlier in the week. She had been reading a book about ADHD, which led to a treadmill conversation on the topic. As it turned out, she was planning an ADHD awareness event and was in great need of possible helpers. Helping to plan a community event isn't a role I would have ever committed to in the past for fear of "the unknown," yet here I sat in the living room of Meg's luxurious, historic district home surrounded by promotional packets, volunteer sheets and signage.

The room reflected her personality—colorful and scattered, yet refined. Her tousled auburn hair fell to her shoulders, framing her lean face. Her physique implied she was either an avid runner or The Energizer Bunny—maybe both. She chattered in a manner once familiar to me, going above and beyond to make me feel welcome, while trying to ignore the countless tasks on her over-whelming to-do list.

"Yes...pretty much everything...except our family photos on the wall," I explained. "They wanted the house and all the details that made it 'ours.' Crazy, right?!"

Meg's eyes seemed to be searching for more.

"But, why?" she questioned.

"Who knows...except maybe the Man upstairs?" I said. "All I know is that the buyer helped fulfill my wish of moving south... without 'things' weighing us down."

Being Meg's "helper" was a new role for me—the reformed over-achiever in me was no longer in search of attention. In fact, attention was the last thing I wanted, but, for some reason, I felt at ease with Meg. As the night progressed, we settled into deep conversation, and her line of questioning grew more and more personal. What surprised me more than her questions were my answers, which were far more truthful and revealing than I ever imagined sharing with *anyone*—especially a person I had only met for the first time earlier in the evening.

For most of the people back in Traverse City who had ques-tioned the reasons for our radical move, I had perfected the story of my trauma and freeing transformation without any mention of Chad. My omission of a few details wasn't to protect myself. It was more to protect selfless Patrick. He didn't deserve the scrutiny that would surely follow the telling of the whole truth.

Today was different.

"That's not what I mean." Meg's eyes squinted, as she contin-ued, "I mean...I could never just walk away from our stable life for the unknown. Why rock the boat?"

"I didn't think I ever would either...but floating through life on a flat, predictable river wasn't enough for me. I wanted to ride the rapids, even if I fell overboard. I thought I had happy figured out, but I was so wrong. I had settled for OK, when God had promised amazing. I had to remember to have faith in His ride and not one I had mapped out for myself."

"Huh?"

The wheels in Meg's head seemed to be churning something. *Should I divulge more?*

"I know I sound crazy...and you'd understand just how crazy, if you knew my old self," I said, snickering.

I shrank at the thought of the empty woman I had once been.

"I doubt that. Look at you." she said gesturing toward me, referencing the organized piles on the table where I was working. "I can't imagine you any other way than put together."

I looked down. The pile of disheveled paperwork she had given me earlier was arranged in neat, alphabetized stacks.

Meg sat on the other end of the long, mahogany dining table, with her portion of the files still a mess.

Not knowing what to do next, I said, "I guess I'm still a Type-A, control freak who can't let go of every bad habit overnight."

I laughed.

"You should be thankful that the 'old me' didn't show up. I may have taken over the whole project, thinking I was being helpful instead of annoyingly controlling!"

Meg shared the laugh. I could tell she was not convinced that the humble woman in front of her was once an over-bearing know-it-all. This must be how a girl feels after losing an significant amount of weight. She still sees herself as obese and not worthy of head turns.

Our two-hour chat turned into an all-day event. As my story unfolded, I shared details about Chad without shame and specifics about 'the incident' were unfiltered.

My mind kept telling me to shut up, yet gruesome details kept tumbling out of my mouth. Meg's questions were probing and my descriptions were unlike any other time I had shared the story—even with family and close friends. In this new, comfortable place, I was who I was—no masks, no pretense and no walls.

My answers were raw. Her reaction was awe.

"I kept thinking my situation wasn't that bad because I wasn't raped," I said. "But my body was holding on to feelings my mind had erased."

I took a breath and continued down my uncomfortable path.

"When I would wake to my husband spooning me, my body would tense...remembering the panic when the Sheriff betrayed my trust. I didn't understand my reaction until PTSD therapy bridged the Sheriff waking me with my feelings of rage when awakened by Patrick's touch," I explained.

Meg's expression changed. Her mouth drooped open, and her hands began to shake.

With a quivering voice, she said, "I left therapy six months ago and never went back after saying your exact words about my own husband to my therapist. My body tenses when I wake to my husband spooning me...that touch triggers horrific memories...." Fighting back tears, she continued, "My father would come into my bedroom at night...put his hands on me...and press into me. I just pretended to be asleep."

I was stunned. I knew just how difficult it must have been for her to say those words out loud. Tears flowed from my eyes, but only swelled in hers. In fact, they never breached her well-built dam. Meg's disclosure to me must have been her first in years. I could relate. She revealed more details from her nightmarish childhood. I focused on her outpouring of secrets, restraining myself from embracing her. She was a strong girl, and I knew better than to physically approach the armor.

I took a deep breath and listened.

When she has finished, I said, "Maybe this is a 'sign' you should go back to therapy. I'm living proof there is light past the darkness."

Meg didn't make eye contact. She sat frozen, staring down as she fussed with her fingers.

"Maybe you're right," she acknowledged.

The bubbliness bounced back into her voice.

"There is no other explanation for you, Kristy. You came into my life like lightning...opening my heart and my mouth. I can't believe what just happened between us. You must be the life preserver I needed to save me from drowning. I've been feeling down, very alone and...BOOM...here you come with your openness. You must be an angel...my angel!"

Meg sniffled with dry eyes.

"You really think things can be different for me?" she asked.

"I KNOW they can, Meg. I didn't deserve to be saved from my mistakes...and if I'm worthy of being set free, so are you," I assured her. "You've done nothing wrong and don't deserve to be stuck in a nightmare."

"Kristy, I don't know what to say...other than you have pulled me out of my living hell. I have been holding onto that...that secret...for so long."

Meg was sensing freedom. She did nothing wrong, yet she had been carrying the "icky" in an attempt to mask it behind a white picket fence.

She continued, "I feel like I've found my long lost sister. I've never felt this connected to anyone...ever!"

I was overwhelmed. Me—"Ms. Unfaithful"—she called an angel.

It was an intense day and quite hard to absorb, but the courage I found to share my story was an answer to my prayers—and Meg's.

I found purpose within my new existence and gained a forever friend that day. By giving up control and not caring how I was perceived, my life changed for the better, and strong friendships—ones I craved my entire only-child life—were developing at a surreal pace.

The more I came out of the shadows, the more women decided to share their secrets with me. More women than I would care to count confided in me about a sexual assault plaguing them and how they deemed their experiences "not that bad," just like Meg and I had. Any assault *is* bad, and everyone deserves to be free from whatever demons are holding their hearts hostage. No one soul is more deserving than another. Every soul is worthy of peace.

I discovered my true calling—sharing this good news of hope with all who will listen.

Sarah was right. I was authentic in my transformation, and being among people didn't mean I would revert back to an empty shell or try to be someone I wasn't.

I had busted beyond my white picket fence.

CHAPTER 67

Getting You Home

"What? Why didn't you tell me earlier?" I asked.

Patrick and I were lounging in short sand chairs after our picnic supper, watching and waiting for the destruction as high tide was approaching the children's sand sculptures, yet they remained dedicated to creating their masterpiece. I was undeterred from interrogating Patrick.

"I can't believe you waited to tell me this kind of news! I thought we were in this life together!"

"I didn't want you to worry after all we have sacrificed to get south," Patrick answered, trying to justify the unjustifiable.

"Haven't you learned anything about the 'new Kristy?'"

I didn't wait for his response.

"I guess not! If I've told you once, I've told you a thousand times since my breakthrough, all I need are you and the children to be happy! I'm not who I once was."

Calm down, Kristy! Deep breathe. At least he told you.

I broke a half smile, fixed my blue eyes on his wilting ones and continued, "A job or a place cannot change who I am or who you are. We will be fine even if you're the one on the chopping block."

"I know, but what if..."

He was prepping for a debate of a plan A, B and C, like old times.

I cut him off.

"I'm not worried about the 'what ifs' anymore, and you shouldn't either. We got this far against all odds. Didn't we? We'll control what we can control, and God will provide the rest...eventually. We just might have to endure a little suffering first."

Patrick breathed in the salty air.

"I've already called a few contacts, just in case I'm one of the 3000 laid off this December," his voice stabilized. "I guess it's a good thing we didn't push to get the house."

"Exactly...Now you're starting to talk like me," I said gloating. "And the good news is our money is tucked in the bank in case we want or need to pick up and move again."

"Really?"

He looked at me with *those* eyes.

"You aren't obligated to a company that announces layoffs just because they paid for a transfer...But, you are obliged to tell your wife when you get that kind of news," I scolded flirtatiously.

"But my wife is crazy. Who knows what feedback I would get? She gave up everything familiar and now this wrench gets tossed in?"

"Not everything," I said.

I smiled as I wrinkled my nose and placed my hand on his.

"Who are we to question the journey after all the amazing that's happened? This is just a hiccup. Remember...it's not what you do, or what you have, but who you are. And you're amazing! We will be fine no matter what," I added, leaning over to kiss him.

My chair sank into the sand and collapsed, trapping me inside.

Patrick dropped his head, trying not to laugh. My clumsiness distracted him from his fearful thoughts, while removing whatever ego I had left.

He extended his hand to pull me from the tangled mess.

Once I was freed, he gave me an "OK, I give" look.

"I should have told you the second my boss called," he confessed. His boyish smile returned.

Brushing off the sand, I said, "Yes. You should have."

Saying one would be patient, and being patient, are totally different stories. My peaceful attitude and the relief of not owning a home relieved Patrick's stress for awhile, until the reality of the potential layoffs took over and the fear of the distressed economy penetrated his psyche.

No more floating with the tide. Patrick had jumped out of the boat and was swimming toward shore...*any* shore.

I was thankful he wasn't anchored by owning "the house." However, he was still tied to the burden named me. He didn't deserve the ego bashing of losing his job. Patrick's father lost his during Patrick's adolescent years, and it made a huge impression on him. I heard the story numerous times about how he started high school wearing discount store jeans instead of the designer versions his buddies wore. His tenacious work ethic was formed by that life-changing event. He was determined not to end up like his father—a man who quit his family—which is probably why he never gave up on me. In his mind he had two months to find something, or face his biggest fear—no job.

Were my life changes at Patrick's expense?

Mentally, I was fearless knowing I would be fine going wherever the wind took us. My heart, however, was another story. I had grown fond of Wrightsville Beach and its fabulous people. My time spent alone was less as I spent more and more time nurturing the roots of strong friendships. Meg and I talked endlessly, growing even closer. Despite her fears, she returned to counseling. Her journey wouldn't be easy. She had lots of questions. She continued to pick my brain and lean on my friendship to remain stable after I helped shake her world. I found purpose in bearing some of the burden she didn't deserve. This amazing woman was as much of a gift to me as she claimed I was to her.

Other meaningful friendships were also blossoming, which included the group of blonde bombshells from the children's school. I divulged more of the real me in social settings. The astonishing part was I wasn't drowning beneath the surface, but breathing fine. Discovering the depths of the people around me eased my nerves about being in public, visible without walls for protection. There is no way around being vulnerable to pain when you have an open heart, and I knew whatever was coming next would probably hurt in one way or another.

After completing my morning walk with Sarah in my headphones, I grabbed a book and ventured outside. The humid days of fall had passed, and the weather was ideal for a tranquil beach reading session. The sound of ocean waves as background helped me focus on the story in front of me, and temporarily ignore concerns about Patrick's restless state of mind, oblivious to time.

I heard my phone ringing.

Had I forgotten to pick up the kids from school?

Reluctantly, I fumbled through my beach bag.

"Hello?" I answered.

"I got it!" shouted an energized Patrick.

My mind raced to recall to which job he could be referring to.

With his network capabilities and never burn a bridge philosophy, he had arranged interviews with multiple companies. I couldn't keep them straight. So, I didn't try. I trusted him.

"That's fabulous, honey! Tell me all about it!" I prodded.

"Looks like we're heading to Charleston after all!"

His voice was in perfect pitch.

Charleston?

My head was spinning. It immediately journeyed to the Catholic school lobby I had once been. The phrase "no way" circled in my mind as I remembered staring in awe at the vast display of snow globes on a large shelf.

Shivers shook my body.

I wasn't surprised he landed a new job *before* those layoffs were announced. However, when the new opportunity was the job he always dreamed of having, *and* it was based in Charleston...my jaw touched the sand.

Last year, I felt the snow globes sighting meant we belonged in Charleston, but logic had won the wrestling match with fantasy. I believed I wasn't supposed to control the journey myself. God would. So, when the Wrightsville Beach offer materialized, I dismissed the idea of Charleston, concluding the "sign" of snow globes in the school was merely wishful thinking.

I was wrong.

The sign was a "sign" after all—just not on a path I could see nor understand.

"You really think we can uproot the children again after only a few months?" I asked.

Guilt was sneaking into my desires.

"Did you just say that?"

I could sense him shaking his head and snickering.

"I know Charleston is where we belong, but I feel bad for the upheaval our children have had to endure."

And all the painful goodbyes I would have to endure. I was struggling in my emotional tug-of-war. For a lifelong control freak who preferred neat, orderly and predictable almost as much as her husband, this situation was almost too crazy to comprehend. But I sensed deep in my heart that this change of direction was God's hand at the wheel, keeping us on His path.

Patrick was being rewarded in the most marvelous way with his dream job. I knew he would have never pursued the fantastic opportunity if layoffs had not have been looming. He was far too loyal, and I was far too crazy not to label the job offer another "sign" our journey was being steered by a higher power.

I don't know why, after all the crazy coincidences the past year, miracles in my mind, that I'm still shocked when my reality surpasses my dreams. I guess I still have a ways to go for letting my faith prevail over logic.

Could this really be happening?

My heart was filled with hope, but my logic was filled with doubt...

CHAPTER 68

I Will

An hour or so behind me, Patrick was driving my Suburban and towing a small U-Haul loaded with a few of the necessities from the storage unit. The children were in Florida with my parents. We would join them Christmas Eve, two days away. With tears blurring my vision, I was struggling to keep his small sporty car on another road to the unknown. The goodbye notes from my new friends in Wrightsville Beach replayed in mind during the three-hour drive to our new home even farther south. Gifts gathered on the passenger seat reaffirmed words written—angel pins, angel cards, angel statues, and even an angel snow globe.

Angels? Me?

I was humbled by the theme playing out, and frankly in disbelief. For a girl who saw "signs" in everything, this was overwhelming.

I didn't deserve these gifts.

The old Kristy prided herself in being righteous and kind, and now that I had fallen flat on my morals, I was being admired in ways I only dreamt. My many years of trying to earn friends of this magnitude had failed. Only when I didn't *need* friends to prove my worth did I find true friends. I made a positive impact on other people's lives not by trying to *do* the correct thing or *say* the right thing to be admired. Instead, I simply learned to *be* an authentic me with all my faults intact.

These gifts and heartfelt messages from an unconnected group of woman were unbelievable to me. The circle of friends who gathered around me during my short time in Wrightsville Beach was a miracle only accomplished through God's hands.

I must be crazy to be giving them up. Would I be as lucky to find friends of this magnitude in Charleston?

I hoped so, but my worries began to fester. The difficulties in finding a home in Wrightsville Beach were following us to Charleston. Fear circled us. Maybe moving again was the wrong decision. All the red flags seemed to be waving. I recalled our conversation about a house in Charleston on which we had a signed purchase agreement. We were planning on moving in a week before Christmas.

I went down for the inspection.

Unfortunately, the results weren't what we had hoped for.

I called Patrick with the news.

"So...?" he asked.

"The pilings under the house are compromised. But the homeowners agreed to pay for the repairs," I said, taking a deep breath. "But who knows what that entails."

"Or how long it will take," he added. "I can't worry about a house, you and focus on a new job."

"But, I swore we wouldn't do another rental after all we've put the kids through. It's too much," I pleaded.

"This is so out of my league. I know nothing about houses and pilings. How can we move in less than two weeks with this?"

Patrick's voice betrayed his feelings of inadequacy. He wanted this move to be seamless. We all did.

My nerves were on the verge of spiraling out of control. I gripped the wheel tighter to regain some sense of control over the direction I was headed—to no avail. There were no comforts of friends where I was driving, no familiar surroundings, and no permanent home. After barely six months in North Carolina, I was driving to an unseen rental in another state. My wish for a permanent home had faded. I had no security blankets.

Not only had it been hard to give up on the purchase of a home before the move, but I also had to give up being neighbors with Darius Rucker, our favorite rock star who had "gone country."

Really? Darius Rucker my neighbor? It was all too much.

After we made an initial offer on the house with pilings issues, we found out the singer lived next door, and I thought his presence was another "sign" we were on the right track. His music and his Charleston upbringing had always been soft spots for us. The *Hootie and the Blowfish* album was my first CD with meaning since it was a gift from Patrick. *Mr. Rucker's* switch to country music happened about the time of my transformation. We had always been enamored by the parallels, yet giving up an opportunity to know him must surely be a "sign" we were evolving—or so I hoped.

I hadn't considered the hiccup with the house being a red flag on the entire move—maybe I was wrong. My fears were turning to panic. The sun was slipping below the horizon, dusk was disappearing. I had no idea where I was going and what would be waiting.

Why had I agreed to leave before Patrick finished loading the trailer?

I called Sarah.

"What were we thinking," I blurted. "Are we crazy to be moving again to the unknown?"

"Probably," Sarah snickered.

"You're not supposed to say that."

I sounded like a pouty teenager wanting her mother's reassurance that all would be OK, even if it wasn't.

"I can't do this. It's pitch black, the houses are crazy close to each other and who knows who, or what, is lurking around. What am I getting myself into?" I whined fearfully.

"Kristy, take it down a notch. You'll be fine. This is where you always wanted to be."

"Not in another rental with someone else's stuff!"

"Quit panicking," she said. "The realtor isn't sticking you in a dump. She wants to sell you a house."

Her unruffled voice spoke volumes to her tolerance of my craziness.

My nerves were somewhat comforted by her rational side—but not enough to let her off the phone until I inspected the joint, which I located more easily than I feared. She humored me. I was lucky to have a wonderful friend who put up with my over-the-top personality. Maybe my new friends in Wrightsville Beach would stick with me the way Sarah has, despite my address changes and roller coaster of emotions.

By the time I thoroughly investigated our new place, calmed my nerves and exhausted Sarah, Patrick had pulled into the single lane drive. As I walked out to greet him, I noticed a package near the front steps, propped against a bush. The box was addressed to me, so I opened the attached card and read the hand written note. It was from one of the blonde bombshells.

"When I think about your brief adventure in Wrightsville Beach, this poem by Mother Teresa seems to fit perfectly. It reminds me of our conversations, and I believe it was the message you brought with you to us. Wishing you and your family lots of blessings on your new journey!"

I unwrapped the box to find a beautifully framed poem. It read:

People are often unreasonable and self-centered.
Forgive them anyway.

If you are kind, people may accuse you of ulterior motives.
Be kind anyway.

If you are honest, people may cheat you.
Be honest anyway.

If you find happiness, people may be jealous.
Be happy anyway.

The good you do today may be forgotten tomorrow.
Do good anyway.

Give the world the best you have, and it may never be enough.
Give your best anyway.

For you see, in the end, it is between you and God.
It was never between you and them anyway.

~Mother Teresa

My fears lessened with each word. I was reminded that it didn't matter *where* I lived. It only mattered *how* I lived. I really was this new, humble woman capable of bringing joy and peace to other people's hearts. This was happiness like I have never known it before. I was truly blessed—not because of things I owned, accomplishments I achieved or status I held—but because I was now able to share my *true* self with others. I was receiving more than I ever could have imagined, and I was shining bright enough to be a beacon for others—even if my lamp had a few blemishes.

Overwhelmed, I wept.

CHAPTER 69

Livin' Our Love Song

My sandals scrunched as we approached the familiar door that I once opened before. Patrick's warm hand held mine as we were buzzed into the school office. Like a true Southern gentleman, he opened the door for me.

There they were—snow globes neatly arrayed with glistening sparks of light beaming from their insides. We walked up for a closer look. Labels on three of them caught my eye—Michigan, Texas and Wrightsville Beach.

I felt an internal peace as never before, despite the goose bumps covering my entire being.

As I looked at them again, I turned to Patrick. He understood and squeezed my hand.

The warmth radiating from his touch and his emerald sparkle said it all. He had shared in this journey, my craziness and all. At times, I was so caught up in *me* that I didn't realize *he* was there—always—with a hand to guide me through the dark times, even when I wasn't willing to grab it.

I didn't feel worthy of such a man. Yet, here he was with me, living our dream in South Carolina.

"This school feels different than the last two," he said, as we left the children at their new school.

"I agree. Something is missing, but I'm not sure what."

My mind was searching to find the answer, but it wasn't able to help me identify what "it" was.

"Maybe this place needs the new you," Patrick said with a wink.

I scrunched my lips.

"I have enough on my plate. It's time to get busy writing."

Patrick leaned in for a kiss in the middle of the sidewalk. He knew what today meant to me, and his logical side continued to sway my direction of crazy. I paused to take an *inventory* of our life *invested* down south thus far.

In less than six months, we had relinquished our dream home, lived in four furnished rentals in three states and now had enrolled our children in their third school—pretty interesting for two people who were rooted in structure and reluctant to risk.

Days in our rental turned into weeks. Weeks became months. Still no house.

Against my character, I remained arm's length from the children's school and avoided making personal connections. This was my time to try and write my story—our story.

The cravings for social interaction of this essential extrovert were reignited in Wrightsville Beach. Yet, I knew that if I made friends in Charleston, I would put off the difficult task of writing. Here, I had no excuses not to write—no house to nest and no friends to distract me, except for Sarah whose voice thankfully still accompanied my morning walks. I tried to write every day at Starbucks where I could be anonymous amongst the usual sea of people and noise. This place kept me from getting lost in my own head and allowed me to focus on the keyboard.

Patrick's patience wore thin, and his interest in real estate became more of an obsession. He was having a hard time with the thought of going backwards in amenities in order to honor our pact. He still wanted a home we could be proud of. He continued to search using out-of-the-box options, since the normal routes were hitting dead ends.

As the winter chill faded and the brown landscape transformed to a more cheerful pallet, Patrick looked for any unturned rock. Frustration was settling into our hearts. He reminded me of an odd outburst by Seth five months earlier, while we were driving through a random neighborhood in Charleston before the South Carolina job offer actually happened. The memory was vivid for me as well.

The cloud patterns were unlike anything I had ever witnessed in Michigan. The sky looked like a large blue bowl with soft serve vanilla ice cream swirling around it. I was commenting on the interesting interplay of clouds and sky when Seth yelled from the backseat, "That's our house! That's the one!"

He had twisted like a contortionist in his seatbelt. His finger pointed out the back window at a big, light-blue box on stilts.

We whipped our heads around like synchronized swimmers. Almost in unison, we all asked, "How do you know?"

His ten-year-old mouth brimmed confidence when he said, "I just do."

I contradicted him logically, saying, "First, we don't even know if we're moving here, second, we don't know how much it is and, third, we haven't even seen it!"

Seth mumbled defiantly, "Well, that's it. That's our house."

We shook our heads at his brashness, brushing his tenacity aside.

When Patrick did receive the offer in Charleston, he figured there was no harm in checking out "Seth's house." It was too late. The house had already been sold.

After more months of frustration, Patrick decided to investigate whatever happened with that house. He didn't recall seeing the property in the sold section of the paper, a place he checked daily. To our surprise, he found out that the house was a short sale still waiting to close due to negotiation problems with the bank. Though the property was technically off the market, our realtor was invited to look at it in case the current deal fell through. She told us not to get our hopes up since it was under contract and the bank deals with just one offer at a time. But, after her tour, her voice couldn't hide her excitement when describing the place.

"The home is fabulous. Two palm trees stand guard on each side of the large staircase to the front porch, just as Patrick envisioned. Two live oaks frame an expansive view of the marsh in the backyard. And the porches are amazing! There are plenty of bedrooms and the kitchen could feed an army. It's so 'y'all!'"

We knew we shouldn't be able to afford this, even forgetting our prior pact. Yet the hope of a short sale, paired with the downtrodden economy, put this house within reach—*if* the first buyer backed out, that was. She told us the amount needed to satisfy the bank requirements. It was much lower than our pact. Patrick crossed his fingers. I relied on the "signs." This wasn't merely any house. It was "Seth's house" on a street named Majestic Roses Court.

Could this be destiny?

A poem I had written well over a year and a half ago—the only poem I've ever written in my lifetime—resurfaced in my memory.

> *After all the rain had stopped,*
> *And the storm had passed,*
> *I took a breath,*
> *And two of the most amazing*
> *Flowers remained.*

The two of them weathered the storm
And awoke to an entirely new and beautiful world.

After that, they knew together
Their love could withstand
All obstacles on this earth,
Because their love was God's love.

The gray—otherwise known as the unexplainable—bombarded me the way the snow globes in the school gave me *that feeling*. Life with gray was far more exciting than my old black and white version—even if it meant exposure to pain and disappointment.

Like a tortoise, three more months crawled by. The first buyer was winning. Our realtor was informed that the buyer came up with the money needed. Fatigue settled in our hearts, and Patrick searched for other options. The odds were not favoring the tortoise, but I continued to pray anyway.

Memorial Day weekends had been life-changing for our family the past two years. I hoped this one would be too.

A parent of one of Seth's friends, who handles short sales, called to say, "A friend told me the bank has moved to the second buyer!"

We were on cloud nine thinking we had reached the finish line first at Majestic Roses.

Monday, our realtor informed us that we were *not* the second buyers. The listing agent had put another offer in front of ours, while telling our realtor the first buyer came up with the money.

Anger consumed us. We trusted the agent. We wanted to fight back. Instead, we remembered the messages in Mother Teresa's poem that was now on our mantle.

Keeping the weekend information to ourselves, our realtor pushed to obtain proper signatures to secure our offer as next in line.

We couldn't control the behavior of others, but we could manage ours.

Patrick's hope for Majestic Roses waned. He wanted to make an offer on another house, and I couldn't blame him for being ready to settle down after our bumpy ride.

Our fate was in God's hands.

CHAPTER 70

True Believers

The smell of plough mud filled the air, as the receding tidewater exposed the grassy marsh. The sun began to slip below the horizon. Even at dusk, the heat embraced my body like a comforting blanket.

I rocked on the porch swing hand-in-hand with *my* rock, *my* true love, *my* Patrick.

We breathed in the salty fragrance of the lowcountry and marveled at the majestic view of the open marsh. Hundreds of snowy egrets were taking flight after enjoying the meal provided by the tidewater. Familiar sounds of wild barking tree frogs interrupted the silence. We hesitated, and then exploded in laughter.

So this is what a home feels like.

"Have I told you how amazing you look?" Patrick asked, caressing my bare leg with one hand and placing his other arm around my shoulder.

Our bodies swayed with the swing.

"A hundred times today," I responded with a look that hinted for more.

"Then I guess I better tell you again."

His boyish grin glowed in the moonlight.

"You can barely see me. It's dark," I teased.

"Got you memorized, girl! You're my sweetheart, and I love you!"

I blushed. The once forward flirt melted, feeling the depth of her husband's words.

Deflecting my squirms, I nudged back, "I bet you say that to all the girls."

"Only my wife...and I'm keeping her."

I was complete. It really didn't matter *where* we lived. I thought I knew the only path to "Happily Ever After." I thought wrong. My journey was never about how many people I could get to fall in love with me through my misguided image of "picture perfect." I learned that *true* joy isn't found in accomplishments, recognitions or pats on the back. *True* joy was, and is, about discovering the power of unconditional love.

"What's up with you?" I asked.

"What?" he responded, playing dumb. "Can't I say nice things to my wife?"

I rolled my eyes, knowing he couldn't even see the gesture.

"Of course you can," I answered. "But I'm still getting used to this verbal you."

"Hey. My wife once told me men are physical and women feel with their mind...so guess what I'm doing?"

He didn't wait for my response.

"Having sex with your mind every chance I get!"

We erupted in unified laughter.

Patrick loves all of me—imperfections and all—not because of how I look or what I do, but for who I am on the inside.

The real me wasn't a strong girl, a confident girl or a righteous girl. I was a wounded person trapped behind a façade of perfection but feeling unworthy of love. I used this façade for my heart's protection, until my "perfect snow globe world" disappeared with one vigorous shake from the unpredictable.

I will never look at snow globes the same again.

Discovering the meaning of unconditional love in the most peculiar of ways was enough for me to trust in the gifts laid out in front of me. My husband and this place, even if only temporary, must be gifts from above. This was God's house. He is just letting us live here for awhile. The perfect place and the perfect family don't exist. Perfect love, however, just might.

The "signs" along the path were simply effective ways to tear down my "walls of logic" brick by brick and free my soul to a deeper faith—a deeper love that can only be found within one's soul, and not in the exterior lure of the perfect mate or the perfect house.

Happiness isn't found in the "picture perfect life," but within imperfect design.

Once we were willing to relinquish the wheel and let faith be our guide, God led us to our Southern comfort, our miracle—Majestic Roses—which houses our love, thorns and all.

As we continued to rock on the porch swing, Patrick grabbed my hand and gently pulled me to his chest.

Kissing me tenderly on half of my lip and half of my cheek he whispered in my ear, "I love you, 'crazy girl.'"

I cradled my hands around his cheeks, burning into his eyes with mine, and replied with an overflowing open heart...

"I love you too, Patrick Dominiak...*Forever and Always.*"

Epilogue

As the writing of this book came to a close, this poem was written for me as a gift for my 42nd birthday by a new friend I met at bliss Spiritual Co-op in South Carolina. Despite her being unaware of the story written within these pages, Sylvia has become acquainted with the "new Kristy." I am blessed to have found her and so many other deep friendships after my transformation. Her words are the inspiration needed for the next chapter of my life—and maybe yours.

Within each mind lies a small switch,
For some that switch is flipped open at birth
For some it is opened as a result of an epochal event
For others that switch may never flip,
Remaining closed for an entire lifetime.

Once that switch has flipped, there is no going back
There is no unknowing
The individual has no choice but to
See with new eyes
Hear with new ears and
Speak with a new voice

The individual may then retreat into fear
Or they may burst forth with the song of a new life,
Changing the lives of others forever.

~Sylvia H. Barnhill

About the Author

Photo: Jennifer Cady

KRISTY DOMINIAK is the president of Bliss Spiritual Co-op, a nonprofit retreat house in South Carolina, and a graduate of the University of Notre Dame. She lives with her husband and three children (all pieces of her soul), who have loved her through the ups and downs of life. Kristy lives each day knowing she is exactly where she needs to be. She has learned through the exploration of life that she is enough. With this new-found insight it allows her to love herself, her husband and family more completely. Kristy believes that self-discovery is never-ending, and she remains open-hearted to life's journey. Visit ShakenSnowGlobe.com to learn more.

Pictured above (left to right): Seth, Kristy, Ally, Brooke and Patrick

Acknowledgments

Had my life not been touched by all of the people within these pages and beyond, I would have never discovered who I really am. Words cannot adequately express my overwhelming gratitude for those individuals who supported me on this incredible journey. They believed in me, even when I didn't. Thank you from the depths of my soul.

To my husband (my "Forever and Always"): This story would not have been possible without your love and support. My love for you is beyond words. I am lucky to have you by my side, intertwined, on this incredible journey of life. You love me despite my flaws and challenge me to dream bigger than logic allows. Through you, I have discovered the true meaning of unconditional love and am blessed beyond my comprehension. I will love you...forever and always.

To my parents and children: You are pieces of my soul, and I am grateful for your acceptance and love. Without your open hearts and willingness to share our family with the world, this story could not have been told. I love you to the depths of my being.

To Sarah (my soul sister): Without you believing in me, I would have exited this story long ago. Thank you for your friendship, encouragement, support and unconditional love. You taught me the meaning of true friendship.

To my spiritual mentors (especially Neil and Linda): You shined a light on my lost soul and liberated my spirit. You believed in me, even when I couldn't see a door to escape my internal prison. I will forever be grateful for your wisdom.

To the singers and songwriters who unknowingly cracked open my heart through their music: Thank you. Your voices awakened my soul from its numb existence. Your gifts of words and melodies connected me to something bigger than myself.

To my editor (and forever friend) Pamela Murphy McCormick: You had the unique gift of being able to weed through my words and assemble the right pieces to complete this puzzle. Through you, this story came to life on paper. I will forever be grateful for your leap of faith on this long and tedious journey of self-discovery.

Thank you to the team at Publish Pros (and the "Richs" in my life): You've challenged and pushed me to remain "fiercely authentic." Your creativity of design has given this book life. The book cover and layout exceeded my imagination.

To all my friends within these pages and beyond: I have appreciated your honest critiques as you've read through the many drafts of this book. Thank you, too, for the "ears you've lent" and the unconditional love and support you've given.

Thank you to Bliss Spiritual Co-op: Through you, I have found connections that nourish my soul and prepare me for life's unknown journey. We are all interconnected, if only we can set fear aside and embrace our own authenticity and worth without seeking external validation.

To the many other hands and hearts that have touched this manuscript, this story wouldn't have been the same without you.

Lastly, thank you to the higher power I call God. I now *know* who I am and what *true* love really is because of you.

When we stop trying to prove ourselves to others, only then can we find our *true* self.

Kristy ♡

Made in the USA
Middletown, DE
26 September 2016